FUNDAMENTALS OF BANK ACCOUNTING

FUNDAMENTALS OF BANK ACCOUNTING

James A. Patten, MBA, CPA

RESTON PUBLISHING COMPANY, INC.
A Prentice-Hall Company
Reston, Virginia

ISBN 0-8359-2119-0

The final typesetting was done on a T$_Y$XSET 1000 system in Reston, Virginia, using a Mergenthaler Omnitech/2100. The galleys and page makeup were also done on the T$_Y$XSET 1000 system using a Canon LBP-10 Laser Printer for page proofs.

T$_Y$XSET 1000 is a trademark of T$_Y$X Corporation.

10   9   8   7   6   5   4   3   2   1

Printed in the United States of America.

CONTENTS

PREFACE

WHO SHOULD READ THIS TEXT?

Are you

1. A college student interested in a career in banking?
2. Currently working for a bank and feel that an increased knowledge of the accounting function would be helpful to your job?
3. A bank officer looking for a basic reference guide to bank accounting that will serve in developing bank training programs and/or policy and procedure manuals?
4. A college teacher looking for a basic text in bank accounting to be used in either a career program in banking or as part of the curriculum for a four-year degree program?

If you answer yes to any of the above, then this text was written for you!

WHY THIS TEXT?

I fit into the number four catagory and that is the reason I wrote this text. You see, I could find *nothing* that would meet my needs. Now, by that I don't mean that I had searched through dozens of comparable texts and was just too fussy to use what I found. What I mean is that there was nothing available at all. Just what were my needs? I had been asked by a community college to teach their course in Bank Accounting. The course had never been taught before. Why? No text. Thus the reason for my search. The course is a sophomore level course for students majoring in the career program in banking. The course is also transferable for those students going on to complete a four-year degree. The prerequisite for this course is one semester of accounting principles or comparable work background. Since not all of the potential users of this text may have that prerequisite, included in the text is a unit on basic accounting to aid you in reaching the level of accounting expertise needed to tackle this text. (By the way, I would think that this unit should be required reading for all bank employees—especially tellers and operations personnel.)

Consider that in today's environment the professional career winds its way through many different companies and industries. The management team of most companies is a "melting pot" of different industry and company backgrounds. The need, therefore, exists in banking, as well as in many other industries, to provide a body of professional literature designed to train tomorrow's management team. Career and college training today gives students high expectations of themselves and technology. Thus, they are confident of their ability to quickly apply their skills to the job market and are not willing to wait ten or even five years before given an opportunity to blow the whistle, move the throttle, or hit the brakes. The knowledgeable user of this text will see that it was written, not to replace what is already there but, rather, to serve as a bridge for the future management team to the vast amount of professional literature that already exists in banking.

HOW THIS TEXT IS ORGANIZED

I have taken a proven path in presenting the material. Many accountants would refer to the style as the "balance sheet" approach. The student is introduced to a skeleton balance sheet showing the major "earning" and "nonearning" asset accounts and the primary liability and capital, or equity, accounts. Through simple yet realistic examples, the basic core of transactions that occur in financial institutions is demonstrated. The student sees how these accounts are interrelated and how to arrive at the resulting profit or loss data. Having established a fundamental knowledge of how the accounting formula applies to financial institutions, the text then takes a detailed look at each major segment of the balance sheet, starting with cash and due from banks and ending with stockholders' equity. As the student is taken into the detail of each major balance sheet category, the additional related income and expense accounts are introduced. With this approach, the student not only has a good grasp of the balance sheet, but also understands the how-to and why of the various approaches to preparing the income statement.

The last five units cover the topics of P&L presentation, internal control, data processing, taxes, and analysis of bank performance.

A major supporting tool used within the text is a microcomputer accounting system. With the 51 entries incorporated into the system, the student has all the benefits of the traditional accounting "practice sets" without all of the pencil pushing. Users can easily interface their data processing systems with the text, if desired.

The instructor will find a wealth of material within the text for classroom and testing use. All users will benefit from the unit review questions and projects. The appendices contain complete answers to the unit review questions and projects along with the complete set of "hard copy" from the computerized general ledger. The call report forms are also reproduced and illustrative bank and nonbank financial statements are provided along with a glossary and bibliography.

This entire text was designed to be presented over a 16-week semester. Concluding this preface is a suggested plan for teaching the covered material. Of course, the material could be used in shorter sessions where only certain topics need to be presented. For example, the material on loans and internal control could be packaged into a two- or three-week program. Also, savings and loan associations could use much of the material with little or no modification.

I have tried to put into this material the best of what I have learned in over 16 years in accounting for various financial and nonfinancial institutions. The last seven of those 16 plus years have been spent in full-time teaching of accounting principles at Harper College in Palatine, Illinois, as well as continuing to maintain an accounting practice on a part-time basis. In this endeavor, I am an accounting professional writing a text on a significant industry's use of accounting. I would appreciate users' comments and impressions of this material.

FUNDAMENTALS OF BANK ACCOUNTING CLASS PLAN

The following is a suggested plan for a class meeting for 16 full 2.5 hour periods. Each period can be considered as two sessions. The following gives you the approximate number of sessions that could be spent on each unit and the planned tests.

In addition to the examinations, a course grade could be based on several take-home-type projects developed from the text material.

UNIT	TOPIC	NUMBER OF SESSIONS
1.	Introduction	1
2.	Debits and Credits Explained	2
3.	Cash and Due from Banks	2
4.	Investments	2
5.	Loans	3
6.	Other Assets	1
—	Test	1
7.	Demand Deposits	2
8.	Savings Deposits	1
9.	Other Liabilities	1
10.	Stockholders' Equity	2
—	Test	1
11.	Review of Bank Income Statements	1
12.	Internal Control	2
13.	Data Processing	2
14.	Taxation of Banks	2
15.	Analysis of Bank Performance	2
—	Test	1
	Unallocated Sessions	3
Total—16 classes, two sessions each		32

ACKNOWLEDGMENTS

My wife, Rita, and our daughter, Sandy, deserve my deepest thanks for their labor (Rita), patience (Sandy), and love (both), in helping put this text together.

I also thank my professional colleagues in teaching and accounting practice who have given their input, as well as the valiant students who used the text material during its development over the last two years.

1
GENERALLY ACCEPTED ACCOUNTING PRINCIPLES AND BANK ACCOUNTING

Generally accepted accounting principles (which we shall forever after call GAAP) are the guiding lights by which accountants determine the form and content of the financial statements of enterprises. It certainly would be nice if you could stop off at the local bookstore and purchase *The Book Of GAAP*. Unfortunately, this is not possible. I do not believe that this is due to a failure on the part of the accounting profession to produce such a document. I also hasten to point out that there does exist a vast amount of professional literature discussing various aspects of GAAP in general terms as well as in terms of how GAAP relates to many specific industries. It is my feeling that we will never see *A Complete GAAP Book* or that, if such a work was produced, it would be out of date before it got off the presses. The reason for such a belief is that GAAP is evolved rather than discovered like the laws of science. The development of GAAP is an evolutionary process because GAAP matures and changes to meet the changing needs of the business enterprises it serves.

There are several factors that make bank accounting or bank GAAP a challenging area:

- Current rapid changes in the industry.
- Oversight and regulatory control of various federal and state agencies which often present conflicting reporting requirements.
- Certain unique provisions of the Internal Revenue Code relative to the banking industry.
- The nature of bank assets which preclude the traditional classifications of current and long-term.

Another point some would add to this list is the absence of GAAP guidelines from the public accounting profession. The American Institute of Certified Public Accountants (AICPA) has prepared an audit guide, *Audits of Banks*, which is currently in draft form. The prior guide is over 10 years old.

OVERVIEW OF THE BANKING INDUSTRY

The following is provided to establish a review of the interplay of the various bodies controlling the banking industry.

Banks can operate under a federal or state charter. All national banks that operate under federal charters are required to be members of the Federal Reserve System. State chartered banks, since they operate under state authority, are not required to be members of the Federal Reserve System but they may become members if they meet "Fed" requirements.

The deposits of national banks must be insured by the Federal Deposit Insurance Corporation (FDIC). Although FDIC coverage is optional for state banks, most do subscribe to the FDIC. The cost of FDIC coverage is paid for by the member banks based on total deposits.

Banks operate in various forms such as unit or single location banks. They can also be organized on a branch basis. That is, there is one controlling, or head, office supervising the operations of multiple locations. Chain banks are separate entities owned by the same set of individual owners while group banking involves the ownership of banks by a holding company.

The structure of banks and the way they operate has and is changing. Since 1934, the number of banks has fallen from around 15,000 to 13,000. In that same time, the number of branches has grown from a few thousand to over 30,000. Branching is controlled by state regulation. Some states allow almost unlimited branching while others greatly restrict branching or do not allow branching at all. Branching across state lines is prohibited by federal law. Many large banks operate overseas branches and become actively involved in international trade. In states that restrict branching, bank holding companies and chain banking have become the growth tool. Under Federal Reserve rules banks and bank holding companies have expanded their services to include many related business services such as leasing and data processing services.

Because banking is such a highly regulated industry, it is important to be aware of the different agencies that control and examine banks. The following chart indicates the controlling agencies for national and state banks.

BANK TYPE	COMPTROLLER OF THE CURRENCY	FDIC	FEDERAL RESERVE BANK	STATE BANKING AUTHORITY
NATIONAL	XXXX			
STATE:				
FED MEMBER			XXXX	XXXX
NONMEMBER:				
FDIC INSURED		XXXX		XXXX
UNINSURED				XXXX

Depending on the number of shareholders and the size of security offerings that they make, banks and their holding companies can also fall under reporting requirements and regulations of the Securities and Exchange Commission.

Of all of the agencies listed, the student should be most aware of the operations of the Federal Reserve System (the Fed). In addition to its regulatory function and its duties as the banker's bank (check clearing, wire transfers, etc.), the student should appreciate the Fed's role in controlling the money supply. Hopefully, this will be a review for the typical student.

The three major controls the Fed uses to control money are:

1. *Reserve Rates*—The Fed controls the percentage of deposits that banks must hold in "reserve". If the reserve rate is, say, 10%, then 90% of deposits can be loaned out. Increases in the reserve rate should then reduce the money supply while decreases should have the opposite effect.

2. *Buying and Selling U.S. Securities*—When the Fed is a buyer of U.S. securities, the supply of money in individuals' hands increases, thus increasing the money supply. Fed sales of government securities, of course, have the opposite effect.

3. *The Discount Rate*—Member banks that are "short" on the amount of their reserves will (usually as a last resort) take temporary loans from the Fed to make up reserve deficiencies. The discount or interest rate is the rate the Fed charges on such loans. Increases in the discount

rate tend to restrict credit and the money supply and decreases should have an opposite effect.

SCOPE OF THIS TEXT

Since this material is designed for college students studying banking or persons at the entry level in their bank accounting studies, I could not tackle the accounting problems of multibillion dollar banks. I have geared the material to the basic transactions that a community bank with under $100 million in footings would encounter. With the basic foundation of transactions built into this material, the student should be able to go on to the more complex areas such as leveraged leasing, foreign operations, branch banking, etc.

The accounting transactions presented in the text are illustrated by use of the general journal form which should be familiar to students who have a bookkeeping background. Unit 2 reviews debits and credits and journal entries. It is a good review if you are proficient with the same and a "must read" if you lack in bookkeeping.

Exhibit 1-1 serves as a useful reference in illustrating the basic sequence of events in the accounting cycle.

REVIEW OF PRIMARY FINANCIAL STATEMENTS FOR BANKS

When an accountant refers to the Financial Statements, or more formally, the Primary Financial Statements, he or she is referring to the following five reports (alternative titles shown).

1. Balance Sheet
   Statement of Condition
   Statement of Financial Condition
2. Statement of Income
   Statement of Earnings
3. Changes in Shareholders'/Stockholders' Equity
4. Statement of Changes in Financial Position
5. Summary of Significant Accounting Policies (Usually included with the notes to the financial statements)

Included in Appendix C are samples of these statements, along with samples of statements of a typical nonbanking firm. You should refer to these statements now since understanding them is what this text is all about.

EXHIBIT 1-1
Bank Accounting Cycle

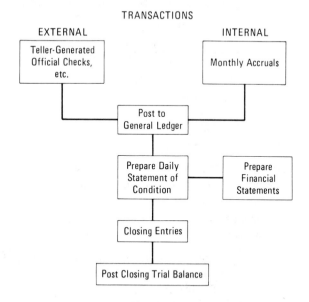

1. The balance sheet is prepared *as of* a point in time. It is sometimes called a "snapshot" of the firm. This is one way to think of the balance sheet.

Earning Assets		Liabilities	
+ Nonearning Assets		+ Equity	
Total Assets (footings)	=	Total Footings	

   Earning and *nonearning assets* are terms in banking jargon to distinguish assets that are earning interest income from all other assets. As we will see, investments and loans are *the* earning assets of a bank.

2. The Statement of Income (which we will call the P&L, short for profit & loss statement) always covers a period of time. The concept of *income* must always be related to a period of time because it is a time flow concept.

   Think of it this way. If I made the statement, "I made an income of $1,000," you could reply, "So what?" But if I stated that the $1,000 was my income for an entire year, you would probably feel very sorry for me. (Despite your feeling of sorrow you probably would not approve my loan request if you were a loan officer.) On the other hand, if my income statement showed that I earned $1,000 per day each day of the year, you no doubt would have an entirely different picture of my earning capacity.

Basically, here is what a bank P&L shows:

Interest Income
$-$ Interest Expense
___
$=$ Net Interest Income (also called Net Interest Margin)
$-$ Operating Expenses
___
$=$ Operating Income
$+-$ Nonoperating Revenues & Expenses
___
$=$ NET INCOME

This is a rather simplified P&L format but it will work very well for now and serve as a good foundation for some of the complications to come.

3. The structure of the Statement of Changes in Shareholders' Equity is as follows:

Shareholders' Equity—beginning of period
$+$ Net Income
$-$ Dividends
$+-$ Other Activity
___
$=$ Shareholders' Equity—end of period

4. The Statement of Changes in Financial Position, or funds statement, is considered by many financial analysts to be the most important of the primary financial statements. It pulls together the most important ingredients of the P&L and balance sheet. Here is the basic layout:

Cash & Due from (or FUNDS)—beginning of period
$+-$ Funds Flow from P&L
$-$ Funds Used for Dividends
$+-$ Funds Flow Effects of Changes in Balance Sheet
___
$=$ Funds—end of period

5. The fifth element of the financial statements is a written document in which the company discloses the major accounting policies in effect and any other data that is considered necessary for the users of the financial statements.

A word of caution here! The financial statements of a bank or any enterprise cannot, will not, are not designed or intended to, tell you EVERYTHING YOU WANTED TO KNOW ABOUT THE COMPANY BUT

WERE AFRAID TO ASK! The informed user should look at the financial statements as an important tool in judging the merits of a particular enterprise in light of the user's particular needs or goals. The informed user will also realize that there are many other factors outside of the basic financial statements that need to be considered in making a financial decision.

SUMMARY

Upon completing this unit, you should also have:

- Inspected the preface and class plan.
- Read the topical outline.
- Reviewed Appendices A and C.

If you are using this as a course textbook, your instructor will not be upset with you if you perhaps have taken a look at other material. (Say, for example, you might even have had the audacity to skim through the entire text.)

REVIEW QUESTIONS

1. A bank's assessment for FDIC coverage is based on
   A. Total assets
   B. Net loans
   C. Total deposits
   D. Total liabilities
   E. None of the above

2. A bank that controls multiple locations through a main or head office could be classified as a
   A. Chain bank
   B. Branch bank
   C. National bank
   D. Group bank
   E. Holding company

3. A non-Fed member state bank with FDIC coverage will be supervised by
   A. Comptroller of the Currency
   B. FDIC and Federal Reserve Bank

C. Comptroller of the Currency and state banking authority

D. FDIC and state banking authority

E. Both B and D

4. The Fed can *decrease* the money supply by

A. Increasing the reserve rate

B. Decreasing the discount rate

C. Selling U.S. securities

D. Both A and C

E. Decreasing the reserve rate

5. If the sum of liabilities and equity is $600 and earning assets add up to $475, then

A. Total assets are $600

B. Nonearning assets are $350

C. Nonearning assets are $125

D. Both A and C are true

E. None of the above

6. Which of the following is in sequential order?

A. Transactions, post closing trial balance, statement of condition

B. Closing entries, financial statements, posting

C. Monthly accruals, posting, financial statements

D. Customer deposit, posting, closing entries

E. Both C and D

7. If shareholders' equity (or capital) was $150 (beginning of period) and $170 (end of period), net income was $30, and dividends are the only other item effecting capital, then the dividends amount to $10.

A. True

B. False

8. If the bank in Question 7 also sold $15 in new stock to its shareholders, then the dividends would have been

A. $25

B. $5

C. $30

D. $10

E. None of the above

9. If, in a given period, loans and deposits increased by $65 and $50, respectively, funds would, therefore,

    A. Increase by $115

    B. Increase by $50 since loans have no effect

    C. Increase by $15

    D. Decrease by $65 since deposits only effect liabilities

    E. None of the above

10. List several important items that could affect the financial condition of a bank but would *not* be found in the financial statements.

2
DEBITS AND CREDITS EXPLAINED

The purpose of this unit is to give you a basic understanding of the use of the *accounting formula* and *debits* and *credits*. Here is the accounting formula:

$$ASSETS = LIABILITIES + EQUITY$$

- ASSETS = Property (tangible and intangible) owned by the company.
- LIABILITIES = Claims of creditors against the assets of the company.
- EQUITY = Claims of the owner(s) against the assets of the company.

One nice thing about the accounting formula or equation is that it is the same for any type of business. An individual or any nonbusiness entity could even maintain a bookkeeping system using the accounting formula. Another nice thing about the accounting equation is that *any transaction*, no matter how complicated, can be expressed in terms of the accounting formula.

Basically, a *transaction* is defined as an exchange of value that can be measured in terms of money. It is handy to keep in mind the two major subdivisions of transactions.

- *External*—A transaction between the firm and entities outside of the firm.
- *Internal*—A transaction affecting only accounts within the books of the firm.

Later in this unit you will see specific examples of external and internal transactions. The basic point to keep in mind now is that external transactions occur and are recorded on a day to day basis while internal transactions must be generated whenever the bank needs to prepare financial statements.

As in any formula, the equals sign in the accounting formula means that the sum of the left side of the equation must equal the sum of the right side of the equation. The terms of the accounting formula are what I like to refer to as *umbrella terms*. Every account in a set of books must fit under one of these broad terms. The second column of the *chart of accounts* that appears in Appendix A gives you the type or classification of each of the accounts in terms of the accounting formula.

Now we are ready to talk about DEBITS and CREDITS and double entry bookkeeping.

True or False? Double entry bookkeeping means that every transaction is recorded twice.

Well, I hope you answered false. If not, please read on. In double entry bookkeeping we look at and record the dual aspect of every transaction— WHAT and WHY!

Let's explain this *what* and *why* approach by considering a typical external transaction for Dr. Doe, M.D. The good doctor has just received $50 from Mr. Smith for Smith's checkup. What happened? The asset cash increased $50. Why did that happen? Because the doctor earned the $50 by performing the checkup. Therefore, the doctor's equity account on the right side of the accounting formula should be increased by $50.

Here is a simple rule for debits and credits:

- Increase the asset or left side of the accounting equation with DEBITS.
- Increase the liability and equity or right side of the accounting equation with CREDITS.

The rule for decreases would be just the opposite. It would be a good idea now if you wrote out the rules for decreases and compared the two sets of rules. If you are doing this as part of a course, you should check with your instructor to be certain that you can handle the convention of debits and credits as it applies to the accounting formula.

Now that you know the rules for debits and credits, you should be able to take the doctor's $50 transaction and say: Debit cash $50 and credit an equity account (probably a temporary income account like "Patient office fees") for $50.

All transactions are recorded on forms called *journals*. Journals take many different forms depending on the type of business. The form of journal that we will be using in this course is called the *general journal*. The use of the general journal in business is limited because it is a very cumbersome tool for recording large volumes of repetitive transactions such as cash disbursements or sales invoices. On the other hand, any type of transaction can be recorded using the general journal form and the entire transaction is clearly displayed, all in one place in terms of debits and credits. The general journal form that we will use is shown in Exhibit 2-1.

Our doctor's $50 transaction is also here, along with six other typical transactions. Before inspecting these transactions in detail, it would be a good exercise to journalize the six transactions described below on your own and then compare your work to the completed entries.

TRANSACTION DESCRIPTIONS	TRANSACTION AMOUNT	JE#
A. Bill patient on account for office visit	85.00	6
B. Purchase supplies on account	450.00	3
C. Receive payment from patient on account	40.00	4
D. Purchase of X-ray machine financed with a bank loan at 12% (principal plus interest on loan due in six months)	10,000.00	2
E. Payment to creditor on account	450.00	5
F. To record one month's interest on note described in transaction D.	?	7

This would be a good time to refer to Exhibit 1-1 on the bank accounting cycle. Now contrast that chart with Exhibit 2-2, which shows the accounting cycle flow for a nonbanking enterprise.

Do the two flowcharts look similar? Of course they do! Remember that this flowchart of the accounting cycle is applicable to any firm, from Mom & Pop's Grocery Store to General Motors, or from the Local Neighborhood Bank to The Bank of America.

To help you understand journals and Exhibit 2-2 let's review Dr. Doe's seven transactions. The first six are all examples of external transactions. Transaction 7 is an example of an internal transaction. As you can see, the

EXHIBIT 2-1

General Journal Form Sample

```
          COMPANY NAME-Dr. Doe              PAGE #
             GENERAL JOURNAL                  -1-
        Accounting Period-Jan.,19X1
```

DATE	JE#	ACCOUNT	DEBIT	CREDIT
MO/DA/YR	1	#### CASH	50.00	
		#### PATIENT OFFICE FEES		50.00
		TO RECORD CASH FEE FROM		
		SMITH-CHECKUP		
MO/DA/YR	2	#### EQUIPMENT	10,000.00	
		#### NOTE PAYABLE		10,000.00
MO/DA/YR	3	#### SUPPLIES	450.00	
		#### ACCOUNTS PAYABLE		450.00
MO/DA/YR	4	#### CASH	40.00	
		#### ACCOUNTS RECEIVABLE		40.00
MO/DA/YR	5	#### ACCOUNTS PAYABLE	450.00	
		#### CASH		450.00
MO/DA/YR	6	#### ACCOUNTS RECEIVABLE	85.00	
		#### PATIENT OFFICE FEES		85.00
MO/DA/YR	7	#### INTEREST EXPENSE	100.00	
		#### INTEREST PAYABLE		100.00

nature of internal transactions is that you must be aware that they need to be made and that the accountant generally has to compute the amount of the entry.

The following is a series of typical bank transactions, for what I have imaginatively called The First Typical Bank, journalized in general journal form. The first nine are external transactions while JE's 10 through 16 are internal. The account numbers and titles are from the chart of accounts in Appendix A. These transactions will be explained in detail as you continue with subsequent units. This is what you should do now:

1. Trace the amounts from each of the journal entries to their inclusion in the *general ledger*. What you are doing here is retracing the steps of the posting process. In this, the posting process has been done electronically using the BPI general ledger accounting noted in Appendix A.
2. Trace the ending (06/30/84) balance in each general ledger account to the trial balance. The *trial balance* is not a financial statement but simply an accountant's tool used to "prove" the equality of the

EXHIBIT 2-2

Accounting Cycle Flow

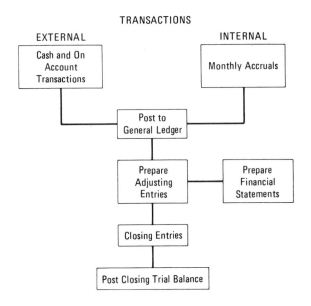

TRANSACTIONS

debits and credits in the general ledger. The trial balance is also a very convenient tool for assembling financial statements. In our case, the financial statements like the general ledger have been prepared electronically.

3. You should now take the time to trace each number on the trial balance for The First Typical Bank to its inclusion on either the June 30 *balance sheet* or the *profit and loss statement* for the month of June.

By performing these three steps, you have essentially gone through the entire accounting cycle outlined in Exhibit 2-2. The particular system that we have used takes a short-cut to the closing process. The *closing* of a set of books is simply the mechanical process of bringing all of the temporary capital accounts to a zero balance. (This is usually only done at the end of the business fiscal year.) If we wanted to close our set of books, all we would do is execute a command that would bring all accounts numbered 4000 and higher to a zero balance. There would be no change in the balances of the accounts numbered 1000 through 3999. If we did this, would our trial balance still balance? To find out, take the time to add up the debit and credit balances on the trial balance for accounts 1000 through 3999 and see if the two totals agree. (On the trial balance, the debit balances are shown as positive numbers while the credit balances are shown as negative. In this fashion the trial balance adds up to a "zero proof". We also save one column width on our trial balance form so it can be printed on standard 8.5 by 11 inch paper.)

GENERAL JOURNAL
AS OF 06/30/84

DATE	JE#	ACCOUNT	DEBIT	CREDIT
06/01/84	1	1000 CURRENCY & COIN	10,000.00	
		3200 COMMON STOCK		5,000.00
		3300 SURPLUS		5,000.00
		SALE OF COMMON STOCK FOR CASH		
06/02/84	2	1101 DUE FROM BANK A---Z	120,000.00	
		2010 DDA-INDIVIDUALS/COS		70,000.00
		2201 SAVINGS & TIME DEPOSITS		50,000.00
		TO RECORD DDA & SAVINGS DEPOSITS		
06/15/84	3	2010 DDA-INDIVIDUALS/COS	3,000.00	
		2201 SAVINGS & TIME DEPOSITS	4,000.00	
		1000 CURRENCY & COIN		7,000.00
		DDA CHECKS CASHED & SAVINGS WITHDR'S		
06/15/84	4	1541 LAND	1,000.00	
		1501 BANK BLDG & IMPR'S-COST	5,000.00	
		1521 FUR & FIX-COST	3,000.00	
		6010 SALARIES & WAGES	1,000.00	
		6040 OTHER EMPLOYEE BENEFITS	500.00	
		6100 OCCUPANCY EXPENSES	300.00	
		2061 OFFICIAL CHECKS (ALL TYPES)		10,800.00
		ISSUE OFFICIAL CHECKS		
06/20/84	5	1000 CURRENCY & COIN	4,000.00	
		1101 DUE FROM BANK A---Z		4,000.00
		CASH TRANS IN		
06/20/84	6	1301 INVESTMENT SEC-FACE	20,000.00	
		1302 UNAMORTIZED PREMIUM-INV	2,000.00	
		2061 OFFICIAL CHECKS (ALL TYPES)		22,000.00
		PURCHASE INVESTMENTS AT A PREMIUM		
06/22/84	7	1401 COMMERCIAL LOANS	40,000.00	
		1421 INSTALLMENT LOANS	15,000.00	
		1423 UNEARNED DISCOUNT-INST LNS		5,000.00
		2061 OFFICIAL CHECKS (ALL TYPES)		50,000.00
		COM'L & INST LN PROCEEDS		
06/22/84	8	1951 PREPAID INSURANCE	3,000.00	
		2061 OFFICIAL CHECKS (ALL TYPES)		3,000.00
		PAYMENT OF INSURANCE PREMIUMS		
06/28/84	9	2061 OFFICIAL CHECKS (ALL TYPES)	85,000.00	
		2010 DDA-INDIVIDUALS/COS	8,000.00	
		1101 DUE FROM BANK A---Z		93,000.00
		CLEARING OF CHECKS ON OUR BANK		
06/30/84	10	1931 INT (& FEES) REC-LOANS	6,000.00	

DATE	JE#	ACCOUNT	DEBIT	CREDIT
		4020 INT & FEES ON LOANS		6,000.00
		TO ACCRUE INT ON COM'L LNS		
06/30/84	11	1423 UNEARNED DISCOUNT-INST LNS	500.00	
		4020 INT & FEES ON LOANS		500.00
		TO RECORD INT ON INST LNS		
06/30/84	12	1901 INT REC-INVESTMENTS	2,000.00	
		4010 INT INCOME-INVESTMENTS		2,000.00
		TO ACCRUE INT ON INVESTMENTS		
06/30/84	13	4010 INT INCOME-INVESTMENTS	50.00	
		1302 UNAMORTIZED PREMIUM-INV		50.00
		TO AMORTIZE PREM ON INVESTMENTS		
06/30/84	14	6200 DEPRECIATION EXPENSE	10.00	
		1502 ACCUM DEPR-BLDG		6.00
		1522 ACCUM DEPR-F&F		4.00
		TO RECORD DEPRECIATION EXP		
06/30/84	15	5000 INT EXP-DEP & DEBT	2,000.00	
		2201 SAVINGS & TIME DEPOSITS		2,000.00
		TO RECORD INT EXP ON SAV & TIME DEP		
06/30/84	16	6900 OTHER OPERATING EXPENSES	600.00	
		2980 ACCOUNTS PAYABLE		600.00
		TO RECORD ACCTS PAYABLE AS OF 6/30		
		TOTAL DEBITS	335,960.00	
		TOTAL CREDITS		335,960.00

ACCT NO	ACCOUNT NAME	FOLIO	FORWARD	MONTH	BALANCE
1000	CURRENCY & COIN		0.00		
	JE # 1	GJ		10,000.00	
	JE # 3	GJ		7,000.00CR	
	JE # 5	GJ		4,000.00	
	CHECKS FOR MONTH	CD		0.00	
					7,000.00
1101	DUE FROM BANK A---Z		0.00		
	JE # 2	GJ		120,000.00	
	JE # 5	GJ		4,000.00CR	
	JE # 9	GJ		93,000.00CR	
					23,000.00
1301	INVESTMENT SEC-FACE		0.00		
	JE # 6	GJ		20,000.00	
					20,000.00
1302	UNAMORTIZED PREMIUM-INV		0.00		
	JE # 6	GJ		2,000.00	
	JE # 13	GJ		50.00CR	
					1,950.00
1401	COMMERCIAL LOANS		0.00		
	JE # 7	GJ		40,000.00	
					40,000.00
1421	INSTALLMENT LOANS		0.00		
	JE # 7	GJ		15,000.00	
					15,000.00
1423	UNEARNED DISCOUNT-INST		0.00		
	JE # 7	GJ		5,000.00CR	
	JE # 11	GJ		500.00	
					4,500.00CR
1501	BANK BLDG & IMPR'S-COST		0.00		
	JE # 4	GJ		5,000.00	
					5,000.00
1502	ACCUM DEPR-BLDG		0.00		
	JE # 14	GJ		6.00CR	
					6.00CR
1521	FUR & FIX-COST		0.00		
	JE # 4	GJ		3,000.00	
					3,000.00
1522	ACCUM DEPR-F&F		0.00		
	JE # 14	GJ		4.00CR	
					4.00CR

18

ACCT NO	ACCOUNT NAME	FOLIO	FORWARD	MONTH	BALANCE
1541	LAND		0.00		
	JE # 4	GJ		1,000.00	
					1,000.00
1901	INT REC-INVESTMENTS		0.00		
	JE # 12	GJ		2,000.00	
					2,000.00
1931	INT (& FEES) REC-LOANS		0.00		
	JE # 10	GJ		6,000.00	
					6,000.00
1951	PREPAID INSURANCE		0.00		
	JE # 8	GJ		3,000.00	
					3,000.00
2010	DDA-INDIVIDUALS/COS		0.00		
	JE # 2	GJ		70,000.00CR	
	JE # 3	GJ		3,000.00	
	JE # 9	GJ		8,000.00	
					59,000.00CR
2061	OFFICIAL CHECKS (ALL TY		0.00		
	JE # 4	GJ		10,800.00CR	
	JE # 6	GJ		22,000.00CR	
	JE # 7	GJ		50,000.00CR	
	JE # 8	GJ		3,000.00CR	
	JE # 9	GJ		85,000.00	
					800.00CR
2201	SAVINGS & TIME DEPOSITS		0.00		
	JE # 2	GJ		50,000.00CR	
	JE # 3	GJ		4,000.00	
	JE # 15	GJ		2,000.00CR	
					48,000.00CR
2980	ACCOUNTS PAYABLE		0.00		
	JE # 16	GJ		600.00CR	
					600.00CR
3200	COMMON STOCK		0.00		
	JE # 1	GJ		5,000.00CR	
					5,000.00CR
3300	SURPLUS		0.00		
	JE # 1	GJ		5,000.00CR	
					5,000.00CR
4010	INT INCOME-INVESTMENTS		0.00		
	JE # 12	GJ		2,000.00CR	

ACCT NO	ACCOUNT NAME	FOLIO	FORWARD	MONTH	BALANCE
	JE # 13	GJ		50.00	
					1,950.00CR
4020	INT & FEES ON LOANS		0.00		
	JE # 10	GJ		6,000.00CR	
	JE # 11	GJ		500.00CR	
					6,500.00CR
5000	INT EXP-DEP & DEBT		0.00		
	JE # 15	GJ		2,000.00	
					2,000.00
6010	SALARIES & WAGES		0.00		
	JE # 4	GJ		1,000.00	
					1,000.00
6040	OTHER EMPLOYEE BENEFITS		0.00		
	JE # 4	GJ		500.00	
					500.00
6100	OCCUPANCY EXPENSES		0.00		
	JE # 4	GJ		300.00	
					300.00
6200	DEPRECIATION EXPENSE		0.00		
	JE # 14	GJ		10.00	
					10.00
6900	OTHER OPERATING EXPENSE		0.00		
	JE # 16	GJ		600.00	
					600.00
	TOTALS		0.00	0.00	0.00

NET INCOME(CR) OR LOSS(DB):   4,040.00CR

RESULTING EARNING AND INCOME TRANSFER ACCOUNTS:

3500	CURRENT YEAR EARNINGS	0.00	4,040.00CR	4,040.00CR
9999	INCOME TRANSFER	0.00	4,040.00	4,040.00

THE FIRST TYPICAL BANK

TRIAL BALANCE
AS OF   06/30/84

ACCOUNT NUMBER	TYPE	ACCOUNT NAME	BALANCE
1000	ASSETS	CURRENCY & COIN	7,000.00
1021	ASSETS	REDEEMED SAVINGS BONDS	0.00
1023	ASSETS	UNPOSTED DEBITS	0.00
1024	ASSETS	TRANSIT ITEMS	0.00
1099	ASSETS	OTHER ITEMS IN COLL	0.00
1101	ASSETS	DUE FROM BANK A---Z	23,000.00
1200	ASSETS	RESERVE ACCT (FED/ST)	0.00
1301	ASSETS	INVESTMENT SEC-FACE	20,000.00
1302	ASSETS	UNAMORTIZED PREMIUM-INV	1,950.00
1303	ASSETS	UNAMORTIZED DISCOUNT-INV	0.00
1398	ASSETS	FEDERAL FUNDS SOLD	0.00
1399	ASSETS	SEC PUR/RESELL AGREE	0.00
1401	ASSETS	COMMERCIAL LOANS	40,000.00
1402	ASSETS	PART SOLD-COM'L LNS	0.00
1403	ASSETS	UNEARNED DISCOUNT-COM'L LNS	0.00
1404	ASSETS	PART PURCHASED-COM'L LNS	0.00
1421	ASSETS	INSTALLMENT LOANS	15,000.00
1423	ASSETS	UNEARNED DISCOUNT-INST LNS	4,500.00-
1440	ASSETS	REAL ESTATE LOANS	0.00
1461	ASSETS	CREDIT CARD LOANS	0.00
1464	ASSETS	IMMEDIATE CR COLL ITEMS	0.00
1465	ASSETS	OVERDRAFTS	0.00
1490	ASSETS	RES FOR POSS LN LOSSES	0.00
1501	ASSETS	BANK BLDG & IMPR'S-COST	5,000.00
1502	ASSETS	ACCUM DEPR-BLDG	6.00-
1521	ASSETS	FUR & FIX-COST	3,000.00
1522	ASSETS	ACCUM DEPR-F&F	4.00-
1541	ASSETS	LAND	1,000.00
1551	ASSETS	LEASEHOLD IMPROVEMENTS	0.00
1552	ASSETS	ACCUM AMORTIZATION-LH IMPR	0.00
1801	ASSETS	REAL ESTATE OWED (NET)	0.00
1840	ASSETS	REPOSSESSIONS	0.00
1850	ASSETS	CASH ITEMS-NOT IN COLL	0.00
1901	ASSETS	INT REC-INVESTMENTS	2,000.00
1921	ASSETS	INT REC-FED FUNDS SOLD	0.00
1922	ASSETS	INT REC-SEC PUR/RESELL	0.00
1931	ASSETS	INT (& FEES) REC-LOANS	6,000.00
1951	ASSETS	PREPAID INSURANCE	3,000.00
1952	ASSETS	PREPAID FDIC ASSESSMENT	0.00
1957	ASSETS	PREPAID RENT	0.00
1979	ASSETS	OTHER PREPAID EXPENSES	0.00
2010	LIABILITIES	DDA-INDIVIDUALS/COS	59,000.00-
2031	LIABILITIES	US TT&L ACCOUNT	0.00
2039	LIABILITIES	OTHER US DDA	0.00
2040	LIABILITIES	DDA-STATE & LOCAL GOVT	0.00
2061	LIABILITIES	OFFICIAL CHECKS (ALL TYPES)	800.00-
2081	LIABILITIES	UNPOSTED CREDITS	0.00
2084	LIABILITIES	UNDISBURSED LOAN PROCEEDS	0.00
2101	LIABILITIES	DUE TO BANK A---Z	0.00
2201	LIABILITIES	SAVINGS & TIME DEPOSITS	48,000.00-
2410	LIABILITIES	FEDERAL FUNDS PURCHASED	0.00

TRIAL BALANCE
AS OF 06/30/84

ACCOUNT NUMBER	TYPE	ACCOUNT NAME	BALANCE
2420	LIABILITIES	SEC SOLD-REPUR AGREE	0.00
2600	LIABILITIES	MORTGAGE DEBT	0.00
2610	LIABILITIES	OTHER LIAB FOR BORROWED MONEY	0.00
2620	LIABILITIES	BORROWINGS FROM FED RES BK	0.00
2820	LIABILITIES	DIVIDENDS PAYABLE	0.00
2841	LIABILITIES	INT PAY-SAV & TIME DEPOSITS	0.00
2931	LIABILITIES	INT PAY-FED FUNDS PUR	0.00
2932	LIABILITIES	INT PAY-SEC SOLD/REPUR AGR	0.00
2935	LIABILITIES	INT PAY ON BORROWED MONEY	0.00
2941	LIABILITIES	INCOME TAXES PAYABLE-FEDERAL	0.00
2951	LIABILITIES	INCOME TAXES PAYABLE-STATE	0.00
2976	LIABILITIES	REAL ESTATE TAXES PAYABLE	0.00
2978	LIABILITIES	OTHER TAXES PAYABLE	0.00
2980	LIABILITIES	ACCOUNTS PAYABLE	600.00-
2990	LIABILITIES	OTHER ACCRUED LIABILITIES	0.00
2999	LIABILITIES	SUBORDINATED DEBT	0.00
3100	CAPITAL	PREFERRED STOCK	0.00
3200	CAPITAL	COMMON STOCK	5,000.00-
3300	CAPITAL	SURPLUS	5,000.00-
3400	CAPITAL	UNDIVIDED PROFITS	0.00
3500	CAPITAL	CURRENT YEAR EARNINGS	4,040.00-
4010	INCOME	INT INCOME-INVESTMENTS	1,950.00-
4020	INCOME	INT & FEES ON LOANS	6,500.00-
5000	EXPENSES	INT EXP-DEP & DEBT	2,000.00
6010	EXPENSES	SALARIES & WAGES	1,000.00
6020	EXPENSES	PAYROLL TAXES	0.00
6030	EXPENSES	GROUP INSURANCE	0.00
6040	EXPENSES	OTHER EMPLOYEE BENEFITS	500.00
6100	EXPENSES	OCCUPANCY EXPENSES	300.00
6200	EXPENSES	DEPRECIATION EXPENSE	10.00
6210	EXPENSES	AMORTIZATION-LH IMPR'S	0.00
6300	EXPENSES	FURNITURE & EQUIP EXPENSES	0.00
6900	EXPENSES	OTHER OPERATING EXPENSES	600.00
8000	INCOME	DDA SERVICE CHARGES	0.00
8010	INCOME	OTHER S/C ON DEPOSITS	0.00
8020	INCOME	OTHER S/C & FEES	0.00
8030	INCOME	OTHER MISC INCOME	0.00
8400	INCOME	SECURITY G/L-(NET)	0.00
8800	EXPENSES	OTHER MISC EXPENSE	0.00
8900	EXPENSES	PROVISION FOR INCOME TAXES	0.00
9999	INCOME	INCOME TRANSFER	4,040.00
	TOTAL		0.00

```
                    THE FIRST TYPICAL BANK
                        BALANCE SHEET
                       JUNE 30, 1984


ASSETS
    CASH & EARNING ASSETS
        CURRENCY & COIN                  7,000.00
        DUE FROM BANK A---Z             23,000.00
        INVESTMENT SEC-FACE             21,950.00
        COMMERCIAL LOANS                40,000.00
        INSTALLMENT LOANS               10,500.00
            TOTAL CASH & EARNING ASSETS                    102,450.00

    FIXED ASSETS
        BANK BLDG & IMPR'S-COST          4,994.00
        FUR & FIX-COST                   2,996.00
        LAND                             1,000.00
            TOTAL FIXED ASSETS                               8,990.00

    OTHER ASSETS
        INT REC-INVESTMENTS              2,000.00
        INT (& FEES) REC-LOANS           6,000.00
        PREPAID INSURANCE                3,000.00
            TOTAL OTHER ASSETS                              11,000.00
                                                        ---------------
            TOTAL ASSETS                                   122,440.00
                                                        ===============


LIABILITIES
    DEPOSIT LIABILITIES
        DDA-INDIVIDUALS/COS             59,000.00
        OFFICIAL CHECKS (ALL TYPES)        800.00
        SAVINGS & TIME DEPOSITS         48,000.00
            TOTAL DEPOSIT LIABILITIES                      107,800.00

    OTHER LIABILITIES
        ACCOUNTS PAYABLE                   600.00
            TOTAL OTHER LIABILITIES                            600.00
                                                        ---------------
            TOTAL LIABILITIES                              108,400.00

CAPITAL
        COMMON STOCK                     5,000.00
        SURPLUS                          5,000.00
        CURRENT YEAR EARNINGS            4,040.00

            TOTAL CAPITAL                                   14,040.00
                                                        ---------------
            TOTAL LIABILITIES & CAPITAL                    122,440.00
                                                        ===============
```

```
                    THE FIRST TYPICAL BANK
                   PROFIT AND LOSS STATEMENT
                       JUNE 30, 1984

                        CURRENT      %      YEAR-TO-DATE    %


INTEREST INCOME
    INT INCOME-INVESTMENTS     1,950.00              1,950.00
    INT & FEES ON LOANS        6,500.00              6,500.00
                            ------------          ------------
        TOTAL                  8,450.00   100.0      8,450.00   100.0

INTEREST EXPENSE
    INT EXP-DEP & DEBT         2,000.00    23.7      2,000.00    23.7
                            ------------          ------------
GROSS PROFIT                   6,450.00    76.3      6,450.00    76.3

OPERATING EXPENSES
    SALARIES & WAGES           1,000.00    11.8      1,000.00    11.8
    OTHER EMPLOYEE BENEFITS      500.00     5.9        500.00     5.9
    OCCUPANCY EXPENSES           300.00     3.6        300.00     3.6
    DEPRECIATION EXPENSE          10.00     0.1         10.00     0.1
    OTHER OPERATING EXPENSES     600.00     7.1        600.00     7.1
                            ------------          ------------
        TOTAL                  2,410.00    28.5      2,410.00    28.5
                            ------------          ------------
INCOME <LOSS>                  4,040.00    47.8      4,040.00    47.8

OTHER INCOME
                            ------------          ------------
        TOTAL                      0.00     0.0          0.00     0.0

OTHER EXPENSES
                            ------------          ------------
        TOTAL                      0.00     0.0          0.00     0.0
                            ------------          ------------
NET INCOME <LOSS>              4,040.00    47.8      4,040.00    47.8
                            ============          ============
```

REVIEW QUESTIONS

1. Normally an asset account will maintain a debit balance.

   A. True

   B. False

2. During a particular accounting period the assets of a bank increased by $488,000. If capital decreased by $50,000 during the same period, then liabilities must have decreased by $438,000.

   A. True

   B. False

3. Balances in temporary capital accounts must be closed out at the end of each business year.

   A. True

   B. False

4. In this unit, only two of the five elements of a complete set of financial statements were illustrated.

   A. True

   B. False

5. Using the columnar headings provided below, show the effect on the accounting equation of each one of the 16 journals given in this unit for The First Typical Bank. You should then add up each column and compare these totals against the balance sheet and profit and loss statement.

JE#	NONEARNING ASSETS	+	EARNING ASSETS	=	LIABIL-ITIES	+	CAPITAL ACCOUNTS PERMANENT	+	(REVENUE-EXPENSE)
1	+10,000						+10,000		

3

CASH AND DUE FROM BANKS

In this unit, I will specifically discuss the following accounts which appear in our Chart of Accounts (Appendix A).

ACC#	TYPE	ACCOUNT NAME	NORMAL BALANCE
1000		CURRENCY & COIN	DEBIT
1021		REDEEMED SAVINGS BONDS	DEBIT
1023		UNPOSTED DEBITS	DEBIT
1024		TRANSIT ITEMS	DEBIT
1099		OTHER ITEMS IN COLL	DEBIT
1101		DUE FROM BANK A—Z	DEBIT
1200		RESERVE ACCT (FED/ST)	DEBIT
2081		UNPOSTED CREDITS	CREDIT
2101		DUE TO BANK A—Z	CREDIT

Before you go on, please fill in the TYPE column above! I will stick to the broad umbrella classifications for other accounts that will be used in this unit (i.e., loans, investments, deposit liabilities, etc.). This will be a consistent policy throughout the text so that you can differentiate accounts that are being introduced, or that have already been introduced, from accounts that are still to be dealt with in detail. This means that by Unit 10 *all* accounts will be displayed with account numbers.

OVERVIEW OF BANK ACCOUNTING OPERATIONS

At this point, we should make an overview of the accounting operations of a bank. The core of a bank accounting system is the *proof department*. Proof receives batches of checks, deposit tickets, etc., from the other bank departments and outside sources like clearinghouses and correspondents. In proof

1. The accuracy of batch totals is "proved".
2. The items are resorted for delivery to subsequent departments where they will be further processed.

In proof, totals are generated for posting to the *general ledger control accounts* with the sorted batches serving as input for posting to the various *subsidiary ledgers*.

Proof operations and sorting procedures will vary from bank to bank depending on the type of equipment used. In one type of operation, the various items coded in proof are sorted into preestablished categories ("pockets"). To give you an idea of the types of documents and sorts, Exhibit 3-1 lists proof sorts for a machine with 24 pockets. The particular bank involved is located in Chicago.

Since the elements of each transaction must be separately sorted and accounted for in proof, including general ledger activity (see pockets 12 and 13 in Exhibit 3-1), single entry tickets must be prepared for every transaction. This expedites the processing and sorting of transactions in proof. This is a fine procedure for teller-generated transactions. Cash is the offsetting debit or credit for all teller transactions. To check that cash on hand agrees with the affect of the other transactions processed, tellers "prove" or balance their individual cash drawers at the end of each day (or shift). In this fashion, the amount of the net change in cash can be posted to the general ledger with only one debit or credit ticket.

These procedures cause some "audit trail" problems in tracing through transactions that do not involve cash; constructing the complete set of debits and credits for such transactions can be a difficult job and may involve the re-creation of the entire set of a day's noncash transactions in order to determine that a particular transaction was properly recorded. To illustrate, just imagine

EXHIBIT 3-1

Example of Proof Machine Pockets

POC #	DEBIT-CREDIT	DESCRIPTION OF ITEMS SORTED TO POCKET
1.	Credit	Deposits and credit memos—checking accounts
2.	Debit	Checks drawn on Chicago banks (FRB 710)—see pocket 14
3.	Debit	Checks drawn on other banks
4.	Debit	On-us check (checks drawn on our bank)
5.	Debit	U.S. Treasury checks
6.	Debit	Tellers' "cash-in" tickets
7.	Credit	Tellers' "cash-out" tickets
8.	Debit	Savings withdrawals
9.	Credit	Savings deposits
10.	Debit	Teller transfer tickets
11.	Credit	Teller transfer tickets
12.	Debit	GENERAL LEDGER DEBIT TICKETS
13.	Credit	GENERAL LEDGER CREDIT TICKETS
14.	Debit	Checks drawn on five specific Chicago banks
15.	Credit	Cashiers checks sold (carbon copies of the checks)
16.	Credit	Money orders sold (carbon copies of the money orders)
17.	Credit	Installment loan payment coupons
18.	Credit	Christmas club deposits
19.	Credit	Golden savings deposits
20.	Debit	Golden savings withdrawals
21.	Credit	New York (Chase bank) drafts (check carbons)
22.	Debit	U.S. savings bonds cashed (redeemed) for customers
23.	Credit	U.S. savings bonds sold to customers
24.	Debit	Mastercard and VISA tickets (from retail stores)

that you had a stack of debit and credit tickets for each one of the 16 typical bank journal entries shown in Unit 2. Take the stack and mix it up in a container and then try to reassemble the tickets for each one of the transactions.

As I pointed out in Unit 2, the use of the general journal form clearly isolates the elements of the transactions that are being discussed, so we will stick with this technique throughout the text.

ACCOUNT DESCRIPTIONS & SAMPLE ENTRIES

1000 CURRENCY & COIN

This is the general ledger control account representing all the currency and coin owned by the bank. Subsidiary ledgers would be as follows:

- vault cash
- teller cash (subledger for each drawer)

SAMPLE ENTRIES:

1000	CURRENCY & COIN	DR	
	#### VARIOUS		CR

To record cash receipts. Main credits, deposit liabilities and loans.

####	VARIOUS	DR	
	1000 CURRENCY & COIN		CR

To record cash payments. Main debits, deposit liabilities.

1000	CURRENCY & COIN	DR	
	1101 DUE FROM BANK A—Z		CR
	or		
	1200 RESERVE ACCT (FED)		CR

To record receipt of cash from correspondent or Fed.

NOTE: Transfer of cash to correspondent or Fed would, of course, be just the opposite.

ACCOUNTS: 1024 TRANSIT ITEMS
1101 DUE FROM BANK A—Z
2101 DUE TO BANK A—Z
1200 RESERVE ACCOUNT (FED/ST)

NOTE: To keep our discussion more straightforward, I am demonstrating the accounting for clearing and correspondent accounts under the "Due From" category.

SAMPLE ENTRIES:

1101	DUE FROM BANK A—Z	DR	
	or		
2101	DUE TO BANK A—Z	DR	
	#### VARIOUS		CR

To record sending of CASH LETTER Main credits—deposit liabilities and loans.

1024	TRANSIT ITEMS	DR	
	#### VARIOUS		CR

To record cash letter to drawee
bank (when collection will take
one or more days).

1101	DUE FROM BANK A—Z	DR	
	1024 TRANSIT ITEMS		CR

To record collection of transit
item.

1200	RESERVE ACCT (FED/ST)	DR	
	#### VARIOUS		CR

To record transfers to the reserve
(federal or state) account.

NOTE: Transfers from would be just the opposite.

ACCOUNTS: 1023 UNPOSTED DEBITS
2081 UNPOSTED CREDITS

The "unposted" accounts usually represent items that will be processed the following day. They are also referred to as holdover items or next day items.

SAMPLE ENTRIES:

1023	UNPOSTED DEBITS	DR	
	1000 CURRENCY & COIN		CR

To record check cashed after
cut-off time.

####	VARIOUS	DR	
	1023 UNPOSTED DEBITS		CR

To record processing of above
check on next work day.

1101	DUE FROM BANK A—Z	DR	
	2081 UNPOSTED CREDITS		CR

To record an unidentified
deposit.

2081   UNPOSTED CREDITS   DR
           # # # # DEPOSIT LIABILITY ACCT   CR
To record above deposit
on next work day.

1021 REDEEMED SAVINGS BONDS

NOTE: This account is given as being representative of the category of cash items in the process of collection. Other items are security interest coupons sent to paying agents for collection, government warrants in collection, etc.

SAMPLE ENTRIES:

1021   REDEEMED SAVINGS BONDS   DR
       1000 CURRENCY & COIN   CR
To record redemption of
US Savings Bonds.

1200   RESERVE ACCT (FED)   DR
       1021 REDEEMED SAVINGS BONDS   CR
To record collection of amount
due on US Savings Bonds from
the US Treasury.

NOTE: Many community banks would handle this entry through their correspondent, rather than directly with the "Fed."

FINANCIAL STATEMENT PRESENTATION

The following GAAP for Cash & Due From is quoted from the proposed AICPA Industry Audit Guide, *Audits of Banks*.

All items included in the...(Cash & Due From)...classifications...are normally included in...(that balance sheet caption). However, material interest-bearing deposits with banks should be disclosed separately in the balance sheet.

Reciprocal due to/from balances should be offset for balance sheet presentation where, under the law, they may be offset in the process of collection or payment. However, before reciprocal balance adjustments are made, due from credit balances should be reclassified as short term borrowings. Similarly, due to debit balances should be reclassified as loans.

Cash items typically include maturing coupons and bonds, petty cash vouchers, returned checks, due bills, unposted debits, and other items temporarily held pending their liquidation. Technically, these items are not in process of collection, and each item requires special handling. Cash items should be recorded in a separate general ledger account, but may be included in the cash-on-hand total in teller funds. In the preparation of financial statements, unposted debits, if material, should be reclassified to the account of ultimate disposition.

INTERNAL CONTROL

There is a complete unit on internal control but before we get there, I will provide a list such as the following for the internal control considerations in each major balance sheet area:

INTERNAL CONTROL POINTS—CASH & DUE FROM

1. Do tellers have exclusive control over their cash funds?
2. Do tellers lock their drawers when away from their stations?
3. Are cash storage facilities adequate?
4. Are cash funds periodically counted on a surprise basis?
5. Are there limits set on teller funds?
6. Is vault cash under dual control?
7. Is the night depository under dual control?
8. Is the holding of noncash items (like petty cash vouchers) limited to a specified teller(s)?
9. Are cash items reviewed daily by appropriate personnel other than the custodian of the items?
10. Is there proper segregation of duties over the issuance of official checks?
11. Are due from/to accounts properly reconciled?
12. Are reconciling items in due from/to accounts promptly and properly followed up on?
13. Are confirmation requests received and answered by an employee other than the one reconciling the account(s)?
14. Are wire transfers controlled by employees other than the ones performing the transaction?

15. Are the "unposted" accounts reviewed by persons independent of the routine handling of the accounts?

This list is not all inclusive. Do you understand why the items listed are important? Could you perhaps add to the list? How about this? On an examination, could you provide say five of the above points and briefly explain the importance of each? Internal control point listings like this are an important tool used by both internal and external bank auditors. You should observe, of course, that a no or negative response to the questions is designed to highlight an undesirable situation.

REVIEW PROJECTS

1. Every industry has its own jargon and banking is no exception. As you should have noted, we have already used quite a bit of jargon. Your understanding of the terms so far will depend on the background you have before getting into this material. What you should do now is prepare a "laundry list" of the terms that you have encountered but are not sure of. Many of the terms should be described in the glossary (Appendix D) while others are detailed in the text material. A good idea would be to write down what you *think* the term(s) mean and then to compare your interpretation with the explanation found in this text or other appropriate reference material. A good starting point for your "other appropriate references" is found in Appendix G.

2. Using your own paper (preferably a two or four column columnar pad) record the following transactions in general journal form. The account numbers and titles should be from the Chart of Accounts (Appendix A) which you should use as your only reference. DO NOT go back into this unit for help now! Do the best you can ON YOUR OWN. After you have made your own best effort, compare your work with the given solutions. A good suggestion would be to highlight your errors in red pencil. DO NOT ERASE your incorrect answers! You will be making many mistakes now (hopefully, fewer as you go on). You will have a project like this at the end of each of the next seven units. You should follow the same procedures described here for each one of these projects!

   A. Record cash deposits of $7,000 to DDA accounts and $4,000 to savings accounts.

   B. Record the cashing of "on us" checks totaling $6,000.

   C. Record the transfer of $3,000 excess currency and coin to correspondent bank.

D. In one journal entry, record a batch of outclearing items which are summarized as follows:

DEBITS

Savings bonds redeemed that will be collected by our correspondent	150
Checks on which the clearing correspondent bank will give immediate credit	12,000
Checks that will take our correspondent several days to collect	1,500
Items that could not be identified for various reasons	200

CREDITS

Savings deposits	3,450
Checking deposits	9,000
Installment loan payments	600
Items that could not be identified for various reasons	800

E. Record the transfer of $8,000 from our correspondent to the "reserve account."

F. Received advice of credit from our correspondent for transit items and savings bonds redeemed submitted in transaction D.

G. Resolved the unpostables from transaction D as follows:

DEBITS

Items on which correspondent will give immediate credit	200

CREDITS

Installment loan payments	300
Checking deposits	350
Savings deposits	150

4
INVESTMENTS

Earning assets are investments and loans. In managing these assets a bank must, of course, maintain sufficient liquidity to meet the obligations to its depositors and other liabilities and be able to adequately meet the loan needs of the community that it serves. Investments in marketable securities are the tools that banks use to maintain liquidity and the vehicles for quickly turning increases in cash and due from accounts into profitable assets.

Here are the accounts from Appendix A that we will be dealing with in this unit.

ACC#	TYPE	ACCOUNT NAME	NORMAL BALANCE
1301	ASSET	INVESTMENT SEC-FACE	DEBIT
1302	ASSET	UNAMORTIZED PREMIUM-INV	DEBIT
1303	ASSET	UNAMORTIZED DISCOUNT-INV	CREDIT

ACC #	TYPE	ACCOUNT NAME	NORMAL BALANCE
1398	ASSET	FEDERAL FUNDS SOLD	DEBIT
1399	ASSET	SEC PUR/RESELL AGREE	DEBIT
1901	ASSET	INT REC-INVESTMENTS	DEBIT
1921	ASSET	INT REC-FED FUNDS SOLD	DEBIT
1922	ASSET	INT REC-SEC PUR/RESELL	DEBIT
2410	LIABILITY	FEDERAL FUNDS PURCHASED	CREDIT
2420	LIABILITY	SEC SOLD-REPUR AGREE	CREDIT
2931	LIABILITY	INT PAY-FED FUNDS PUR	CREDIT
2932	LIABILITY	INT PAY-SEC SOLD/REPUR AGR	CREDIT
4010	INCOME	INT INCOME-INVESTMENTS	CREDIT
5000	EXPENSE	INT EXPENSE-DEP & DEBT	DEBIT
8400	INC/EXP	SECURITY G/L – (NET)	CREDIT/DEBIT

TYPES OF INVESTMENT SECURITIES

Bank investment portfolios may be categorized as follows:

- U.S. Treasury bills, notes, and bonds
- Other U.S. Government Agency Obligations—Government National Mortgage Association, TVA, etc.
- State and Local Government Obligations—bonds, debentures, notes.
- Other Bonds, Notes, and Debentures.

LIQUIDITY OF INVESTMENTS

Since there is a ready market for the types of investments that banks make, they can be quickly (one would hope) converted into cash. Later in this unit, I will discuss the resulting gains or losses (frequently substantial) that can result in selling securities. The point I am making here is that it is much easier to manage the size of the investment portfolio than it is to control the changes and size of the amount of loans. Therefore, the investment portfolio can be viewed as the "buffer" between more or less uncontrollable or unforeseen changes in loan demand and deposit liabilities.

Take the time now to review those components of the Call Report that relate to investments (Appendix B—Schedules B, D and E of the Call Report). You should also read Note 2 on Investment Account Securities that appears in the financial statements for SAMPLE BANK (Appendix C).

Having taken the time to review the above material, you have an idea of the type of subsidiary record detail that must be maintained for regulatory, financial, and managerial accounting purposes. You can also see from Note 2 in Appendix C that some of the investments must be pledged. Therefore, the "buffer" aspect of investments would really be the unpledged portion of the portfolio.

THE ENTRIES

Enough of investment strategy. Now let's get down to making entries. Let's assume that our bank runs its books on a calendar year. On 7-1-80 it purchases a bond of the local sanitary district with a face value of $100,000. The bond is dated on that date and has a term of 10 years. Interest is paid at the end of each calendar quarter at the stated annual rate of 12%. We'll also assume that these are coupon bonds that we will be sending to a correspondent (due from bank—a 1101 account).

7-1-80
1301 INVESTMENT SEC–FACE   DR
         1101 DUE FROM BANK A–Z   CR
         To record the purchase of Clean City
         SD bond through a correspondent bank.

NOTE: The credit also could have been to an "Official Check" liability account or a deposit account of the SD (sanitary district) at our bank. In the case of the purchase of U.S. Treasury securities, the credit could also be directly to our reserve (1200) account.

7-31-80
1901 INT REC–INVESTMENTS   DR
         4010 INT INCOME–INVESTMENTS   CR
         To record interest earned for July
         on SD bond.

Now, this entry bothers many newcomers to accrual accounting. They say, "How can you record anything as earned when you haven't received anything?" The answer is that we certainly have earned the interest and the right to collect it. The above entry reflects this fact. In terms of the accounting equation, this entry is showing an increase in an asset account and an increase in the temporary capital account (4010).

There are two ways to proceed in the accounting for this entry which would, of course, be made on a monthly basis. My preference is to avoid reversing entries at all costs so I won't even explain what a reversing entry is at this time. If you are using this book as a course text, your instructor may love reversing entries. Then, too, many banks may use them so I will leave the topic for classroom discussion. The point I am making is that although there are two simple ways to handle accrual entries, in practice, the two methods should not be mixed. My teaching experience has proven to me that the best thing to do is to present only one of the two methods.

Following my chosen path, the above entry would be repeated each month (until sale or maturity). Therefore, the balance in account 4010 would be $3,000 as of 9-30-80. (Note—It is also very nice to pretend that this was our only investment for purposes of illustration.) The 9-30-80 balance in account 1901 will be   ?

Did you fill in an answer? Also, recall that someone would have to remember to have clipped that first coupon so that the following entry could be made.

9-29-80
1099 OTHER ITEMS IN COLL   DR
      1901 INT REC–INVESTMENTS   CR
      To record the submission of 9-30-80
      interest coupon to collection agent
      for payment (amount $3,000).

So now you know that the balance in 1901 as of 9-30-80 should be ZERO!

Try this little matching quiz just to make sure you have it. The balance in 1901 as of the following dates is:

1. 10-31-80		A. $2,000	
		B. $1,000	
2. 11-30-80		C. $3,000	
		D. $ -0-	
3. 12-31-80		E. $6,000	

Your answers should have been B, A, and D, respectively. If they were, that's good. You are ready to go on!

SECURITIES PURCHASED BETWEEN INTEREST PAYMENT DATES

To demonstrate the case of purchasing securities other than on an interest payment date (which is usually the case), let's assume that the Clean City bond was not purchased until 9-1-80. We will also continue to assume that the bond sold at face value.

9-1-80

1901	INT REC–INVESTMENTS	2,000	
1301	INVESTMENT SEC–FACE	100,000	
	1101 DUE FROM BANK A–Z		102,000

To record purchase of Clean City
SD bond through a correspondent bank.

The $2,000 debit represents the accrued interest on the bond as of the purchase date. The seller is the one who has earned this amount but, since we are buying the coupon, we will be the ones that will collect on the coupon. Now, of course, one way to solve this problem would be to have "fractional coupons" so that the seller would tear off his portion and leave the buyer with the remainder of the coupon. This would tend to make the bond market very unmanageable. The way the problem is solved is simply to have the buyer pay the seller his accrued interest as of the date of purchase and allow the buyer to redeem the next coupon in full.

NOTE: This accrued interest that the buyer pays to the seller is often referred to as "purchased interest." An account bearing this title is often used. When it is used, this account would be debited for the accrued interest at the time of purchase. When using a "purchased interest" account, the redemption of the first coupon could be recorded as follows:

9-29-80

1099	OTHER ITEMS IN COLL	3,000	
	1901 INT REC–INVESTMENTS		1,000
	####"PURCHASED INTEREST"		2,000

Since there is no difference between the nature and balance sheet classification of 1901 and "purchased interest", my preference is to just use the 1901 account. I think you might agree with me that just using the 1901 account is easier. My bank audit experience has also shown me that the "purchased interest" account, when used, is one of the most likely accounts to be handled improperly.

BOND PREMIUM AND DISCOUNT

With the Clean City bond we made the simplified, but unusual, assumption that the bond sold at its face amount. This means that the interest rate in the bond market for that type of security happened to be the same as the stated rate of interest on the bond instrument. Had the market rate of interest been in excess of the stated rate the bond would have sold for an amount less than the face value. This amount is referred to as the *discount*. If the bond market rate of interest had been less than the stated rate, the bond would have sold for an amount greater than the face of the bond. This amount in excess of the face value is (you guessed it!) called the *premium*.

To understand *bond premium* and *discount* you must also appreciate that bond issuers have no control over the market rate of interest that they will have to pay in order to sell their bond issues. The bond market, much like the stock market, establishes the rates of interest that determine the ultimate purchase price of the securities.

You also have to appreciate that a bond is nothing more than a long-term promissory note. Since it is long term, the bond or note must stipulate the times (semi-annually, quarterly, etc.) at which interest will be paid and indicate or state a rate of interest. (The amount of each interest payment is, of course, determined by multiplying the stated rate times the face or principal amount of the bond.)

A bond, therefore, creates two obligations for the issuer:

1. To pay the face or principal amount of the bond at maturity.
2. To pay fixed amounts of interest on a periodic basis over the life of the bond. All of you mathematical geniuses will instantly recognize this obligation as an ordinary annuity. For the other 99% of us, an *annuity* is a string of payments of equal amounts made at regular intervals. Therefore, the interest payments on our Clean City bond can be considered an ordinary annuity of 40 periods (quarters) with a payment amount of $1,000.

We could demonstrate, by reference to appropriate mathematical tables for present values, that the initial price of a bond can be determined by computing the present value of the payment of the face value of the bond and the present value of the annuity represented by the interest payments. If we go through these computations using the stated bond interest rate, the total of these two amounts will be equal to the face value of the bond. If we use an interest rate greater than the stated rate, the total will be *less* than the face value of the bond (a discount). Alternatively, using an interest rate of less than the stated rate will give you a bond price *in excess* of the face value (a premium).

The premium or discount is simply an adjustment in the selling price of the bond necessary to compensate for the difference between the market and stated rates of bond interest. Both the buyer and issuer of the bond must contend with the premium and discount on their books. To the buyer or purchaser of the bond, the amount of premium or discount affects the reported amount of interest income. To the issuer, the premium or discount is an adjustment to the reported amount of interest expense.

The following entries illustrate the accounting for premiums:

```
7-1-80
1301  INVESTMENT SEC–FACE              100,000
1302  UNAMORTIZED PREMIUM–INV            1,800
      1101 DUE FROM BANK A–Z                        101,800
      To record the purchase of Clean
      City bond–Market rate under 12%.
```

The entry to "write off" or amortize bond premium is:

```
XX-XX-XX
4010  INT INCOME–INVESTMENTS               DR
      1302 UNAMORTIZED PREMIUM–INV                    CR
```

Premiums should be amortized over the remaining life of the bond issue, based on the fixed maturity date or the estimated life of the contract, such as in the case of GNMA modified pass-through certificates.

The two methods of amortizing both premiums and discounts are the straight-line method and the interest or effective rate method. The interest method is the preferred method since it results in showing a constant yield (the market interest rate at the time of purchase) over the holding period of the security. The straight-line method has the merit of being simple, but should not be used if it would give income materially different than the preferred interest method.

Since the two methods of handling premiums and discounts are the same from a bookkeeping viewpoint, we'll leave the joys of the interest method for potential classroom discussion and continue here with the straight-line method.

Under the straight-line method, and assuming the bank is making monthly adjusting entries, how much of the Clean City premium would be amortized each month? Check your answer against this entry.

```
7-31-80
4010  INT INCOME—INVESTMENTS                $15
      1302 UNAMORTIZED PREMIUM—INV                    $15
      To amortize bond premium for
      July 80.
```

The *carrying value* of the bond as of 7-31-80 would be computed as follows:

Balance account 1301	$100,000
PLUS Balance account 1302	1,785
Carrying Value 7-31-80	$101,785

It is the difference between the carrying value and the (net) selling price of the security that determines the amount of gain or loss upon sale of the security. Therefore, any time a security is sold, the related premium or discount must be amortized to the date of sale.

Let's assume that we held the Clean City bond until maturity.

1. What would be the carrying value as of 6-30-85?
2. How much interest income was reported on the bond in 1980?
3. How much interest income was reported on the bond in 1981?
4. How much interest income was reported on the bond in 1990?
5. How much interest was earned on the bond over the ten years?
6. Does this look like a good entry to record the collection of the maturity value?

1101 DUE FROM BANK A–Z	100,000	
1301 INVESTMENT SEC–FACE		100,000

Here are the answers. How did you do?

1. $100,900
2. $ 5,910
3. $ 11,820
4. $ 5,910
5. $118,200
6. This is a good entry.

DISCOUNTS

To illustrate discounts, let's assume that the Clean City bond was purchased when the market rate of interest was higher than 12%.

7-1-80

1301	INVESTMENT SEC–FACE	100,000	
	1303 UNAMORTIZED DISCOUNT–INV		2,400
	1101 DUE FROM BANK A–Z		97,600

To record purchase of bond
at a discount.

NOTE: Historically, regulations did not permit recognition of bond discounts. The thought was that this was an increase in assets and earnings that may never be recognized. This thinking is now changed, and banks with footings over $25 million must recognize discounts. The amount of such discount (which is part of interest income) must be separately disclosed when material. (*material* being 5% or more of total investment income). Many bank accounting systems refer to the accretion of discount. Under this procedure, the investment account is debited for the initial cost of the bond and a separate balance sheet account is debited for the amount of the discount taken into income. The procedure illustrated here is more common to the practice of nonbanking firms. This procedure is adopted here since it is consistent with the approach shown for premiums and should, therefore, be more straightforward for the newcomer.

7-31-80

1303	UNAMORTIZED DISCOUNT	DR?	
	4010 INT INCOME–INVESTMENTS		CR?

To record amortization of discount
for July.

Take the time now to figure out the carrying value of the bond *before* looking at the computation that follows.

The carrying value of the bond as of 7-31-80 would be $97,620 computed as follows:

$100,000	7-31-80 balance-account 1301
2,380	LESS 7-31-80 balance in account
	1303 (2,400-20)
$ 97,620	

Here are some other questions for you to check out. (I hope they look familiar.)

1. What would the carrying value be as of 6-30-85?
2. How much interest income was reported on the bond in 1980?
3. How much interest income was reported on the bond in 1981?

4. How much interest income was reported on the bond in 1990?

5. How much interest was earned over the ten years?

6. What would be the entry to record the redemption of the bond at maturity?

As in the previous questions for premiums, STOP NOW and work out your own answers before checking these out.

1. $ 98,800
2. $ 6,120
3. $ 12,240
4. $ 6,120
5. $122,400
6. The entry would be the same as the entry given for the premium example!

SECURITY GAINS AND LOSSES

Security gains and losses come about when the bond or other investment is sold prior to maturity. Let's go back to the Clean City bond example where a premium was involved and assume the bond was sold on 7-31-85, at 106.

1101	DUE FROM BANK A–Z	107,000	
	1901 INT REC–INVESTMENTS		1,000
	1302 UNAMORTIZED PREMIUM–INV		885
	1301 INVESTMENT SEC–FACE		100,000
	8400 SECURITY G/L (NET)		5,115

To record sale of bond at a gain.

Now it's your turn! Assume that the Clean City bond we purchased with a 2,400 discount was sold on 7-31-85 at 95. Prepare the entry to record the 7-31-85 sale at 90.

8400	SECURITY G/L (NET)	8,800	
1101	DUE FROM BANK A–Z	91,000	
1303	UNAMORTIZED DISCOUNT–INV	1,200	
	1301 INVESTMENT SEC–FACE		100,000
	1901 INT REC–INVESTMENTS		1,000

To record sale of bond at a loss.

FEDERAL FUNDS AND REPURCHASE/REVERSE REPURCHASE AGREEMENTS

The "federal funds" market is a result of the Federal Reserve System. It provides a means for banks with excess reserves to lend those funds to banks needing additional reserve balances. The Fed funds market thus helps to efficiently distribute the reserve balances of the member banks of the Federal Reserve System. The following write-up on federal funds is from Chapter 9 of the proposed AICPA audit guide for banks.

The following types of federal funds transactions are commonly used:

UNSECURED LOAN.
The selling bank sells federal funds on one day and is repaid on the following day, or at the maturity of the term, whichever is applicable.

COLLATERALIZED TRANSACTION,
OTHER THAN BY REPURCHASE AGREEMENTS.
A bank purchasing federal funds places U.S. Government securities in a custody account for the seller until the funds are repaid.

REPURCHASE/REVERSE REPURCHASE AGREEMENTS.
The bank selling federal funds does so by buying U.S. Government securities from the borrowing bank or dealer in U.S. securities for immediate cash delivery. On the agreed date, usually the following day, the borrower repurchases the securities at the same price plus interest at a predetermined rate. These transactions are referred to as securities sold under agreements to repurchase (repos) by the borrowing banks, and securities purchased under reverse repurchase agreements (reverse repos— also known as resell agreements) by the lending bank.

In addition to buying and selling funds to meet their own needs, banks with correspondent banking relationships absorb or provide funds as a service or accommodation to their correspondent banks. The larger accommodating banks operate on both sides of the market on the same day. Transactions between correspondent banks usually clear through the Federal Reserve System.

Many banks, particularly banks that maintain trading accounts, . . . use repo/reverse repo transactions for purposes other than the purchase and sale of federal funds. Since the sale of securities under a repo agreement is, in substance, a loan to the selling bank collateralized by the securities that are repurchased, it is not unusual for a bank to use this tool for financing its trading portfolio and for other purposes, depending on prevailing interest rates. Conversely, banks may enter into reverse repos as a lending accommodation to their corporate customers.

ACCOUNTING.
Separate general ledger control accounts are usually maintained for federal funds sold, federal funds purchased, securities purchased under reverse repo agreements, and securities sold under repo agreements. Depending on the extent of these transactions, the control accounts are supported by some form of subsidiary records. These records normally include: (1) written repo/reverse repo agreement, (2) names of the banks involved in the transactions, (3) interest rates, (4) methods of payment, (5) settlement dates, and (6) identification of securities is subject to repo/reverse repo agreements. Accounting for repo and reverse repo transactions is currently being studied by certain AICPA committees. Any pronouncement ultimately issued is expected to be applicable to banks.

When federal funds transactions occur, no physical transfer of funds takes place. The Federal Reserve merely charges the seller's reserve balance and credits the buyer's reserve balance. The respective banks then charge or credit federal funds sold/purchased, offsetting the entry by a charge or credit to their reserve accounts with the appropriate Federal Reserve Bank.

FINANCIAL STATEMENT PRESENTATION.
Federal funds transactions should be stated gross rather than net in the balance sheet. Since securities sold/purchased subject to repo/reverse repo agreements are, in substance, short-term loans borrowings, it is permissable to combine federal funds sold with securities purchased under reverse repo agreements and federal funds purchased with securities sold under repo agreements.

Following are the journal entries that would be involved on both sides of a federal funds transaction. The principal amount is $1,000,000 and we will assume the interest for the day the funds were out was $500.

ENTRIES TO RECORD FEDERAL FUNDS LOAN

9-1-X1	BORROWING BANK		
1200	RESERVE ACCOUNT (FED/ST)	1,000,000	
	2410 FEDERAL FUNDS PURCHASED		1,000,000
9-1-X1	LENDING BANK		
1398	FEDERAL FUNDS SOLD	1,000,000	
	1200 RESERVE ACCOUNT (FED/ST)		1,000,000

ENTRIES TO RECORD SETTLEMENT OF FEDERAL FUNDS LOAN

9-2-X1	BORROWING BANK		
2410	FEDERAL FUNDS PURCHASED	1,000,000	
XXXX	INTEREST EXPENSE (5000 series account)	500	
	1200 RESERVE ACCOUNT (FED/ST)		1,000,500
9-2-X1	LENDING BANK		
1200	RESERVE ACCOUNT (FED/ST)	1,000,500	
	1398 FEDERAL FUNDS SOLD		1,000,000
	4010 INT INCOME–INVESTMENTS		500

FINANCIAL STATEMENT PRESENTATION OF INVESTMENTS

Investment account securities are usually carried at cost rather than the lower of cost or market. The reasoning is that it is assumed that securities will be held until maturity and, therefore, interim changes in the market values should not be disclosed. The entire area of valuation of investments for all types of firms is a very controversial issue in GAAP. It suffices to say for the scope of this text that the debate will probably continue, thus, leaving this area in limbo. Observe in Appendix C that the 12-31-78 carrying value of SAMPLE BANK's investments is $609,000 below the market value. This is over 6% of stockholders' equity.

The "NET" in account 8400 means that security gains and losses are reported after (or net) of taxes. This is another approach that is customary industry practice. If you look at the Statements of Income for SAMPLE BANK in Appendix C, you will see that it had security gains of $65,000, net of tax, in 1978. The pretax gain was $131,000. This text has complete units on both the income statement and bank taxation so we will be seeing more of these aspects of income reporting later.

Many banks provide supplemental data on their investments to further aid the users of the financial statements. Among these items could be:

1. Average maturities
2. Book value
3. Yields on a tax-equivalent basis
4. Concentration of investments by industry/issuer or other major classifications

INTERNAL CONTROL POINTS—INVESTMENTS

1. Are security purchases approved by the board of directors or other appropriate group?
2. Is the board provided with informative reports on investment activity and status?
3. Is there proper segregation of duties relative to accounting entries and the related investment transactions?
4. Are securities under dual control?
5. Are proper physical inventories of securities taken?
6. Is there appropriate segregation of bank and nonbank securities, such as collateral or trust securities?
7. Are securities held in safekeeping by others periodically verified and inventoried?
8. Is there adequate follow up exercised over individual security transactions?
9. Is there sufficient testing of recorded earnings and accrued interest receivable?

REVIEW PROJECT

Record the following transactions in general journal form.

A. Purchase a 12% bond with a face value of $10,000 at 90 plus accrued interest of $100. The purchase was made through our correspondent.
B. Accrue two months interest on the bond purchased in transaction A.
C. Amortize six months of discount on the bond purchased in transaction A. Assume the bond has a 10 year term.
D. Record the submission of the coupon for collection of one quarter's interest on the bond purchased in transaction A.
E. Assume the bond purchased in transaction A was sold at 95 immediately after collecting all interest due thereon. Don't forget to zero out the balance in account 1303 related to the bond. (See transactions A and C.)

5
LOANS

Clearly, the most significant bank assets are its loans. In today's economic environment, it is difficult to talk about the typical bank loan. In order to meet the competition of nonbank lenders and the needs of their loan customers, banks have to be flexible and creative in putting together loan packages. This would be a good time for you to review Schedule A of the Call Report that is reproduced in Appendix B. For our purposes, we will classify loans according to the following breakdown:

1. Single payment at maturity.
2. Installment-type loans.
3. Real estate loans.

Here are the accounts that we will review from our Chart of Accounts:

ACC#	TYPE	ACCOUNT NAME	NORMAL BALANCE
1401	ASSET	COMMERCIAL LOANS	DEBIT
1402	ASSET	PART SOLD—COM'L LNS	CREDIT
1403	ASSET	UNEARNED DISCOUNT—COM'L LNS	CREDIT
1404	ASSET	PART PURCHASED—COM'L LNS	DEBIT
1421	ASSET	INSTALLMENT LOANS	DEBIT
1423	ASSET	UNEARNED DISCOUNT—INST LNS	CREDIT
1440	ASSET	REAL ESTATE LOANS	DEBIT
1461	ASSET	CREDIT CARD LOANS	DEBIT
1464	ASSET	IMMEDIATE CR COLL ITEMS	DEBIT
1465	ASSET	OVERDRAFTS	DEBIT
1490	ASSET	RES FOR POSS LN LOSSES	CREDIT
1931	ASSET	INT (& FEES) REC—LOANS	DEBIT
4020	INCOME	INT & FEES ON LOANS	CREDIT

THE OPERATING CYCLE

Accountants think of the operating cycle in *any* business as the cycle of the conversion of cash into goods or services that are then sold to customers, hopefully, for a profit. The customers will then (again, we hope) pay for the goods or services, which completes the operating cycle. An understanding of the operating cycle of a business is essential to anyone attempting to understand its accounting system. Exhibit 5-1 illustrates the operating cycle in banking.

EXHIBIT 5-1

Bank Operating Cycle

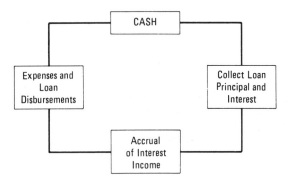

Before we get into specific accounting procedures for loans, you should review and keep in mind the following terminology and regulatory considerations.

- *Regulations* set limits on the maximum amount of a loan. Good management of the loan portfolio should dictate limits on loans to individual borrowers, as well as limits on loans within geographic areas and or individual industries.
- *Liability ledger* is banking jargon to describe records that are maintained summarizing the loan status (past and present) of individual borrowers.
- *Collateralized loans* are supported by borrowers' signature and specific assets of the borrower and are referred to as "secured". Collateral can take many forms, such as negotiable securities, inventory, growing crops, etc.
- *Noncollateralized loans* are supported only by the borrowers' signature and are referred to as "unsecured".
- *Guaranteed loans* are loans that are endorsed by third parties.

SINGLE PAYMENT LOANS

Single payment loans may be either on a short-term basis (60 to, say, 180 day maturities) or on a long-term basis. Long-term loans would provide for the periodic payment of interest as well as the payment of the loan principal at maturity just like bonds described in Unit 4.

The following series of entries for single payment loans forms the basic pattern of entries for all types of loans. You should also observe where these entries would fit in the bank operating cycle (Exhibit 5-1).

ENTRY TO RECORD DISBURSEMENT OF LOAN PROCEEDS

1401 COMMERCIAL LOANS	DR	
####VARIOUS*		CR

*Account credited would depend on the mode of the disbursement.

INTERNAL ENTRY TO RECORD ACCRUAL OF INTEREST

This entry could be prepared on a daily, weekly, or monthly basis. All accruals of interest should be brought up to date whenever financial statements are to be prepared.

1931 INT (& FEES) REC—LOANS   DR
    4020 INT & FEES ON LOANS   CR

ENTRIES FOR THE COLLECTION OF LOAN PRINCIPAL & INTEREST

On long-term loans, the periodic interest payments would be recorded as follows. (**NOTE:**   As in Unit 4, we are not utilizing reversing entries.)

VARIOUS*   DR
    1931 INT (& FEES) REC—LOANS   CR

The next entry is to record receipt of loan principal and interest at maturity as in the case of a short-term, single payment loan.

VARIOUS*   DR
    1401 COMMERCIAL LOANS   CR
    1931 INT (& FEES) REC—LOANS   CR

*Account debited would depend on the mode of payment.

PARTICIPATION LOANS

Banks may find it necessary, due to loan limits, or desirable, due to loan concentration considerations, to sell off a portion of a loan to another bank(s). Take the case of a large corporate borrower who is dealing with a local community bank located near a new plant site. The community bank is asked to lend $3 million to finance the construction of the plant. Assuming the community bank had a lending limit of $500,000, it would have to "participate out" at least $2.5 million. Depending on the bank's liquidity and/or the make up of its existing loan portfolio, it may participate out more than the $2.5 million.

We will further assume that the community bank will serve as the "lead bank" in this loan. It will, therefore, service the loan and be responsible for the documentation required of the loan customer. Although various types of loans can be "participated in or out", the basic accounting can be illustrated by assuming that our loan here is a six-month, single-pay-type loan.

The accounting for the bank(s) participating in the loan is very straightforward. Just go back to the previous entries illustrated under single payment loans and substitute account 1404 (participations purchased) for 1401.

The accounting for participations sold (1402) goes like this:

1401 COMMERCIAL LOANS	$3 million	
1402 PART SOLD—COM'L LNS		$2.5 million
####VARIOUS		.5 million

This entry shows the net effect on the books at the time the loan proceeds are disbursed. Actually, several transactions occur at this time.

1. Funds are transferred to the lead bank by the participants ($2.5 million in our example).
2. The lead bank disburses the full loan proceeds to the customer.

Here is the entry to record the accrual of interest on the loan:

1931 INT (& FEES) REC—LOANS	DR	
2101 DUE TO BANK A—Z		CR
4020 INT & FEES ON LOANS		CR

True or False? If the debit in the above entry was $60,000, the credit to 4020 would be $10,000.

If you said true, you have the idea. If not, consider how much of the total interest on the loan the lead bank has a claim to. Well, it sold off $2.5 million or 5/6ths of the loan so, therefore, it retained a 1/6th interest in the loan, and 1/6th of $60,000 is $10,000.

This is what happens at maturity.

#### Appropriate "CASH" account	DR	
1401 COMMERCIAL LOANS		CR
1931 INT (& FEES) REC—LOANS		CR
To record receipt of maturity value of loan from customer.		

Now, of course, we need to pay off the participating banks.

1402 PART SOLD—COM'L LNS	DR	
####Appropriate "CASH" account		CR

DISCOUNT LOANS

So far we have been considering single payment loans where the borrower pays both the principal and interest either in periodic payments or at maturity. A discount or discounted loan is one on which both the maturity value and the face, or principal, amount of the loan are the same. At the time of the disbursement of the loan, the interest is computed on the loan for its term and deducted from the principal amount of the loan to arrive at the "net proceeds" to be paid to the borrower. This means that, although the borrower is paying interest on the full amount of the loan, he only has use of the net proceeds over the term of the loan. Because of this feature of discount loans, the actual or effective interest rate will always be greater than the stated rate of interest on the note. This difference between stated and effective interest rates will be more fully discussed in the section on installment lending since that is where the difference is most significant.

For purposes of illustration, we will use a discount note with a principal amount of $100,000 at a stated rate of 12% for one year. The bank updates its interest accruals on a monthly basis.

7-1-XX
1401 COMMERCIAL LOANS $100,000
          1403 UNEARNED DISCOUNT—COM'L LNS $12,000
          ####VARIOUS $88,000
      To record discount loan proceeds.

7-31-XX
1403 UNEARNED DISCOUNT—COM'L LNS $1,000
          4020 INT & FEES ON LOANS $1,000
      To record amortization of unearned
      discount for July.

This entry would be repeated each month for 11 more months. When the loan was paid off at maturity, the following entry would be made.

6-30-XX
VARIOUS $100,000
          1401 COMMERCIAL LOANS $100,000

If the loan permitted early payment, the "pay-off" balance would be the principal less the portion of the discount that was still unearned as of the pay-off date. You will see more of this in the next section on installment loans.

INSTALLMENT LOANS

An installment loan is nothing more than a discount note that calls for the borrower to pay off the face of the note in equal monthly installments over the life of the loan. Installment lending can be made to both businesses and individuals but the prevalent use of installment lending is at the retail or consumer credit level. Individuals will make installment loans to finance purchases of many types of products but, as is probably the case with most of the users of this text, it is the acquisition of an automobile for which most individuals take out installment loans. Usually, then, these loans are secured loans. When the customer comes in "off the street" to apply for the loan, we have an example of what the banker calls direct paper, or a direct loan. Many banks have agreements with auto dealers by which the car buyer can make all the arrangements for the loan with the dealer. It should be no surprise that we call such loans *indirect paper*.

When banks accept indirect paper arrangements with auto dealers, they will also frequently finance the dealer's car inventory. This is called *floor plan financing*. Since the inventory is the collateral for the loan, the repayment agreement will stipulate that the floor plan loan be paid off as each unit is sold from inventory.

This narrative gave you a general understanding of installment lending and showed how lending terms are designed to meet the needs of specific customers. Now let's move on to the accounting—

Installment Loan Situation

Amount to be financed	$1,200
"Add-on" rate 10%	
One year term	
Finance charge	120
Amount of loan	$1,320

Annual percentage rate (APR)	approx.	20%

I have deliberately kept this example very simple to get across the basic concepts of the accounting for unearned discount and the approximate computation of the APR. The alternative is to keep an eye on mathematical detail and, consequently, lose sight of the basic theory.

This is the entry to record the disbursement of the loan:

```
6-1-XX
1421  INSTALLMENT LOANS                        $1,320
         1423 UNEARNED DISCOUNT—INST LNS                 $120
         ####VARIOUS                                   $1,200
```

Let's assume that the first payment date is $7-1-XX$. The entry to record that payment, as well as the other 11 payments, would be as follows:

VARIOUS $110
      1421 INSTALLMENT LOANS $110

The form of the entry to amortize, or take into income, the amount of unearned discount looks like this:

1423 UNEARNED DISCOUNT—INST LNS   DR
      4020 INT & FEES ON LOANS   CR

Easy so far? Now the only problem is to figure out the dollar amounts for the last entry. One thing you know is that if we add up all 12 entries, they total $120. Now, if we used the straight-line method that we used in Unit 4 to amortize bond premium and discount, the monthly amount would be $10. However, what did we say about the straight-line method for bond premiums and discounts? You cannot use it if the method would yield income materially different from the effective interest method.

The effective interest or APR on our sample loan is approximately 20%. How? Look at Exhibit 5-2.

EXHIBIT 5-2

Approximated Computation of APR on Installment Loan

The customer borrowed	$1,200
The customer is paying interest of	$120
If the customer had the use of the $1,200 over the full term of the loan, the $120 would represent	10%
The amount that the customer had the use of was	$600
The APR is, therefore, approximately	20%

Based on the facts presented in Exhibit 5-2, I will next explain *The Rule of 78's*, which is nothing more than a simple way of computing the amount of unearned interest to be "taken into income". The use of this method gives results that do approximate the APR being earned on installment loans. Look at the following to understand this point:

For the month of June the bank has
this invested in the loan $1,200

Therefore, the amount to be recorded
as income in June based on the
APR would be 1,200 X 20% X 1/12 $20

In July the bank would recover 1/12
of the amount it has invested,
and the July interest earned would be approximately. $18

Using The Rule of 78's the interest income to
be recorded for June and July would be—

JUNE ($120 x 12) / 78 = $18.46

JULY ($120 x 11) / 78 = $16.92

In many states, banks are allowed to compute the pay-off balance on installment loans by using what has been traditionally called The Rule of 78's. Under this procedure, the customer who pays off an installment loan early is rebated unearned interest on a sliding scale rather than on a prorata basis.

For example, on a prorata basis the customer in our loan example would be rebated $110 if he paid off the loan after one month. This would leave the bank with earnings of $10 for the month on the loan or only 10%. Under the 78's method, the bank's earned portion of the interest is computed by multiplying the total interest on the loan times a fraction. The denominator is the sum of the total of months of the loan. If you do it the long way by adding $1+2+3$...etc. $+12$, you get 78. (Now you know why they call it The Rule of 78's.)

If you have a 36- or 48-month loan, it is handy to have the formula for getting the sum of a string of digits starting with the number one. Here it is, but please don't worry, I will not give or expect you to know the derivation. Just use the formula as a handy tool.

$$\text{The sum of 1 through } N = N \times (N+1) / 2$$

N is the last number in the string or series of digits.
Here it is with 1 through 12:

$$78 = 12 \times (12+1) / 2$$

Try it with 1 through 36 and 1 through 48. You should get 666 and 1176, respectively.

The numerator of our earnings fraction is the sum of the expired months, in reverse order that is. In our one month pay-off example, the fraction would, therefore, be 12/78. For the first month, then, the bank would be allowed to earn $18.46 (12/78 x 120). The 18.46 works out to just over 18% earnings for the bank on the $1,200 it had invested in the loan.

Many people (especially loan customers) feel that the 78's method of rebating is unfair. Hopefully, truth-in-lending legislation and increased borrower understanding have reduced abuses in interest rate disclosures and manipulation. The customer in our example would have had the 20% interest rate on the loan disclosed to him at the time the loan was made. Hopefully, consumers know that APR is the true cost of borrowing. Under the 78's method, the customer wound up paying just over 18%, almost two points less than he or she signed up for. My last comment on the social implications of The Rule of 78's is that some states and banks dropped "add on interest" types of loans altogether, apparently, in the realization that the day of advertising 3% auto loans and really earning twice that is gone forever.

Now, if you understand the 78's method, in the second month of the loan (July) the bank will record 11/78 of the $120 as interest income on the loan. For the two months, or on a cumulative basis, 23/78's of the interest is considered earned by the bank and 55/78's is still considered as unearned.

REAL ESTATE LOANS

With today's rapidly changing interest rate structures and "creative financing" (as realtors call it) of real estate, it seems like an exercise in ancient history to discuss real estate loans. It is the traditional real estate loan with its long-term and fixed rate of interest that places financial institutions with large portfolios of these loans into financial difficulty. What happens, of course, is that inflation drives the cost of funds for financial institutions over the yield of the loan portfolio. What we have today as a replacement for the traditional real estate loan are floating rate mortgages and mortgages with renegotiable terms. I have provided here the basic accounting for the traditional mortgage loan. Accounting for the newer types of mortgages would be variations on this basic accounting.

```
6-1-XX
1440    REAL ESTATE LOANS                          DR
####    (balance due from buyer)                   DR
          ####(escrow funds)                              CR
          ####(loan fees/points)                          CR
          ####(balance due seller and/or others)          CR
        To record disbursement of real estate
        loan.
```

EXHIBIT 5-3

Loan Amortization Schedule

LOAN PRINCIPAL $10,000
TERM   18 months
INTEREST RATE   18%
MONTHLY PAYMENT $638.06

PMT #	INTEREST	PRINCIPAL REDUCTION	MONTH END BALANCE
1	150.00	488.06	9511.94
2	142.68	495.38	9016.56
3	135.25	502.81	8513.75
4	127.71	510.35	8003.40
5	120.05	518.01	7485.39
6	112.28	525.78	6959.61
7	104.39	533.67	6425.94
8	96.39	541.67	5884.27
9	88.26	549.80	5334.47
10	80.02	558.04	4776.43
11	71.65	566.41	4210.02
12	63.15	574.91	3635.11
13	54.53	583.53	3051.58
14	45.77	592.29	2459.29
15	36.89	601.17	1858.12
16	27.87	610.19	1247.93
17	18.72	619.34	628.59
18	9.43	628.63	−.04

To continue our illustration, Exhibit 5-3 shows a loan amortization schedule. As you can see, the loan amount is for $10,000 over 18 months at 18%. (Please forgive the .04 rounding on the final payment.)

Assuming that these were the terms of the loan we booked on 6 – 1, here is how we could record the interest for June.

6-30-XX
1931 INT (& FEES) REC—LOANS $150
      4020 INT & FEES ON LOANS $150
      To record June interest—see
      above amortization schedule
      for detail.

To continue, if the first payment was on 7-1-XX, here is how we could record it.

7-1-XX

(payment) $638.06
      1440 REAL ESTATE LOANS $488.06
      1931 INT (& FEES) REC—LOANS $150.00

Here we have given just the basic overview of accounting for real estate loans. Other points that might be explored in the classroom environment are as follows:

1. Timing of collection of interest.
2. Capitalization of interest and other charges.
3. Escrow accounts
    a. Maintenance of current insurance and taxes on property.
    b. Interest on escrow.
4. Foreclosure

CREDIT CARD LOANS

In the early 1960s, banks entered the consumer credit market by issuing their own system of personal credit cards. According to some researchers in banking, if the industry had to make the decision to enter this market again, it probably would not do so. It took years of red ink to learn how to manage consumer credit. Here are some of the problems of managing this business.

1. Control over issuance of cards.
2. Control of fraudulent use of cards.
3. Deliquency follow up.

Unlike other types of loans, banks have found that it is difficult to manage the size of this loan category. Consequently, credit card loans can present liquidity problems to banks.

Fortunately, the accounting for these loans is not as complex as the management problems they present. The basic features of these cards are:

1. Each cardholder has a credit limit.
2. Minimum payments are required on a monthly basis.
3. Interest (finance charges) are charged monthly on unpaid balances.
4. Merchants are required to obtain authorization for sales over stipulated amounts

5. Merchants deposit charge sales slips into checking accounts, receiving immediate credit (less a service charge).

Following are the entries:

1461	CREDIT CARD LOANS	DR	
	####(merchant DDA)		CR
	####(service charge)		CR
	To record sales slip deposited by merchant.		
1461	CREDIT CARD LOANS	DR	
	4020 INT & FEES ON LOANS		CR
	To record finance charge.		
####	(payment)	DR	
	1461 CREDIT CARD LOANS		CR
	To record customer payment		

OTHER LOANS

Immediate credit collection items (1464) and overdrafts (1465) are classified as loans for GAAP and the Call Report.

LOAN FEES

The timing of the recognition of fee income on loans is an area in which there are varied approaches. In the case of loan commitment fees, following are some alternatives.

1. Cash basis.
2. At expiration of commitment.
3. Over the commitment period.
4. Over both commitment and loan period.

The criteria to be followed in deciding when the fee income should be recorded depend on the nature of the fee. If the charges are designed to recover direct costs of making the commitment, then immediate recognition would be indicated. If the fee is designed to compensate the bank for earmarking funds, then it should be recognized over the commitment period.

LOAN LOSSES

Would a bank make a loan that it thinks will never be repaid? Will all loans that a bank makes be fully repaid? The answer to both of these questions is NO. Uncollectable loans are simply risks of doing business for banks.

Valuation of Assets

GAAP tells us that any asset that is expected to be converted into cash should be recorded at its "net realizable value."

Timing of the Loan Loss

The entry to record the estimated amount of loan losses is:

4020   INT & FEES ON LOANS   DR
      1490 RES FOR POSS LN LOSSES   CR

Throughout this unit, I have been using 4020 as a general ledger control account. In the case of the loan loss provision, this emphasizes that uncollectable loans are a reduction of the amount of interest income earned by a bank.

The 1490 or "reserve" account is what accountants call a *valuation account*. By netting the balance in the valuation account against the balance of the other loan accounts, we accomplish the feat of stating loans at their net realizable value (that is, provided that the loss is determined based on a reasonable educated guess of the amount of uncollectable loans).

For tax purposes, banks compute the loan loss, or "bad debt" deduction, using either the experience (educated guess) method or the percent-of-outstanding-debt method. Under the latter method the percentage is 0.6 for 1983 through 1987. After 1987, only the experience method will be allowed.

Writing Off a Loan

When it has been determined that a specific loan is uncollectable, the following entry is made:

1490   RES FOR POSS LN LOSSES   DR
      ####(appropriate loan account)   CR

Loan Status

The status of a loan will determine if it is a write-off candidate. Here are the general classifications for loan status determination.

- *Full Accrual*—Loans upon which full collection of both principal and interest is expected would fall under this classification. This, hopefully, would be the normal status of most of the loan portfolio.

- *Nonaccrual*—Loans upon which the collection of the interest is in doubt would be put on a nonaccrual status. This means that the loan principal would remain as receivable but that the recording, or accrual, of the interest thereon would be discontinued. See Note 3 for SAMPLE BANK in Appendix C for the suggested disclosure of such loans.

- *Problem Loans*—This is my designation for loans that have full or partial loss potential. See Loan Classifications Used by Supervisory Agencies in Appendix D for subdivisions of this category.

At the risk of oversimplification, I have presented only the two basic entries affecting account 1490. The reader should be aware that the control over and accounting for loan losses is one of the more challenging areas in banking.

INTERNAL CONTROL POINTS—LOANS

1. Are all loans made according to written board policy?
2. Are credit reports required on new loans?
3. Are definitive loan limits established and adhered to?
4. Is there adequate segregation of duties between loan approval, disbursement, collection, and bookkeeping?
5. Are cash disbursements of loan proceeds prohibited?
6. Is there adequate physical control over loan notes, collateral, and files?
7. Are subsidiary loan ledgers properly balanced to the general ledger control accounts?
8. Are paid notes canceled and returned to the borrowers?
9. Are independent reviews made of loan file documentation?
10. Is there adequate control over:
    a. Deliquency?
    b. Loans written off?
    c. Provision for loan losses?

REVIEW PROJECT

Record the following transactions in general journal form.

A. Record the making of a single payment loan of $10,000. The proceeds are to be disbursed as follows:

To customer's DDA account	9,500
Undistributed	500

B. Per customer instructions, the undisbursed portion of the loan in transaction A is to be disbursed as follows:

Cashier's check to ABC Company	500
Cashier's check fee to be charged to customer's DDA account	5

C. Accrue six months' interest on the loan in transaction A, assuming that it was at 18%.

D. Record "on us" check for payment of loan from transaction A at maturity. Payment includes principal plus six months' interest.

E. Management estimates that there should be a valuation account established for the loan portfolio of $1,500.

F. The $500 commercial loan to Deep Well Corporation has been on a nonaccrual basis since about one week after the loan was made. Deep Well has now gone down the drain and the loan should no longer be on the books.

G. Record installment loans for indirect paper from Super Auto Sales. The loans amount to $3,000 and the interest thereon is $600. The net proceeds of the loans are to be credited to Super's DDA account at the bank.

H. Record interest income of $4,000 earned on installment loans.

6
FIXED AND ALL OTHER ASSETS

In this unit, we will complete our review of the left half of the accounting equation for banks. When you think of the asset side or left half of the balance sheet, these are the major "umbrella" categories that you should think of:

CASH & DUE FROM BANKS	(Unit 3)
INVESTMENTS	(Unit 4)
LOANS	(Unit 5)
FIXED ASSETS	(Unit 6)
OTHER ASSETS	(Unit 6)

Exhibit 6-1 on page 74 is a summary of these major captions in balance sheet format. Grouped under each caption are the general ledger chart of account numbers that relate to it.

The accounts that will be reviewed in this unit are as follows:

ACC #	TYPE	ACCOUNT NAME	NORMAL BALANCE

FIXED ASSETS

1501	ASSET	BANK BLDG & IMPR'S—COST	DEBIT
1502	ASSET	ACCUM DEPR—BLDG	CREDIT
1521	ASSET	FUR & FIX—COST	DEBIT
1522	ASSET	ACCUM DEPR—F&F	CREDIT
1541	ASSET	LAND	DEBIT
1551	ASSET	LEASEHOLD IMPROVEMENTS	DEBIT
1552	ASSET	ACCUM AMORTIZATION—LH IMPR	CREDIT
6200	EXPENSE	DEPRECIATION EXPENSE	DEBIT
6210	EXPENSE	AMORTIZATION—LH IMPR'S	DEBIT
6300	EXPENSE	FURNITURE & EQUIPMENT EXPENSES	DEBIT

REO & REPOSSESSIONS

1801	ASSET	REAL ESTATE OWNED (NET)	DEBIT
1840	ASSET	REPOSSESSIONS	DEBIT

PREPAID EXPENSES

1951	ASSET	PREPAID INSURANCE	DEBIT
1952	ASSET	PREPAID FDIC ASSESSMENT	DEBIT
1957	ASSET	PREPAID RENT	DEBIT
1979	ASSET	OTHER PREPAID EXPENSES	DEBIT

FIXED ASSETS

Fixed assets can be generally defined as being tangible assets, having a useful life of over a year, which are used in the business to produce a product or provide a service. Now try this. TRUE or FALSE? A building is always considered a fixed asset.

The answer is false since, although a building should have a useful life of over a year, it may not be utilized in the conduct of the business. Such would be the case with a building acquired through foreclosure. The accounting history of a fixed asset may be summarized as follows:

1. The fixed asset is acquired.
2. The fixed asset is DEPRECIATED or AMORTIZED over its estimated useful life.

3. The fixed asset is "retired."

Here are the entries:

15XX	APPROPRIATE FIXED ASSET	DR	
	####VARIOUS (i.e., official checks)		CR
6200	DEPRECIATION EXPENSE	DR	
	or		
6210	AMORTIZATION—LH INPR'S	DR	
	15XX APPROPRIATE ACCUMULATED DEPRECIATION		
	or AMORTIZATION ACCOUNT		CR
15XX	APPROPRIATE ACCUMULATED DEPRECIATION		
	or AMORTIZATION ACCOUNT	DR	
	15XX APPROPRIATE FIXED ASSET		CR

NOTE: This entry assumes that the fixed asset was retired at the end of its useful life when it was fully depreciated, and that no scrap or salvage value was received.

An interesting historical note here is that banks used to follow the "conservative" policy of writing fixed assets down to one dollar. Basically, what they were doing at that time was showing only cash and earning assets on the balance sheet, realizing that all other assets would ultimately become an expense and thus a reduction of bank capital. This was an extreme over-application of the accountant's concept of conservatism. The (often misunderstood) theory of conservatism goes basically like this: When the existence of an asset or a liability is in reasonable doubt, the situation should be handled so as to avoid the overstatement of assets or the understatement of liabilities. When a bank acquires a $10 million building to conduct its operations in or computers and furniture to conduct its business with, the theory of conservatism clearly does not apply.

DEPRECIATION/USEFUL LIFE/BENEFIT PERIOD

Depreciation expense is accounting jargon for the recognition of the cost of fixed assets as expense. *Benefit period* is another piece of jargon that you should understand. A clear example of what we mean by "benefit period" is the issuance of weekly paychecks to employees. If payday is Friday for the five days then ended, the benefit period to the employer is Monday through Friday. One of the tenets of accrual accounting is that expenses should be recognized (i.e., recorded as expenses) over their benefit period, regardless of when paid! This means that if a financial reporting period ends on a Thursday, an adjusting entry would have to be made to recognize the four days of wages that are unpaid. We will see more of this type of transaction in Unit 9.

Now, consider for a moment, what is the benefit period of a fixed asset? Well, if you thought that it is the useful life of the asset, you were correct. (See, you may become an accountant after all.) The useful life of an asset is obviously an estimate. The method of recording depreciation is what the Internal Revenue Service calls an "election," or choice, among several allowable accounting procedures. Since we are assuming some basic accounting as a prerequisite, we will only list the allowable methods:

- Straight Line
- Double Declining Balance (or 125% or 150% DB)
- Sum of the Digits

For GAAP, a firm may use any one or any mixture of the three methods. Once a method has been selected for a particular asset, the firm must use that method exclusively for that asset. As firms acquire large quantities of fixed assets, they may be "pooled" or grouped into "composites" (groupings) for purposes of depreciation computation and recordkeeping. Although pooling facilitates bookkeeping for fixed assets, it is important to maintain adequate physical inventories of fixed assets for good internal control.

There are major changes in the depreciation rules for taxes under the Tax Reform Act of 1981. Basically, these new tax depreciation procedures (ACRS—for accelerated cost recovery system) allow a firm to write off fixed assets over periods substantially less than their benefit periods.

Regardless of the method of depreciation chosen, the point to keep in mind is that the function of depreciation accounting is to allocate the cost of fixed assets to expense over their useful lives. The new ACRS tax depreciation method does cause some fancy accounting for income tax expense which we will tackle in Unit 14.

Another important point in fixed asset accounting is the tax consideration of the "investment credit." Taxpayers are allowed a credit against their tax liability of up to 10% of the cost of "qualifying" fixed assets purchased and placed in service during a year. All firms should have competent tax advisors review their fixed asset expenditures for qualifying property expenditures. In taxes, a credit ignored is gone forever.

COST BASIS/LAND AND LEASEHOLDS

The accumulated depreciation accounts are referred to as *contra asset accounts*. Unlike the 1490 loan loss allowance contra account, the accumulated depreciation accounts are *not* valuation accounts. The cost basis, or theory, states that assets should be recorded at original cost less any allowances for declines in value below cost, or accumulated depreciation, or amortization. Thus, under the cost theory or principle, any gain on the sale of an asset should not be recorded until the point of sale. The accounting profession, the business world, and government regulators (both bank and nonbank) are beginning to question the advisability of this theory. In banking we see an exception to the cost principle in the area of valuation of the trading account at market. In fixed asset accounting we have long recognized that inflation has caused the cost principle to be about as realistic as the old $1 policy for fixed assets.

Since land is the only fixed asset that is not subject to depreciation, it will make a good illustration of the cost principle. Let's assume that in 1950 a bank located in the heart of a major city acquired 10 acres of land in Typicalville, a small farming community outside the major city. The bank acquired the land with the idea that someday it might like to build a branch in Typicalville. At the time the board of directors thought that the branch was highly unlikely but at $200 an acre, what's the difference?

It is now 1983 and the bank is about to have the grand opening of its new main office in Typicalville. The 10-acre site happily turned out to be right next to one of the nation's largest shopping centers located in Typicalville. Typicalville is now the home of the corporate offices of over 35 major corporations and the population of the town is over one hundred thousand and growing. The old downtown building is being used as a warehouse for dormant trust department records.

Is this a familiar story? Sure, it is. What about the land values of the downtown and Typicalville locations? In terms of market values, it is apparent that there must have been dramatic movements in both properties (in opposite directions). In terms of book values under the good old cost principle, the downtown land would still be at its original cost and so would the Typicalville land. The whole point is that the word *value* in the term "book value" of fixed assets has *no* relationship to the economic *value* of the fixed assets.

Leasehold improvements are items of fixed assets, installed in leased or rented facilities, whose useful lives are limited to the term of the leases. Thus, special wall or floor coverings, electrical work, or special counters that would not be removed at the expiration of the leases are included in this classification. Leaseholds are amortized on a straight-line basis.

The 6300 account for Furniture and Equipment Expenses was included in this section of this unit since the maintenance and repair and other upkeep expenses associated with fixed assets, along with the associated depreciation expense, is a major expense to a bank. Charges to account 6300 would usually come about through disbursements of official checks or the recording of accounts payable or accrued liabilities. Charges to 6300 could also come from adjusting entries to record the expiration of prepaid costs which we will cover in the next section.

PREPAID EXPENSES

The concept of the benefit period also applies to prepaid expenses. Accountants define *expenses* as expired costs. In the case of prepaid expenses, the benefit period occurs *after* the item was paid for. At the time the item is paid for, the appropriate prepaid expense account (an asset account) is debited. At the end of each reporting period it is, therefore, necessary to transfer the expired portion of the prepaid expense to the appropriate expense account, leaving the unexpired portion in the asset account.

Here are these two entries:

19XX	PREPAID INSURANCE, ETC.	DR	
	####official checks		CR
	Journal for external transaction for the payment of insurance premiums.		

####	Appropriate Expense Account	DR	
	19XX PREPAID INSURANCE, ETC.		CR
	Journal for the internal transaction (adjusting journal entry) to transfer the expired portion of insurance premiums to expense.		

REAL ESTATE OWNED

The 1801 account, Real Estate Owned, would include the cost of real estate owned by the bank that is not currently being used in the operations of the bank. Also carried in this category would be the value of real estate acquired through foreclosure. The valuation of foreclosed real estate would be the lower of its fair market value or the unpaid mortgage balance plus the costs of foreclosure.

Real estate owned, or REO, as it is not so fondly referred to by institutions holding such property, is subject to depreciation and you would, therefore, have accumulated depreciation accounts for REO. All expenses and income associated with REO should be under control of separate general ledger control accounts.

Repossessions

The 1840 account, Repossessions, represents the fair market value of personal property aquired upon default of a secured loan. Any excess of the loan balance and repossession expenses over the fair value of the collateral would be charged (debited) to the 1490 account, Loan Loss Allowance. If the reverse was the case (which it, hopefully, would be), a miscellaneous liability account would be credited for the excess of the value of the collateral over the loan and repossession costs.

INTERNAL CONTROL POINTS—FIXED AND OTHER ASSETS

Fixed Assets

1. Do purchases of fixed assets require authorization by appropriate officer or board approval?
2. Are fixed asset accounting procedures adequately documented and followed?
3. Are periodic physical inventories made of bank fixed assets and are they compared to the general ledger record of fixed assets?
4. Are insurance values of fixed assets periodically reviewed with appropriate changes made in insurance coverages?
5. Are all investment tax credit property purchases identified to assure claiming of the credit?
6. Are depreciation schedules properly maintained and reviewed?

Prepaid Expenses

1. Are routine periodic entries formatted to record the expiration of prepaid expenses?
2. Does the internal auditor test and verify entries and schedules maintained on prepaid expenses?
3. Is there sufficient control over the purchasing and usage of bank supplies?

Real Estate Owned and Repossessions

1. Are acquisitions (foreclosures) and sales of real and personal property authorized by board approval?

2. Are real and personal property owned under control of appropriate officers?

3. Are periodic independent appraisals and inspections made of real and personal property?

4. Are real estate owned income and expense accounts properly reviewed and controlled?

REVIEW PROJECTS

1. This unit completes your study of the left half of the accounting equation. This project will review and test your understanding of the material that you have covered so far.

   INSTRUCTIONS: Prepare the asset portion of the balance sheet based on the trial balance in Appendix F. Use a copy of Exhibit 6-1 on page 74 as your working paper.

2. Prepare entries in general journal form for the following transactions.

   A. Record depreciation expense on bank fixed assets as follows:

Bank building	250
Furniture and fixtures	300

   B. Record official check payment of FDIC assessment of $180 for a 12-month period.

   C. Record five months of FDIC assessment from transaction B as expired cost.

EXHIBIT 6-1

The First Typical Bank Financial Statement Project

ASSETS

CASH & DUE FROM BANKS:
```
        1000                                        $
        1021
        1023
        1024
        1099
        1101
        1200                                                        $
                                            --------
```

INVESTMENTS
```
        1301                            $
        1302
        1303                        (           ) $
                                    ---------
        1398
        1399                                                        $
                                            --------
```

LOANS
```
        1401                            $
        1402                        (           )
        1403                        (           )
        1404                                        $
                                    ---------
        1421                            $
        1423                        (           ) $
                                    ---------
        1440                                        $
        1461
        1464
        1465
                                            --------
                                            $
        1490                                (       ) $
                                            --------
```

FIXED ASSETS
```
    COST                                        $
    LESS ACCUMULATED DEPRECIATION               (       ) $
                                            --------
```

OTHER ASSETS
```
    1800 & 1900 ACCOUNTS                                    $
                                                    ----------
            TOTAL ASSETS
                                                    ==========
```

7
DEMAND DEPOSITS

In this unit, I will cover the procedural and internal control considerations relative to demand deposits. Be aware that many of these points, of course, are also applicable to savings deposits.

The DDA accounts that we will be specifically considering are as follows:

ACC#	TYPE	ACCOUNT NAME	NORMAL BALANCE
2010	LIAB	DDA—INDIVIDUALS/COS	CREDIT
2031	LIAB	US TT&L ACCOUNT	CREDIT
2039	LIAB	OTHER US DDA	CREDIT
2040	LIAB	DDA—STATE & LOCAL GOVT	CREDIT
2061	LIAB	OFFICIAL CHECKS (ALL TYPES)	CREDIT
8000	INCOME	DDA SERVICE CHARGES	CREDIT
8010	INCOME	OTHER S/C ON DEPOSITS	CREDIT

OPERATING PROCEDURES

In order to support the large volume of customers and transactions, all financial institutions use some form of automated data processing. We will look at these systems in Unit 13. Here we will consider the operating controls necessary regardless of the extent of automation.

1. New accounts should be opened by persons independent of teller or bookkeeping functions.
2. Tellers should be discouraged from preparing deposit/withdrawal tickets for customers.
3. Limits should be set for tellers on the amount of cash disbursed to customers via check cashing or withdrawals. Related to this would be guidelines on account balance and signature verification.
4. Specific controls should be established to identify dormant accounts and monitor any activity in such accounts.
5. If "no mail" accounts are accepted, controls should be provided to maintain that status.
6. Significant changes in individual account balances should be reviewed by management. Related to this would be a review of closed accounts and accounts going to a zero balance.
7. There should be adequate control over the mailing of customer statements. Returned customer mail should be followed up.

OVERDRAFTS

As noted in Unit 5, overdrawn checking accounts are classified as loans on the balance sheet. No matter what the viewpoint on overdrafts, there should be specific review procedures on such accounts.

In my experience, the opposite ends of the spectrum of viewpoints on overdrafts are:

- No overdrafts will be allowed!

  vs.

- Overdrafts are our most profitable loans!

DDA SUBDIVISIONS AND U.S. TT&L ACCOUNT

Accounts 2010 through 2040 in your example Chart of Accounts are given as a representation of the categories of DDA accounts. Schedule F of the Call

Report given in Appendix B also gives you the regulatory classifications. The U.S. TT&L account is a special account maintained by banks in their role of acting as a depository for federal income taxes. Credits to this account are initiated by the deposits of corporate and small business taxpayers of their income and payroll tax liabilities. The deposits are accompanied by specially coded remittance advices which are provided by the Internal Revenue Service. These remittance advices are forwarded to the IRS. Charges or debits to the TT&L account are offset by credits to the Reserve (1200) account when the U.S. Treasury "calls," or transfers, funds from the TT&L account.

OFFICIAL CHECKS

The 2061 account is provided in our Chart of Accounts as being representative of several accounts that we can refer to, in general, as being "official check" accounts. These accounts represent the unpaid balances of checks written by the bank to pay expenses, disburse dividends, etc. Examples of the various categories are:

- Certified checks
- Cashier's checks
- Expense checks
- Money orders
- Dividend checks
- Club account checks
- Trust checks

Good internal control would dictate that reconciliations of official checks be performed by employees independent of initiating or recording official checks.

UNCOLLECTED FUNDS

Many bank customers do not appreciate that their bank is acting only as their agent in the process of collecting checks that they have deposited with the bank. If it takes three-days for a bank to collect a check, then the bank collecting the check does not have use of the funds for that three-day period. If the bank does allow its customer to make a withdrawal against uncollected funds, then it does so, not as an obligation, but rather as an accommodation to its customer. Financial institutions should have a definitive policy as to disbursements against uncollected funds.

SERVICE CHARGES/BUDGETING

The tremendous volume of paperwork associated with demand deposit accounts makes them one of the most costly aspects of conducting bank operations. Banks usually attempt to recover some of their DDA operating expenses by levying services charges on customer accounts. Many factors influence the determination of service charges, not the least of which is competition among banks for deposits by offering low-cost or free checking services. Exhibit 7-1 provides a typical example of a service charge structure.

BUDGETING AND SERVICE CHARGE EXAMPLE

The following hypothetical situation is provided to give you some insight into the concepts of budgeting and some strategic thinking relative to the control over deposits and the determination of service charges.

FACTS

1. Your bank is considering offering a new type of no minimum balance checking service to senior citizens and students in the local college.
2. The loan department believes that all lendable funds generated from the new accounts could be loaned out at 14%.
3. Assume that there would be a reserve requirement of 6% on these deposits.
4. The monthly costs of maintaining each account are estimated as follows:

A. Postage	.80
B. Forms	.20
C. Service bureau costs	.50

5. In addition to the above costs, management believes that additional customer service employees will have to be hired, increasing payroll expense by $25,000 annually. The annual depreciation expense for the floor space that will be needed within the existing lobby is computed to be $4,000.
6. The marketing department estimates that 3,000 such accounts would be opened.

EXHIBIT 7-1

Example Schedule of DDA Service Charges

CHECKING

Checks written	.14ea
Items deposited	.08ea
Monthly maintenance	$6.00
Credit toward charges based on daily average collected balance	Equal to monthly average of 6 mo. Treasury Bill
Coin, currency, etc., received or purchased	Quoted on request, subject to volume and handling costs

ACCOUNTING SERVICES

Stop payments	$10.00ea
Extra statement of account	$ 5.00ea
Bookkeeping inquiry	$ 2.00ea
Overdrafts	
Checks returned	$10.00ea
Overdraft paid	$10.00ea
Returned items	$ 2.00ea
Copies	
Microfilm	$ 1.50ea
Photo	.25ea
Account reconcilements	$10.00ea
Wire transfer of funds	$10.00ea
Customer account research	$30.00/hour

SPECIAL TELLER SERVICES

Money orders	$ 2.00ea
Cashier's checks	$ 2.50ea
Certified checks	$ 5.00ea
Collection items	$ 5.00ea
New York draft	$ 5.00ea
Foreign draft	$10.00ea
Travelers' checks	$1.00/100

SOLVE FOR THE FOLLOWING:

What would the average balance in each account have to be in order for the bank to break even:

    A. Assuming no service charges were made.

    B. Assuming a flat service charge of $2.00 per month per account.

Try to work out the answers for yourself before checking the solution. The answers, to the nearest dollar, are:

A. $200.00
B. $ 18.00

SOLUTION:

The break even point can be generally defined as the level of activity where total revenue exactly equals total expenses. The quickest way to proceed is to determine our total costs.

Monthly maintenance costs	
(.80 + .20 + .50) x 12 x 3000	$54,000
Additional payroll costs	25,000
Total expense without service charge	$79,000
Annual service charge	72,000
Total expense with service charge	$7,000

NOTE: The depreciation expense is NOT a relevant factor in this case. You notice that I stated in the facts that we would be using *existing* lobby space. The $4,000 of depreciation is a "sunk cost". That is, the bank will incur the depreciation regardless of the proposed operations. This demonstrates one of the problems in budgeting, which is picking out the relevant data necessary for your solution.

Now that we know our total costs, we can compute the amount of interest income needed to break even. Since we must reserve 6% of any deposits, only $94 of every $100 can be loaned out at 14%. For each $100 of deposits, we can earn $13.16 (94 x .14 = 13.16). For computation ease we will, therefore, use an effective rate of 13.16%.

A. Total deposits necessary to earn $79,000 interest income

$$79,000/13.16\% = \$600,304$$

B. Total deposits necessary to earn $7,000 interest income

$$7,000/13.16\% = \$53,191$$

The average balance per account is each case would be

    A. $600,304/3000 accounts = $200
    B. $ 53,191/3000 accounts = $ 18

SUMMARY

If you are in a classroom environment, your instructor may have lots of fun with the example by adding other factors, changing the facts, or both. One way to use the data that we generated here is to assume that our bank decided to go with the service charge and that 3,000 accounts were opened, each carrying a $200 average balance. You should be able to see that our bank would have a pretax profit of $72,000 from these accounts.

$$(600,304 \times 13.16\%) - 7,000 = 72,000$$

REVIEW PROJECTS

1. This unit contains the major internal control considerations for DDA. Incorporating these, and your own background, prepare a list of internal control points for DDA. You should follow the format of the internal control points provided in previous units. Compare your points to the suggested listing found in Appendix E.

2. Prepare entries in general journal form for the following transactions.
   A. Record "on us" checks deposited into the bank's TT&L account—Total $3,000.
   B. Reclassify DDA accounts with debit balances amounting to $170.
   C. Record service charges on DDA accounts, $60.

8

SAVINGS AND TIME DEPOSITS

In Unit 7, I covered the procedural and internal control aspects of DDA, noting that many of the points covered were also applicable to savings deposits. This unit will concentrate mainly on those matters related to savings.

The accounts for this unit are:

ACC#	TYPE	ACCOUNT NAME	NORMAL BALANCE
2201	LIAB	SAVINGS & TIME DEPOSITS	CREDIT
2841	LIAB	INT PAY—SAV & TIME DEPOSITS	CREDIT
5000	EXPENSE	INT EXP—DEP & DEBT	DEBIT

These accounts are, again, used as general ledger control accounts. You should refer to Schedule F of the Call Report (Appendix B) for a detail of the categories that would be included in the 2201 account.

The distinction between savings and time deposits is that time deposits usually have a fixed maturity date while savings accounts are subject to withdrawal at any time. Although banks can insist on, say, a 30-day waiting period before notices of withdrawals against savings deposits are honored, this right would rarely be exercised. So again, for all practical purposes, savings deposits are subject to withdrawal upon demand. I recently brought our five-year-old to a rerun of Disney's "Mary Poppins" and I couldn't resist recalling here the run on the Fidelity-Fiduciary Bank caused by the refusal of the chairman (Dick Van Dyke) to return young Michael's tuppence.

Operating Procedures

To continue with serious business, I have included a review of the operating procedures for savings from the AICPA *Proposed Audit Guide—Audits of Banks.*

> When a savings account is opened, many banks provide the depositor with a passbook, providing a record of deposits, withdrawals, interest, and account balance. Normally, the bank's rules and regulations affecting the conduct, use, and privileges of savings accounts are also shown in the passbook. The passbook is usually presented each time a deposit or withdrawal is made. As a result of increased utilization of EDP equipment there has been a growing tendency to eliminate passbooks and provide periodic statements of savings activity.

> Regulations of state and federal authorities define the various categories of time deposits, govern interest rates that may be paid, and specify from whom they may be accepted and the reserve requirements that must be maintained against deposit balances. One of the most important regulations is Regulation Q of the Board of Governors of the Federal Reserve System. While this regulation sets maximum interest rates, it also recognizes the rate limitation set by each individual state for its local banks and applies the state limitation, if lower, to all banks within jurisdiction in the state.

> Methods of computing interest and periods used for compounding vary from bank to bank. The methods currently in use vary from a policy that requires amounts to be on deposit for the entire interest period to earn any interest to a policy of allowing interest for the exact number of days on deposit.

> DORMANT ACCOUNTS The classification of accounts as dormant varies depending on individual bank policy. The required period of inactivity before savings accounts are classified as dormant is normally longer than for checking accounts because savings accounts records are usually less active. It is preferable that dormant accounts be kept under the control of individuals independent of the teller and bookkeeping functions.

CLOSED ACCOUNTS When an account is closed, the signature card should be removed from the file of active accounts and placed in a closed account section. Generally, if a passbook is used it is perforated in a cancelling machine and returned to the customer.

INTEREST EXPENSE

The 5000 account, as we are using it, would be broken down on the income statement as shown in Exhibit 8-1. The numbers used are from SAMPLE BANK's income statement in Appendix C. As you can see, the interest on deposits is, by far, the largest element of total interest expense.

EXHIBIT 8-1

Detail of Interest Expense

Interest on deposits:		
Savings deposits	$A	
Time deposits	B	
Time deposits (over $100,000)	C	
Deposits in foreign offices	D	$3,946,000
Interest on bank debt:		
Short-term debt interest		33,000
Long-term debt interest		80,000
TOTAL INTEREST EXPENSE		$4,059,000

INTERNAL CONTROL FOR SAVINGS DEPOSITS

As noted in Unit 7, the level of automation will determine the extent and nature of many of the operating procedures over deposits, but the following internal controls over savings deposits should be present, regardless of the extent of automation.

1. All types of accounts should be under prenumbered control.
2. Unissued passbooks and certificates should be under control.
3. Savings trial balances (both automated and manual) should be reconciled to the general ledger control account(s).
4. All withdrawal tickets should be canceled at the close of each business day.

5. "No-passbook" transactions, if allowed, should be adequately controlled.

6. Tests of interest paid should be made on an overall basis and on a test basis for individual accounts. (This is applicable even with automated systems!)

ACCRUAL OF INTEREST EXPENSE

I am suggesting that the recording of interest expense be handled in the same manner used for the recording of interest income on single payment loans. That is, like this:

5000	INT EXPENSE—DEP & DEBT	DEBIT	
	2841 INT PAY—SAV & TIME DEPOSITS		CREDIT
	Adjusting entry to record the accrual of interest expense.		

The payment of the accrued interest would then be as follows:

2841	INT PAY—SAVE & TIME DEPOSITS	DEBIT	
	####Appropriate savings or official check account		CREDIT
	To record payment of interest on savings accounts.		

There are various methods for computing interest on savings deposits. Brief descriptions of two (LIFO and FIFO) are found in Appendix D.

Detailed explanations of the variations on interest computation are beyond the scope of what I feel needs to be covered here; however, if you are using this text in the classroom, your instructor may give you some examples. For our text discussion, three experiences from my bank auditing background are apropos.

1. The bank had its savings accounts maintained by a service bureau. Bank policy was to compute interest on a FIFO basis; however, LIFO was the actual method used by the service bureau.

2. The bank's actual interest computation was done as called for under its stated rules; however, customer service personnel were describing another method to customers opening accounts.

3. The bank's computerized system properly computed interest on each of its certificates of deposit and had the capability of generating interest checks. The accounting department used the interest accruals and

payments indicated per the computerized system. The check preparation ability of the automated system was not utilized and personnel in charge of official checks computed the interest *manually* when preparing the interest checks. Of course, there were differences between the manual and computerized amounts.

The lessons to be learned from these experiences are:

1. Make sure your automated system is doing what you want it to do.
2. Be sure all personnel are aware of what the system is doing and that they can explain same to customers.
3. Utilize automated systems properly to obtain their full benefit.

REVIEW PROJECTS

1. Prepare a listing of internal control points for savings and time deposits like the one requested in the first project in Unit 7 on DDA. As in the Unit 7 project, compare your points to the suggested listing found in Appendix E.
2. Using the Chart of Accounts from Appendix A, prepare entries in general journal form for the following transactions.

   A. Accrue interest on savings deposits amounting to $2,600.

   B. Pay interest on savings accounts as follows:

Credit customer accounts	800
Issue checks to customers	400

9

OTHER LIABILITIES

In Units 7 and 8, I reviewed the accounting and internal control aspects of the major elements of bank liabilities. I will take a somewhat different format in presenting the accounts that we will be considering since we have already seen most of these accounts in other units.

ACC#	ACCOUNT NAME	NORMAL BALANCE
ACCRUED LIABILITIES:		
2841	INT PAY—SAV & TIME DEPOSITS	CREDIT
2931	INT PAY—FED FUNDS PUR	CREDIT
2932	INT PAY—SEC SOLD/REPUR AGR	CREDIT
2935	INT PAY ON BORROWED MONEY	CREDIT
2941	INCOME TAXES PAYABLE—FEDERAL	CREDIT
2951	INCOME TAXES PAYABLE—STATE	CREDIT

ACC #	ACCOUNT NAME	NORMAL BALANCE
2976	REAL ESTATE TAXES PAYABLE	CREDIT
2978	OTHER TAXES PAYABLE	CREDIT
2990	OTHER ACCRUED LIABILITIES	CREDIT

OTHER LIABILITIES:

2600	MORTGAGE DEBT	CREDIT
2610	OTHER LIAB FOR BORROWED MONEY	CREDIT
2620	BORROWINGS FROM FED RES BANK	CREDIT
2820	DIVIDENDS PAYABLE	CREDIT
2980	ACCOUNTS PAYABLE	CREDIT

SUBORDINATED DEBT:

2999	SUBORDINATED DEBT	CREDIT

ACCRUED LIABILITIES

The term *accrued* can be used in reference to either a liability or an asset account. As we saw on the asset side of the balance sheet, accrued interest receivable represents the increase in assets that results from the earning of interest over time. Accrued liabilities represent the recognition of expenses that have been incurred but not yet paid. What, you might ask, is the difference between accrued liabilities and accounts payable? In essence, they are exactly the same but, in the case of accounts payable, you have a creditor's invoice in hand while, with accrued liabilities, you must compute the amount of the liability. In many cases, the amount may be an estimate (such as in the case of real estate taxes) or it may be a fixed amount that will not be billed until a subsequent period.

ACCRUALS/REVERSING ENTRIES AND INCOME TAXES

In prior units, I noted that it is my policy to avoid reversing entries at all costs. In practice, reversing entries are optional. Here I will show you the same example with and without reversing entries and the mechanics of the payment of federal income taxes. It would be a good idea to go over this material again before you start Unit 14.

INCOME TAX PROCEDURES

ESTIMATED TAXES

Like individuals, corporations are subject to federal income taxes. Unlike most individuals, corporations must pay their tax liability directly to the IRS. Most individuals, who are wage earners, have their tax payments made for them through payroll withholding. In any case, all taxpayers are obligated to satisfy their tax liability on a pay-as-you-go basis. All taxpayers that estimate that they owe taxes at the end of each quarter must pay at least 80% of those taxes on a quarterly basis. The payment dates for calendar year taxpayers are 4-15, 6-15, 9-15, and 1-15. These do not look like "quarterly" dates to me but you'll have to ask your Congressman for the reason.

THE TAX RETURN

Individuals must compute their final tax liability and pay any balance due, or request a refund, when they file their individual tax returns (Form 1040) by April 15th of each year. Calendar year corporations must do the same by March 15th when they file their corporate income tax returns (Form 1120).

CORPORATE TAX SITUATION

Let's assume that a bank estimates its tax liability for 19X1 to be $200,000. Assuming that our bank, like any other taxpayer, wants to hold on to its assets as long as possible, it would make four estimated tax payments amounting to $160,000 (80% of $200,000). The entry to record three of the four payments required during 19X1 would look like this.

XX-15-X1
8900 PROVISION FOR INCOME TAXES   40,000
      2061 OFFICIAL CHECKS (ALL TYPES)   40,000
      To record estimated income tax payment.

To further simplify our example, we will assume that the bank only records adjusting entries once a year.
    On December 31, 19X1, the following adjusting entry would have to be made.

12-31-X1
8900 PROVISION FOR INCOME TAXES   80,000
      2941 INCOME TAXES PAYABLE—FEDERAL   80,000
      To record accrual of taxes payable
      as of 12-31-X1.

On the income statement for 19X1, the 8900 account would show $200,000 and the 12-31-X1 balance sheet would show a balance of federal income tax payable (account 2941) of $80,000. In the 19X1 year-end closing procedures, the 8900 account would be closed (zeroed) out to retained earnings (undivided profits). The balance in account 2941 would, of course, remain open.

FINAL PAYMENT OF TAX—WITH REVERSING ENTRY

If we record a reversing entry in January of 19X2, it would look like this:

```
1-1-X2
2941  INCOME TAX PAYABLE—FEDERAL          80,000
         8900 PROVISION FOR INCOME TAXES             80,000
         To reverse 12-31-X1 adjusting entry
         for 12-31-X1 accrued taxes.
```

Immediately after the entry is posted, the balance in account 2941 would be zero and account 8900 would have a *credit* balance of $80,000.

NOTE: If our bank was preparing monthly financial statements, it would be necessary to adjust the balances in accounts 2941 and 8900 at the end of January and February 19X2 since $40,000 is still payable at the end of each of these months.

The $40,000 payments on 1-15-X2 and 3-15-X2 would be recorded as follows:

```
XX-15-X2
8900  PROVISION FOR INCOME TAXES          40,000
         2061 OFFICIAL CHECKS (ALL TYPES)            40,000
         To record payment against 19X1 taxes.
```

Starting with the end of March 19X2, no further adjusting entries would be necessary for accounts 2941 and 8900 since the balance in both accounts would be zero. (I am ignoring any provision for 19X2 taxes for purposes of this discussion.)

FINAL PAYMENT OF TAX—NO REVERSING ENTRY

With no reversing entry, the payments due on 1-15-X2 and 3-15-X2 would look like this:

```
XX-15-X2
2941  INCOME TAX PAYABLE—FEDERAL          40,000
         2061 OFFICIAL CHECKS (ALL TYPES)            40,000
         To record payment against 19X1 taxes.
```

After the 3-15-X2 payment was recorded, the balance in account 2941 would be zero and we would be ready to start the cycle all over again. The advantage of this approach is that the bank would only have to make adjusting entries in interim months for the accrual of additional income taxes payable. The unadjusted interim income statement accounts would reflect pretax profits without having to back out the reversing entry to determine this amount.

You will see more about the determination of income taxes in Unit 14 so we will leave this topic now, letting it stand as your basic introduction to corporate taxation.

Accounts Payable

As noted earlier, it is the presence of a vendor's invoice that distinguishes accounts payable from accrued liabilities. In banks, these unpaid invoices would include purchases of bank supplies; utility bills; bills for legal, accounting, and other professional services; bank equipment; and various other assorted items. There are two ways to handle the recording of accounts payable.

Accounts Payable Set-Up and Reversal

At the end of each accounting period, the unpaid invoices would be accumulated, summarized, and journalized in a compound journal that might appear as follows:

XXXX >		5,000
XXXX >		3,000
XXXX >VARIOUS ACCOUNTS		2,500
XXXX >		1,600
XXXX >		1,400
2980 ACCOUNTS PAYABLE		13.500

At the start of the next accounting period, this entry would be reversed and the invoices would be charged to the applicable expense account when paid.

This is a convenient method of handling accounts payable when their volume is reasonably small as is the case in smaller banks.

Accounts Payable—No Reversal

As the number of vendors and outstanding invoices increases, it becomes practical to handle the recording of accounts payable in the manner in which retail stores account for credit purchases of merchandise. Under these procedures, invoices are recorded (probably as approved) as liabilities as in the entry above. Subsidiary ledgers for major vendors may also be maintained or the bank may even establish a voucher system. In any case, under this procedure, no reversing entries are needed since the payments of the invoices are charged to accounts payable.

SUBORDINATED DEBT

The equivalent of subordinated debt in nonbanking firms is long-term bonded debt. Just as nonbanking firms see it, long-term debt effectively becomes part of the permanent capital structure of a bank. National banks may include subordinated debt in "capital" for calculating lending limits on unsecured loans. (State banks are somewhat more limited here.)

This debt must have minimum seven-year maturities to be excluded from legal reserve requirements. FDIC approval is also required before these securities are repaid. The subordination of this debt to the claims of the depositors is the feature that tends to make it similar to an equity security. In the next unit on bank capital, I will discuss the concept of leverage. At this point, it will be handy to have this prioritized list of bank creditors and equity holders.

- CREDITORS:
    DEPOSITORS
    NONSUBORDINATED DEBT HOLDERS
- EQUITY HOLDERS:
    SUBORDINATED DEBT
    PREFERRED STOCK
    COMMON STOCK

There is more discussion of bank equity and leverage in Unit 10.

INTERNAL CONTROL POINTS—OTHER LIABILITIES

NOTE: These points only include the other liability accounts not covered in previous units.

ACCRUED LIABILITIES

1. Are all noninterest accruals appropriately documented?
2. Are supporting working papers for noninterest accruals tied into the applicable general ledger accounts?

ACCOUNTS PAYABLE

1. Are purchase orders, requisitions, vouchers, or some other form of written documentation used for purchases of bank supplies, etc.?

2. Are all vendors' invoices checked for accuracy and agreement to the purchase terms?

3. Are there periodic reviews made of source vendors and comparisons made against alternative vendors?

4. Are persons authorized to make purchases different from those who can authorize disbursements?

BANK DEBT (SUBORDINATED AND NONSUBORDINATED)

1. Is there evidence of board approval of bank debt?

2. Are all applicable regulatory requirements met on bank debt?

REVIEW PROJECTS

1. Now that you have almost completed your review of the right half of the accounting equation, you should be able to complete this project, which is essentially a continuation of project 1, started in Unit 6.

   INSTRUCTIONS: From the trial balance in Appendix F prepare the liability and equity portions of the balance sheet. Use a copy of Exhibit 9-1 as your working paper.

2. Prepare entries in general journal form for the following transactions.

   A. Record reversal of 6-30-84 accounts payable. (See journal entry #16 for THE FIRST TYPICAL BANK in Unit 2.)

   B. Record the official check payment of 6-30-84 accounts payable.

   C. Record accounts payable as of 12-31-84 which are recapped as follows:

Employees' group insurance	30
Occupancy expense	65
Office machine repair	15
Other expenses	90

   D. Record 9-15-84 payment of estimated taxes for the year, $300.

E. Record 12-31-84 accrual of income taxes for the year of $550. The provision is to be allocated as follows:

Tax on security gains	$ 50
Tax on all other income	$500

NOTE: Don't forget that $300 of the provision was already recorded in transaction D.

EXHIBIT 9-1

The First Typical Bank Financial Statement Project

LIABILITIES

```
DEPOSITS
      2010-2101                           $
      2201                                           $
                                              --------

SHORT-TERM BORROWINGS
      2410 & 2420                                    $

ACCRUED INTEREST & OTHER LIABILITIES
      2600-2990                                      $

SUBORDINATED DEBT
      2999                                           $
                                              ---------
                 TOTAL LIABILITIES                   $
```

SHAREHOLDERS' EQUITY

```
      3100                                 $
      3200
      3300
      3400                                           $
                                   --------  ---------
      TOTAL LIABILITIES & SHAREHOLDERS' EQUITY       $
                                            =========
```

10
STOCKHOLDERS' EQUITY

In the sample Chart of Accounts, I have chosen to use the traditional account titles for the equity section. Here I have, again, listed the same account titles along with their more layperson-oriented titles.

STOCKHOLDERS' (SHAREHOLDERS') EQUITY

ACC#	ACCOUNT NAME	NORMAL BALANCE
3100	PREFERRED STOCK	CREDIT
3200	COMMON STOCK (at par or stated value)	CREDIT
3300	SURPLUS (paid-in-capital in excess of par or stated value)	CREDIT
3400	UNDIVIDED PROFITS (retained earnings)	CREDIT
3XXX	TREASURY STOCK—AT COST (account not in original chart of accts)	DEBIT

I believe that it is most appropriate to begin this unit with the concept of leverage since banking is one of the most highly leveraged of all industries. I have heard it noted that if a potential loan customer was as highly leveraged as the typical bank, the customer would never get the loan. The term *leverage* is simply jargon in referring to the relationship, or ratio, of the amount of owner's equity, or capital, to the amount of debt. The term is also referred to as "trading on the equity."

To see how it works, use this illustration:

- A business person has $10,000 to invest.
- He or she has a product that can be sold for a 40% mark-up.
- He or she is in the 50% marginal income tax bracket.

You should see with the following two subtle scenarios that:

LEVERAGE CAN BE VERY PROFITABLE

LEVERAGE CAN BE VERY RISKY

"My goodness," you say, "If leverage is risky, why allow banks, of all places, to get into such a risky situation?" Well, now I guess you really know why we have all those bank regulations!

On with the leverage illustration (Exhibit 10-1).

As you can see, in both of the scenarios in Exhibit 10-1 we started with the same amount of owner investment. In the first case, which is NO LEVERAGE, the owner enjoyed a 20% growth in equity, or capital. Now that is an after-tax increase so, even in today's inflationary times, that is an excellent return.

On the other hand, the owner in the second case enjoyed an after-tax increase in equity of 120%! By working with a little bit of capital and a lot of money from debt (that's leverage and that's how banks operate), the owner did *five times* better in the second case vs. the first case. If you remember the dynamics of a lever from physics, you can see why they call this leverage. As would be expected, since leveraging is the more profitable approach, the higher the leveraging, the higher the risk.

CREATING AN INTANGIBLE LEGAL PERSON

This section's title may sound like a chapter title from a science fiction novel, but it simply states what a corporation is in the eyes of the law. All corporations are simply risk-spreading devices that were created from the growth of the size of business entities that came with the Industrial Revolution. For

EXHIBIT 10-1
Leverage

Scenario #1	Cash	+ Inventory	=		Capital
Invest $10,000 captial in inventory		10,000			10,000
Sell all inventory at 40% mark-up	14,000	<10,000>			4,000
Pay tax at 50%	<2,000>				<2,000>
ENDING BALANCES	12,000	-0-			12,000

Scenario #2	Cash	+ Inventory	=	Debt	+ Capital
Invest $10,000 capital and proceeds of loan into inventory		110,000		100,000	10,000
Sell all inventory at 40% mark-up	154,000	<110,000>			44,000
Pay off loan plus 20% interest	<120,000>			<100,000>	<20,000>
Pay tax at 50%	<12,000>				<12,000>
ENDING BALANCES	22,000	-0-		-0-	22,000

example, in its era, the Cutty Sark was one of the largest and fastest clipper ships ever to sail. At the time there were very few individual businessmen who could or would want to take on the risk of financing even a single voyage. By forming a corporation (or a corporate joint venture) several businessmen could consolidate their capital to come up with the requisite cash needed to finance a voyage and, at the same time, limit their risk to the amount invested. Since the return to the individual stockholders is simply based on their proportionate ownership of stock, there is no problem with disputes arising relative to the division of corporate profits, as can occur with the partnership form of business. Since the corporation is a separate entity, the shareholders may be compensated as employees of the corporation. In today's environment, this is one of many tax advantages of the corporate form of business.

I should hasten to note that the corporate form is not desirable for every business. There are numerous tax and operating advantages to the corporate form as well as some considerable disadvantages that could outweigh the merits of the advantages depending on the circumstances of a particular business. Among these disadvantages are the double taxation of corporate earnings that occurs when cash dividends are paid, the increased regulatory reporting required of corporations, and the relative inflexibility of the corporate form.

Unlike other businesses, banks have no choice as to the form of business. That is, banks must be organized in the corporate form.

THE NATURE OF CAPITAL

EXHIBIT 10-2
Shareholders' Equity

Paid-in capital:		
Capital stock	$1,500,000	
Surplus	4,500,000	$6,000,000
Retained earnings		4,028,000
TOTAL SHAREHOLDERS' EQUITY		$10,028,000

In Exhibit 10-2, I have taken the shareholders' equity section of the balance sheet from SAMPLE BANK (Appendix C) and restated it to show the two components of shareholders' equity. *Paid-in capital*, as the term indicates, is capital paid directly into the corporation by its shareholders when they purchase its stock. The capital stock account represents the par value of the shares sold. Par value is not to be construed as representative of the market value of the stock. Par value is only of legal significance. In most states, corporations cannot sell previously unissued stock below par value. Once the stock is sold, the corporation cannot return any of the par value to shareholders as a "liquidating" dividend. (This term is explained later in the unit.) The concept is that this is a protection to corporate creditors that prohibits the board of directors from reducing corporate equity below the par value (or, whatever amount is defined as legal capital in the state of the corporation) of the issued stock through dividends.

If stock is sold for an amount in excess of its par (or, as it is sometimes called, stated value), the excess is credited to an account variously called:

1. Paid-in capital in excess of par (or stated value).
2. Premium on common stock.
3. Surplus.

The surplus account is unique to the banking industry. GAAP attempts to discourage use of the term *surplus* for general purpose financial statements, so its use in banking is an exception to the general rule because of the industry's long traditional use of the term. As GAAP literature points out, surplus is not to be construed as an unnecessary, or excessive, amount. Federal banking regulations require that the amount of premium, or surplus, must be equal to (or exceed) the par value of the stock issued. The amount of loans that can be made to an individual borrower is based on a percentage of capital and surplus. We'll assume that this percentage is 10% for purposes of discussion.

Let's make the following assumptions relative to SAMPLE BANK (Appendix C).

1. All of the stock was initially sold in 1976 (the first year of bank operations) at $35.
2. The board of directors decided to transfer $750,000 of retained earnings to surplus to increase the bank's legal lending limit.
3. We will further assume that net income for the year was $2,654,000. (This would be an astronomical feat for a new bank but the assumption is needed to tie this example into SAMPLE BANK'S numbers.)

The journal entries to record these transactions would be

```
XX-XX-76
XXXX   Appropriate cash account              5,250,000
         3200 COMMON (or capital) STOCK                     1,500,000
         3300 SURPLUS                                       3,750,000

XX-XX-76
3400   UNDIVIDED PROFITS (retained earnings)   750,000
         3300 SURPLUS                                         750,000
```

After this entry, the bank's legal lending limit would increase from $525,000 to $600,000.

```
12-31-76
3500   CURRENT YEAR EARNINGS*               2,654,000
         3400 UNDIVIDED PROFITS                            2,654,000
         Final closing entry to transfer
         current year earnings to
         undivided profits.
```

*Also variously called income summary or revenue and expense summary account.

As you see, we have used the undivided profits and the retained earnings accounts interchangeably. *Undivided profits* is the old traditional banking term. The title of *retained earnings* is the preferable term since it does a much better job of describing the account, especially for the layperson user of financial statements.

EXHIBIT 10-3

Sample Bank Capital Statement For 1976
in thousands of dollars

	TOTAL	CAPITAL STOCK	SURPLUS	RETAINED EARNINGS
Initial sale of stock	$5,250	$1,500	$3,750	
Net income	2,654			$2,654
Transfer of retained earnings to surplus	-0-		750	(750)
Balance, 12-31-76	$ 7,904	$ 1,500	$ 4,500	$ 1,904

Observe NOW how the ending balances from Exhibit 10-3 tie into the Statement of Changes in Shareholders' Equity presented in Appendix C for SAMPLE BANK. Also, observe how the capital statement serves as the linking statement between the balance sheet and the income statement.

DIVIDENDS

Dividends can be categorized as:

1. Ordinary cash dividends.
2. Liquidating cash dividends.
3. Stock dividends.

All dividends must be authorized by the board of directors of the corporation. Dividend policies are a very sensitive area of corporate life. The owners of a corporation, its shareholders, are compensated for their risk taking in the form of dividends and the appreciation in the market value of corporate stock. Of the two methods, appreciation is probably the most beneficial to the individual shareholders. Nonetheless, the frequency and amount of dividends is an important element of corporate management.

All dividends go through a three-step process which can be depicted in journal form as follows:

2-15-X1

3400 UNDIVIDED PROFITS	DEBIT	
2820 DIVIDENDS PAYABLE		CREDIT

To record the declaration of
a $1.50 per share cash dividend
on the 100,000 shares of common
stock issued and outstanding.
The dividend will be payable to
owners of record as of 3-15-X1.

3-15-X1

This is called the *record date*.
No journal is required since the
record date simply establishes
who owned the stock on that date.

One of the jobs of the corporate stock transfer agent (a service performed for other corporations by many banks) would be to provide the bank with a listing of the shareholders of record so that the dividend checks can be properly prepared.

4-15-X1

2820 DIVIDENDS PAYABLE	DEBIT	
2061 OFFICIAL CHECKS (ALL TYPES)		CREDIT

To record the payment of the
cash dividend.

The amount received by each shareholder would, of course, depend on the number of shares he or she held. The job of preparing dividend checks is one well suited to commercial banks. (I've often wondered what the postage bill alone must add up to for mailing AT&T dividends.)

Liquidating cash dividends (which are very rare) are paid out of the surplus account. The entries to record a liquidating cash dividend would be the same as those illustrated above for ordinary cash dividends (just substitute account 3300 for account 3400). Since they represent a return of capital, they are not taxable income to the shareholders.

Ordinary cash dividends are, of course, taxable income to shareholders since they do represent a distribution of profits. The profits of a bank, or any corporation, are what is left over after corporate income taxes have been paid. The taxation of ordinary cash dividends to corporate shareholders is, therefore, the second time taxes have been paid on corporate profits. This is why it is said that corporate income is subject to "double taxation." It is one of the factors that makes appreciation in stock market value more attractive than dividends for all types of corporate stockholders.

Stock dividends, like ordinary cash dividends, reduce retained earnings. However, unlike cash dividends, they do not reduce total stockholders' equity. Stock dividends and stock splits (splits only involve a reduction of the par value of the stock and require no journal entries) are made, basically, to decrease the market value of the corporate stock. By doing so, more investors are financially able to acquire a corporation's stock. Thus, splits and stock dividends broaden the market for a corporation's stock.

Stock dividends, since they do reduce retained earnings, also limit the amount available for distribution of ordinary cash dividends. In general, corporations cannot declare dividends that would cause the retained earnings account to go into a debit (or deficit) balance. This means that corporations that already have a deficit balance in retained earnings cannot pay any cash dividends. (In banking, the regulatory agencies would act long before such a condition occurred.) Banking corporations are even more restricted in the dividend area. Look at Note 11 for SAMPLE BANK (Appendix C) to see what I mean here.

The reduction of the market value of corporate stock, which usually occurs with stock dividends and splits, does not adversely affect the existing shareholders since the market values of their holdings, before and after the stock dividend or split, are usually comparable. For example, say that you purchased 100 shares of Bank X stock in January at $30. In March you received a 5% stock dividend so now you own 105 shares of Bank X stock. Let's further assume that the market value of the stock went to 28 and 5/8's after the stock dividend. Are you happy or sad? I suppose you would be only slightly happy since the total market value of your shares went to $3,005.63 after the stock dividend as opposed to their original cost, or basis, to you of $3,000. Of course, you would have been even happier if the market value had simply stayed at $30, which it may very well have. In either case, you would have NO taxable income stemming from the stock dividend since your percentage ownership of the corporation remained unchanged. Even the Internal Revenue Code recognizes that in order to have taxable income, you must have had an increase in your equity, or wealth; and, of course, there is no increase in wealth from stock dividends or splits.

The per share value of a stock dividend on the corporate books is determined by the market value of the stock at the time of the stock dividend. Without going through all of the technical steps involved, this would be the effect of our 5% stock dividend on Bank X's books:

XX-XX-X1

3400	UNDIVIDED PROFITS	120,000	
	3200 COMMON STOCK		40,000
	3300 SURPLUS		80,000

To record 5% stock dividend on
the 80,000 shares of $10 par
common stock outstanding
(market value $30).

TREASURY STOCK

Corporations will frequently reacquire their own shares of stock from their shareholders. Among the primary reasons could be to help support the price of the corporate stock or the acquired shares may be used for employee profit sharing or pension plans. The accounting for treasury stock is very straightforward under the "cost approach" which we will illustrate here.

1-10-X1

3XXX	TREASURY STOCK—AT COST	130,000	
	2061 OFFICIAL CHECKS (ALL TYPES)		13.30,000

To record the purchase of 5000 shares of
the bank's own $10 par common at $26.

2-15-X1

3XXX	Appropriate "CASH" account	30,000	
	3XXX TREASURY STOCK—AT COST		26,000
	3300 SURPLUS		4,000

To record the sale of 1000 shares
of treasury stock which were
originally acquired 1-10-X1 at $30.

The $4,000 credit to the surplus account is not income to the bank for either tax or GAAP. The theory is that a corporate entity cannot show a profit or loss on the sale of its own securities.

The treasury stock account is a contra account within stockholders' equity. It would be presented immediately after the undivided profits, or retained earnings, account on the balance sheet. The unit review questions should help further your understanding of the mechanics of this account.

PREFERRED STOCK

All corporations must have at least one class of stock which would be its common stock. Beyond that, they may have as many classes of stock as they can sell. All these additional classes would be varieties of preferred stock. Basically, the "preferred" stock class means that this class of stock will receive dividends before any dividends are paid to the common stock.

From an investor's viewpoint, preferred stock has a return similar to a bond in that it has a fixed dividend rate. Unlike bonds, preferred stock may be subject to wide changes in the market value, similar to common stock, so an investor may get the best of debt security income protection and stock appreciation potential in preferred stock. (Of course, it's still stock so the investor could get into trouble, too.)

Since banks have used the financial tool of preferred stock very infrequently, we will not expand on the topic other than to note that the liquidation value of preferred stock must be subtracted from stockholders' equity to arrive at the equity per share of the common stock. Also, the amount of the preferred dividends must be subtracted from net income in arriving at earnings per share for the common stock.

EQUITY PER SHARE

Assuming there was no preferred stock, equity per share on common stock is simply arrived at by dividing total shareholders' equity by the number of shares outstanding. For SAMPLE BANK in Appendix C, this works out to $66.85 for the current year and $59.43 for the preceding year. Does this mean that the market values of the stock were those amounts at the end of each year? Does this also mean that the market values of the stock increased during the current year? The answer to both of these questions is, "Maybe but, then again, maybe not." Well then, if equity per share isn't the same as market value, what good is it? The answer here....."Very little good."

The reason for the little question and answer game above is that financial analysts have long abandoned equity per share as a realistic measure of anything, while many laypeople to financial statements believe that equity per share means something. Perhaps, in banking, the effect of several generations of inflation on the balance sheets is less dramatic than in other businesses but I know of very few bankers who would agree to sell their banks for the equity, or book value, per share nor would they make loans to customers based on the customers' book value. The only merit that I can see in equity per share computations is that they are good academic exercises for students so you will be asked to do some in the unit review questions and projects.

EARNINGS PER SHARE

Earnings per share (EPS) is quite another story (as opposed to equity per share). Increases and decreases in EPS on common stock tend to cause similar increases and decreases in the market value of the stock. EPS is the denominator in the all important price/earnings ratio which I will explain in Unit 15.

EPS on Net Income is computed as follows:

$$\frac{\text{Net Income available to the common shareholders}}{\text{\# of shares of common stock outstanding}} = \text{EPS}$$

In a corporation with no preferred stock, the numerator would simply be net income. Where preferred stock is outstanding, the numerator would be net income minus the amount of preferred dividends. In a "simple capital structure," which I will stick to here, the denominator would be the number of shares of common stock outstanding. Of course, if there were changes in the number of shares outstanding during the year, one would use the weighted average.

Armed with the EPS formula, you should be able to go back to SAMPLE BANK in Appendix C and see how they arrived at the EPS numbers. As we will more fully discuss in Unit 11, two after-tax income numbers are shown on the income statement and so, therefore, two EPS numbers are shown.

INTERNAL CONTROL POINTS—STOCKHOLDERS' EQUITY

1. Are all board actions promptly and accurately reflected in the corporate minutes book?

2. Are shares of treasury stock and shareholder ownership records adequately controlled?

3. Are all journal entries affecting stockholder equity accounts properly authorized and controlled?

REVIEW QUESTIONS

1. A bank with 500,000 shares of $20 par common stock authorized issued 310,000 shares. Subsequently, the bank reacquired 10,000 shares. How many shares are

A. Authorized and unissued?

B. Issued and outstanding?

2. If the bank in question 1 above declared a $2 per share dividend, what entry will be made
   A. On the declaration date?
   B. The record date?
   C. The payment date?

3. If the bank in question 2 subsequently declared a 5% stock dividend when the market value is $30 per share,
   A. What will be the increase in paid in capital resulting from the dividend?
   B. What will the effect be on total assets, total liabilities, and total stockholders' equity?

4. During the year, a bank's assets increased by $10 million and its liabilities increased by $8 million. The bank also paid dividends totaling $1 million. There were no transactions during the year affecting bank stock. What was the amount of net income for the year?

5. Had the bank in question 4 sold stock for $2,500,000 and purchased treasury stock for $500,000, what would have been the amount of net income?

6. A bank issued 50,000 shares of its $10 par common stock in exchange for fixed assets having a fair market value of $1,500,000. How would this transaction be recorded?

7. The stockholders' equity of a bank appears as follows:

10% Preferred stock—$50 par	500,000
Common stock—$10 par	1,100,000
Additional paid in capital	4,000,000
Retained earnings	5,000,000
Treasury common—10,000 shares at cost	300,000

The preferred stock is entitled to receive par in the event of liquidation. What is the equity per share of the common stock?

8. In question 7, if the net income was $1,500,000, what would the earnings per share be?

9. Assume the bank in question 7 sold 5,000 shares of the treasury stock at $40.
   A. How would this transaction be recorded?
   B. What would this transaction's effect be on total assets, net income, and shareholders' equity?

10. Using the illustration in question 7 as the beginning balances and assuming that the items in questions 8 and 9 occurred during the current year, prepare a statement of changes in shareholders' equity. Further assume that the regular dividend was paid on the preferred stock and that a $6 per share cash dividend was declared on the common stock. The common dividend occurred after question 9 and after selling an additional 10,000 shares of previously unissued common at $45. The common dividend was not paid until January of the following year.

REVIEW PROJECTS

1. Prepare entries in general journal form for the following transactions.

   A. Record declaration of cash dividends on common stock, $500.

   B. Prepare the final closing entry for the year to close out the balance in the current year earnings account of $4,230.

2. Prepare a capital statement for THE FIRST TYPICAL BANK in Appendix F. Use the format of Exhibit 10-3 as a guide for your working paper. The information necessary to prepare the capital statement is found in the 16 entries in the general journal from Unit 2 and the 35 entries in the general journal in Appendix F.

11
REVIEW OF
BANK INCOME STATEMENTS

THE BALANCE SHEET APPROACH

As stated in the Preface, I have taken the "balance sheet" approach for your study of bank financial statements. This is often an approach taken by CPA's in auditing. That is, if you know and have tested the reasonableness of the beginning and ending balances of the balance sheet accounts, the resulting change in retained earnings (plus any dividends) must be the amount of net income. The preparation of the income statement, or P&L, only consists of logically portraying the elements that go together to comprise the net income amount.

In Unit 1, I showed you the basic format of the P&L for banks. This format concentrates on the amount of interest margin. The *interest margin* is the spread between interest income and interest expense. Interest margin is the equivalent of gross profit for a nonbanking concern like TYPICAL NONBANK, INC., in Appendix C.

P&L FORMATS

The general term used to refer to the "interest margin" type format is the *multiple step* income statement. This is the format of SAMPLE BANK's income statement (Appendix C). Most analysts feel that the interest margin format is superior to the "single step" P&L format, since it specifically sets forth and isolates the significant elements of net income. On the other side of the coin, there is also a school of thought that argues that the multiple step P&L tends to clutter up the P&L with data and that the various subtotals and captions could potentially be used to mislead the reader. The data in Exhibit 11-1 are presented in "single step" format.

Financial statements can also be prepared only in terms of percentages. These are referred to as *common size* statements and are very useful for comparative analysis. These common size statements are also called "vertical analysis" since all data in a given column are shown as a percentage of a base such as net interest margin or total interest income. You could say that the percentage data in Exhibit 11-1 are a vertical analysis of the P&Ls of all FDIC-insured banks. The data for SAMPLE BANK in Appendix C could be restated in the format of Exhibit 11-1 and you could compare the resulting percentages for SAMPLE BANK against the industry percentages.

DETAILED INCOME AND EXPENSE ACCOUNTS

As you can see, the P&L is a summarization of detail that may come from numerous general ledger accounts. In the Chart of Accounts for this text, I followed the summarization technique to highlight the major areas of bank income and expenses. Previous units of this text provide a detailed breakdown of the major balance sheet and P&L accounts covered in those units. The major operating expense accounts, which have not been covered in previous units, are those accounts that do not bear direct relationships to the major balance sheet accounts. In terms of the Chart of Accounts used in this text, those accounts are:

6010 SALARIES & WAGES
6020 PAYROLL TAXES
6030 GROUP INSURANCE
6040 OTHER EMPLOYEE BENEFITS
6100 OCCUPANCY EXPENSES
6300 FURNITURE & EQUIP EXPENSES
6900 OTHER OPERATING EXPENSES

Exhibit 11-2 provides suggested subcategories for each of these accounts.

RESPONSIBILITY ACCOUNTING

In addition to what we might call the "generic" breakdown of income and expense accounts (i.e., interest income/expense, salaries, rent, etc.), many banks go one step further. That step would be to associate all major areas of income and expense to the functional areas of the bank. (Exhibit 12-1 in Unit 12 provides a good outline of these functions.)

With income and expense data by types of expense and by function or areas of responsibility, the board of directors and bank management have the tools necessary to judge the effectiveness of each area of bank operations and a good data base for forecasting and budgeting. More of this area is covered in Unit 13.

P&L PRESENTATION OF INCOME TAXES

Again, look at SAMPLE BANK's income statement in Appendix C and determine the total amount of income taxes for that year. Hopefully, you came up with $146,000. In terms of income tax return terminology, which we will be discussing in detail in Unit 14, the 1978 data could be summarized as follows:

TAXABLE INCOME	$1,581,000
INCOME TAX LIABILITY	146,000
INCOME AFTER TAX (net income)	$1,435,000

NOTE: For the benefit of those of you who may have peeked into Unit 14, I am assuming here that there was no difference between pretax book income and taxable income.

Now for the point of this section! Although the amount of income tax liability or expense is a single amount, it is necessary to allocate that total to the components of the income that we are reporting on the multiple step income statement. Here is the same schedule we started above showing that allocation. (By the way, this is what accountants refer to as intraperiod tax allocation. Aren't you glad I didn't label this section with such a frightening bit of jargon?)

	TOTAL	=	SUBTOTAL	SUBTOTAL
TAXABLE INCOME	1,581,000		1,450,000	131,000
INCOME TAX LIABILITY	146,000		80,000	66,000
INCOME AFTER TAX (NI)	1,435,000		1,370,000	65,000

HOW MANY SUBTOTALS?

SAMPLE BANK's P&L required only two pretax subtotals to arrive at net income. (Can you see now why net income is always an after-tax number? This is why we also say that dividends are paid out of after-tax dollars.) I like to refer to SAMPLE BANK's P&L as a "clean" income statement. I use this term since in a more complex P&L, there could be up to five such subtotals plus a sixth amount related to retained earnings. I will begin a brief discussion of these amounts starting with the last one noted which is called a prior period adjustment.

Prior Period Adjustment

For many years, the theory of income determination held that net income was a rather sacred number and that the amount of net income should reflect a firm's ability to generate income in the ordinary course of business. (The formal title assigned to this theory that was just introduced is "The current operating theory of income determination.") Under this theory, anything unusual in the way of revenue or expense that occurred during the year was charged or credited directly to the retained earnings or surplus account. (In nonbank entities, *surplus* used to be a synonym for retained earnings. See why many people do not understand what *surplus* is on bank financial statements?) To avoid a long discussion here, let's simply say that the problems with this approach far outweigh its merits.

Today's theory of income determination is called "The Clean Surplus Theory." For us, it would perhaps be better to call this the Clean Retained Earnings or the Clean Undivided Profits Theory. Basically, this theory says that if an item of revenue or expense relates to the current year, then it belongs on the income statement! This means that the retained earnings account will only be affected by:

- *Most common*
    Net income or loss
    Dividend declarations
    Prior Period adjustments
- *Uncommon or downright rare*
    Some treasury stock and stock retirement transactions
    In banking—required transfers to paid in capital
    Perhaps a quasi-reorganization

Very simply, then, a *prior period adjustment* is an item of revenue or expense that is recorded in the current period but has actually taken place in some prior period. Want an example? Well, about the only thing that I can really give you without turning this into an advanced accounting theory course is the correction of an error. Let's assume that we forgot to record depreciation expense in 19X1 and caught up with the error in 19X3. The entry would look like this.

```
XX-XX-X3
3400  RETAINED EARNINGS                    10,000
        15XX ACCUMULATED DEPRECIATION                    10,000
```

"Now wait a minute!" you say. "Isn't depreciation deductible in determining taxable income? If we forgot to record depreciation in 19X1, then the 19X1 financials were wrong and we overpaid the income tax in 19X1."

Well, if that's what you said, welcome to the real world. We do make mistakes and things do pop up in subsequent periods that we didn't even dream of when they actually happened. Relative to the income tax consequences of prior period adjustments, here is how they would be recorded for our depreciation goof:

```
XX-XX-X3
2941  INCOME TAXES PAYABLE                 5,000
        3400 RETAINED EARNINGS                            5,000
        To record the reduction in income
        tax liability (and expense) due
        to the adjustment for 19X1 depreciation.
        (50% tax rate assumed).
```

The "net of tax," or after-tax, effect of this prior period adjustment is a decrease in retained earnings of $5,000.

Other P&L Items Given Net of Tax Treatment

Following is a listing of the other three items on the P&L that are handled on a net of tax, or after-tax, fashion.

- Discontinued Operations
- Extraordinary Items
- Income Effect Due to a Change in GAAP

A detailed discussion of each of these items is beyond the scope of this text. It will suffice to say that each of them, like security gains and losses, is looked at as an item that should be isolated on the income statement in order to determine the profitability of the bank without these "unique" occurrences.

SUMMARY

This unit is not lengthy since you should have a fairly good concept of the form and content of the P&L by the time you completed Unit 10. Also, a good deal of what you need to learn about putting together the income statement will be learned by *doing the unit review project* for THE FIRST TYPICAL BANK (an old friend if you have worked through the text to this point). After completing Unit 9, you put together TYPICAL's balance sheet; in Unit 10, you prepared TYPICAL's capital statement; and now—

REVIEW PROJECT

Prepare a multiple step income statement from the trial balance for THE FIRST TYPICAL BANK in Appendix F.

NOTE: Because of the high degree of summarization used (deliberately) in TYPICAL'S chart of accounts, your income statement will be a highly condensed version of SAMPLE BANK's income statement (Appendix C), which you should use as your format guide. In order to conform to the SAMPLE BANK format, you will also have to "reclassify" (break out) the following.

1. The provision for loan losses needs to be pulled out of loan interest and shown separately.
2. The provision for depreciation needs to be allocated between occupancy and furniture and equipment expense.

EXHIBIT 11-1
Annual Income of FDIC Insured Banks

OPERATING INCOME

Interest & fees on loans	$58,991	65.3%
Interest on balances with banks	4,888	5.4
Income on fed. funds sold and sec purchased under resell agreements	2,476	2.7
Interest on U.S. Treasury securities	6,395	7.1
Interest on U.S. Government securities	2,469	2.7
Interest on state and local securities	5,365	5.9
Interest on other securities	859	1.0
Dividends on stock	110	.1
Income from direct lease financing	699	.8
Income from fiduciary activities	1,980	2.2
Service charges on deposit accounts	1,807	2.0
Other service charges, commissions, and fees	2,409	2.7
Other income	1,910	2.1
TOTAL	$90,358	100.0%

OPERATING EXPENSES

Salaries and employee benefits	16,346	18.1
Interest on time certificates of deposit of $100,000 or more issued by domestic offices	6,763	7.5
Interest on deposits in foreign offices	10,216	11.3
Interest on other deposits	21,833	24.2
Expense of federal funds purchased and securities sold under agreements to repurchase	4,543	5.0
Interest on other borrowed money	818	.9
Interest on subordinated notes and debentures	392	.4
Net occupancy expense	3,603	4.0
Furniture and equipment expense	1,931	2.1
Provision for possible loan losses	3,301	3.7
Other expenses	9,599	10.6
TOTAL	$78,792	87.2%
Income before income taxes and securities gains or losses	11,566	12.8
Applicable income taxes	2,832	3.1
Income before securities gains or losses	8,734	9.7%
Securities gains or losses, net of income taxes of 43	99	.1
Income before extraordinary items	8,833	9.8%
Extraordinary gains, net of taxes of 9	46	nil
NET INCOME	$ 8,879	9.8%

Source: FDIC, *Annual Report,* 1977. Reported in millions of $. *Note:* Detail may not add to totals because of rounding.

EXHIBIT 11-2

Sample Detail of Major Operating Expense Categories

6010 SALARIES & WAGES
 Officer salaries
 Employee salaries
 Employee overtime

6020 PAYROLL TAXES
 Employer's FICA
 Unemployment comp
 Workman's comp

6030 GROUP INSURANCE
 Life
 Medical
 Other group ins

6040 OTHER EMPLOYEE BENEFITS
 Profit/pension plans
 Education
 Employee relations

The above salary and employee benefit costs represented 18.1% of operating income for the banks reported in Exhibit 11-1.

6100 OCCUPANCY EXPENSES
The detail for accounts 6010–6040 relating to building employees would fall under this category along with account 6210. Other detail for Occupancy would be—
Rent
Building repairs and maintenance
Building supplies
Utilities
Property taxes
Property insurance
Building depreciation (included in account 6200)
Rental income received from building (a "contra" account)

6300 FURNITURE AND EQUIP EXPENSES
Depreciation on "F&F" (included in account 6200)
Equipment rental
Equipment repairs and maintenance

6900 OTHER OPERATING EXPENSES
Advertising
Armored carriers
Clearinghouse fees
Examination fees
Freight expense
Legal and accounting
Office supplies
Postage
Service bureau/data processing costs
Telephone
Travel and entertainment

12
INTERNAL CONTROL

Internal control and auditing are two concepts that are frequently misunderstood by laymen. Here are two common misconceptions which often make life difficult for the auditor and can lead to lackluster internal control.

1. Internal control is something that management concerns itself with out of a fear of the auditors.
2. The function of auditors is to try to prevent all fraud and to make sure that fraud of any sort that does occur is detected and that corrective action is taken.

MISCONCEPTION #1

To answer misconception #1, refer back to the Internal Control Points that were provided (or that you were asked to generate) for Units 3 through 10. Now imagine that these "points" are all listed by functional area without the yes/no response format. The first "POINT" then under CASH & DUE FROM in Unit 3 might read as follows:

1. The person responsible for a cash fund should be the only one having physical control over that fund.

Other negative type questions asked by auditors are:

- Does the firm have an organization chart?

- Are procedure manuals kept current?

These can be restated like this.

- Organization charts and procedure manuals should be maintained on a current basis to provide a visible record of management structure and firm policies.

Stated in the more positive structures shown above, internal control can be seen more clearly for what it really is—just good sound business and management procedures.

Accountants define internal control as the plans and all of the methods and procedures in effect (1) to safeguard the assets and insure the accuracy of the accounting records, and (2) to promote efficiency and adherence to management policies. As a student of business, I always have to smile when I see this definition, since each separate discipline in business seems to have its own version of this concept. For example, in marketing you might hear it called "The Action Plan." A management major would call this the methods and procedures in the planning-organization-and-control cycle. A professor of finance might talk about the financial structure goal, while an economist might refer to the micro-model of the firm for optimal profit equilibrium or whatever. The point is that all students of business agree that any firm has to do some planning and see to it that the job of running a business gets done in an efficient and legal manner.

In the business of banking, good sound management with a fine system of checks and balancing points (i.e., good internal control) has always been of utmost importance.

In summary response, it can be said that internal control is the accounting profession's jargon for what management is all about.

MISCONCEPTION #2

To respond to this thought, we must, first of all, point out that *auditor* is an umbrella term.

The audit function can be characterized by an analogy to major league professional sports. Auditors can be seen as the umpires or referees of business. The internal auditor is a member of the management team and should share in the development of the "game plan." Regulatory agency auditors are there to determine if the "game plan" is in conformance with legal regulations, which we might equate to the "league rules." The CPA, in the role of independent auditor, shares the concern of both the internal and the regulatory auditors. The CPA must be reasonably satisfied that the firm under examination is operating within the limits of the laws. The CPA is also expected to satisfy himself or herself that all facts are disclosed which may influence the decisions of the users of the firm's financial statements.

Given the above breakdown of the different types of auditors and auditing, it is clear that all auditors would be concerned with fraud but that the problem of fraud is only a portion of the total scope of auditing.

The second part of misconception #2 assumes that if fraud is not prevented, the auditors will, sooner or later (and probably sooner), find out about it and stop the fraud. Certainly, fraud reduction is a goal of the auditor just as crime prevention is a goal of police work. Fraud, like any other type of crime, will never be completely prevented and some crime will always go on unpunished. How much fraud/crime prevention/detection goes on is a function of the effort put behind those aspects of internal control that involve fraud protection.

How much internal control against fraud?

Many authors talk about "simply" applying the law of diminishing returns to determine how much resources are to be put into internal control. This is the correct theory, but its application is just not that simple. Here is a classroom story I tell about Charlie, my hypothetical neighbor.

Charlie decided to buy a puppy for his family and so one day he came home with Max. Knowing that young shepherds like to run and exercise, Charlie built a fence around his lot so Max would not annoy the neighbors. Charlie knew that Max would not be a puppy forever so he made the fence eight feet tall so that when he was full grown, Max would not annoy the neighbors by eating them. As it turned out, Max did indeed grow up to be a BIG healthy dog. Charlie's neighbors enjoyed watching Max, as a puppy, try to scale the fence and, as Max grew up, it was amazing to see him scale the fence with four or five feet to spare. Fortunately, Max would only scale the fence on command from Charlie. Also, fortunately, Max was so well trained that he would not have crossed his own lot line without command, even if there had been no barrier.

Charlie's fence can be viewed as an internal control system. Clearly, in Max's puppyhood Charlie spent too much money on internal control. But, as it turned out, even the eight-foot fence wasn't sufficient to contain Max. Happily, when this happened, Charlie's commands became the system of internal control.

This story of Max illustrates several points:

1. A firm's system of internal control will never reach perfection.
2. Internal control that remains static will become useless.
3. It is possible to spend too much as well as too little on internal control.
4. The last point is that people can be far more devious than Max may ever become. The biggest of frauds occur at the very top levels of management. This type of fraud is almost impossible to detect and if it is, it is usually too late. Such was the situation in the Equity Funding case which resulted in losses of over $300 million to shareholders in a firm whose securities were traded under SEC regulations.

FOREIGN CORRUPT PRACTICES ACT

Background

The Foreign Corrupt Practices Act was enacted in 1977. The law was instituted due to questionable or illegal payments by many U.S. companies to foreign governments and firms. These payments and the practices that fostered them were the source of much comment in the press and of embarrassment to many of those involved.

One of the embarrassments that came out of this public discussion was the fact that illegal payments, amounting to hundreds of thousands, and even millions, of dollars, went unnoted and undetected by the CPAs auditing the firms in question. This led the accounting profession to respond that auditors' examinations are done on a test or sample basis. Further, although the illegal payments involved were substantial, they were not material when viewed within the context of the operations of the multibillion-dollar firms involved and, therefore, did not require disclosure. As to the issue of lack of discovery of the payments by auditors, it was pointed out that the very size of the payments and the political sensitivity involved required the closed-mouth, discrete handling of top management. These are the same ingredients that were required in the Equity Funding case noted above. As such, these payments were the type of fraud (if you agreed that they indeed constituted fraud) least susceptible to detection in an ordinary audit situation.

Many firms defended these "questionable practices." Their logic was that "bribes" to foreign officials and firms were accepted modes of international business dealings. They further pointed out that legislating such "bribes" as illegal would place U.S. firms at a competitive disadvantage. The attitude of many congressmen was that the political sensitivity created by major U.S. multinational firms in making international bribes payments made these payments material, regardless of the dollar amounts involved. The sponsers of the bill felt that, without legislation, the financial integrity of U.S. firms would be impaired.

The Act

The resulting legislation (the Act), which retained the title Foreign Corrupt Practices Act, makes bribing an offense which is punishable to firms by fines of up to $1 million. Further, individuals (including corporate management and directors) face fines of up to $10,000 and/or imprisonment of up to five years.

The Act does not include "grease" or "facilitating" payments to relatively low-level foreign government employees in the definition of bribery. The other provisions of the Act tend to make its title misleading since it also amends the Securities Exchange Act of 1934 by requiring ALL publicly held companies to maintain accurate records and adequate systems of internal control. These accounting provisions of the Act apply regardless of a firm's international affairs.

At the time of its enactment, the SEC staff made it clear that the Act greatly expanded the Commission's authority to regulate public companies' internal affairs. This attitude was made clear when the SEC entered suits against companies based solely on the Act's accounting provisions. More recently, the SEC has taken other avenues outside the Act relative to internal control, but the attitude of SEC and other regulatory agencies' influence over a firm's internal control remains.

One of the weaknesses of the Act is that it contains many uncertainties relative to how to conform to its provisions. Here are examination procedures that were adopted by the Comptroller of the Currency in reviewing the work of internal auditors relative to the Act as well as the Federal Election Law.

a. Determine whether:
- The auditor is aware of their provisions.
- Specific audit programs have been developed to check compliance with them.
- General audit programs remind auditors to be alert for any unusual entries or charges which might be in violation of the acts.

b. Review the results of specific and general programs for indications of improper or illegal payments to persons or organizations covered by the acts.

Similarly, when reviewing directors' compliance with their duties and responsibilities, the national bank examiners will:

Determine compliance with the Foreign Corrupt Practices Act (PL 95-213) by:

a. Reviewing the bank's policy prohibiting improper or illegal payments, bribes, kick-backs, etc. to any foreign government official or other person or organization covered by the law.
b. Determining how that policy has been communicated to officers, employees or agents of the bank.
c. Reviewing any investigation or study done by, or on behalf of, the board of directors of the bank's policies and operations concerning the advance of funds in possible violation of the act.
d. Reviewing the work done by the examiner assigned, "Internal/External Audit" to determine whether internal/external auditors have established routines to discover improper/illegal payments.
e. Analyzing the general level of internal control to determine whether there is sufficient protection against improper/illegal payments being inaccurately recorded on the bank's books.
f. Requesting examiners performing other programs to be alert for any transactions that might violate the provisions of the act.
g. Compiling any information discovered throughout the examination on possible violations.
h. Performing procedures on suspected criminal violations contained in section 503.3.

How To Demonstrate Good Internal Control

The Act requires all firms, including banks, subject to SEC regulation to:

1. devise and maintain a system of internal control sufficient to provide reasonable assurance that assets are safeguarded and that transactions are properly authorized and recorded; and
2. keep reasonably detailed records which accurately and fairly reflect financial activities.

Note how the above provisions of the Act are essentially a restatement of the accountant's definition of internal control noted at the start of this unit. In Unit 1, I noted that there is no definitive reference detailing GAAP. The same situation exists with internal control. There are no criteria for evaluating internal control either in the Act or in professional literature. In the absence of such definitive criteria, the following "laundry list" is provided as suggestive of what a bank can do to demonstrate compliance with the accounting provisions of the Act as well as its commitment to good internal control in general.

1. Maintain a written program calling for an ongoing review and evaluation of existing internal control. Such a program should be monitored by senior management and the board of directors.

2. Maintain current written documentation on bank policies and procedures as well as documentation on the effectiveness of these procedures. Such documentation would include

   a. Flowcharts

   b. Policy and Procedure Manuals

3. Maintain records of management and board meetings when the Act and internal control were specifically addressed. Such memos or minutes should include statements of intent to conform to the provisions of the Act and records of discussion with appropriate employees showing that the Act's provisions were properly disclosed and explained.

4. Maintain letters and reports from independent auditors evaluating the bank's internal control. These records should be cross-referenced to documentation showing how the bank corrected any deficiencies noted in these reports.

As you can see, it is important to have a well-documented plan of internal control. (Let's use I/C from now on.) It is also important to be able to demonstrate that the plan is working. In planning any I/C program, the auditor must have a clear understanding of the operating cycle of the business (discussed in Units 1 and 2) and a good idea of the structure of the organization. Exhibit 12-1 contains a summary of the operating functions of a typical community bank. This will serve as a good discussion and reference tool.

Once the objectives of each functional area have been identified, the audit program should be designed to evaluate whether these goals are being met. Besides the traditional I/C points (i.e., segregation of duties, check and balance points, etc.), the I/C program should also encourage innovation. Following is an excerpt from a sample issue of *Internal Auditing Alert* by Warren, Gorham & Lamont, Inc., to illustrate this point.

AUDITING INNOVATION: HOW TO SPOT IT, HOW TO GROW IT

Innovation is at the root of every successful business, whether it shows up as new product development or improvements in company procedures and systems. Management-minded internal auditors know this and, when conducting repeat examinations of a given area, they include a review of innovations implemented since the last audit. Here's how.

DOES THE COMPANY ENCOURAGE NEW IDEAS? Leave innovation to chance, and chance may pass you by. To avoid that sad fate, look for "yes" answers to these questions:

IS RESPONSIBILITY FOR INNOVATION SPECIFICALLY ASSIGNED? Don't conveniently assume that department managers automatically take on this responsibility if it is not part of their job description. Managers focus their energies where top brass is looking, and if no other direction is given, this too often seems to be a maximum short-term return achieved by playing by the book.

IS THERE ROOM FOR CREATIVE BEHAVIOR? Innovators are often mavericks. You're going to benefit from their ability to think differently—always assuming that creative behavior is never confused with disruptive behavior.

IS LACK OF INNOVATION ACTIVELY QUESTIONED? One aluminum company found a good way to follow up: Where a process cannot be improved at least once every five years, the responsible manager must justify—in a written report to higher management—the decision to stick with older methods. Older methods aren't inherently suspect; the idea is to make sure they aren't maintained solely out of habit.

ARE EMPLOYEE SUGGESTIONS ACTIVELY SOUGHT? You may laugh at suggestion-box cartoons, but an articulated policy soliciting ideas from all employees will pay off—not only in innovation but in heightened morale as well.

DO YOU SPREAD GOOD IDEAS AROUND? In reviewing like operations at diverse locations, internal auditors observe local improvements with universal applications. Different operations should not have to reinvent the wheel. Make sure innovative approaches are shared with other departments performing similar functions. Your interal audit manual should make this part of the auditor's job.

POINTER: Spread the word about the innovators, too. Alert company executives to the potential abilities of subordinate managers. People who find new and better ways to handle their current tasks can be expected to carry this same ability into positions of greater responsibility.

DON'T FORGET INNOVATIONS IN AUDITING. Innovative responsibility is a direct part of your own job. What new and creative practices can you adopt? Innovation may take the form of auditing in pioneer areas, expanded use of statistical sampling techniques to reduce sample size or establish a higher degree of reliability for audit findings, or adoption of methods to expand coverage in familiar areas without increasing examination costs.

EXAMPLE: The payment of transportation invoices by the S.C. Johnson Co. (Johnson's Wax) illustrates innovation in the common function of cash disbursements. A few years ago, Johnson manufactured all of their products in Racine, Wis. Since the company's market embraced the entire United States, it incurred numerous and sizable transporation bills. In addition, ICC regs required that these bills be satisfied within a very few days. To meet this requirement and also save considerable clerical effort and cost, Johnson sent blank sight drafts to regular transportation suppliers, who were expected to complete the drafts for reimbursement. The original sight draft was so arranged that any recordings on it were imprinted on an envelope preaddressed to Johnson. The transportation supplier then inserted all documents supporting his reimbursement in the envelope. Envelopes received by Johnson were sorted by amounts involved; all payments exceeding a specified amount were spot audited, the frequency of examination decreasing as the amount went down.

At first glance, this scheme may appear to violate all the principles of good internal control. But Johnson believed they had one of the strongest controls working in their behalf—the carriers' desire to retain Johnson business. Johnson's audits supported this belief: In the few cases where errors occurred, 90 percent penalized the carriers. [*]

KEEPING THE I/C PROGRAM CURRENT

An I/C program that becomes stagnant is a failure. The audit committee of a bank should be constantly reviewing the thrust of its programs to maintain the good safeguards and to use the I/C program to save costs and/or increase profits. The following two articles, also from the *Internal Auditing Alert*, highlight both of these points.

HOW TO DECIDE WHAT TO AUDIT

No matter what your industry, you want operational audit efforts to focus on areas offering the greatest potential yield. Easy to say in theory, but how do you identify those areas in practice?

First, give top priority to requests from the company president or directors. Evaluate all other requests on two scales: (1) reason for the request and its overall importance and (2) anticipated company benefits. Four good candidates for a benefits "payoff" are:

- Areas of greatest corporate expenditures;
- Areas suspected of having faulty controls;
- Questionable areas identified from ratio and trend analysis; and
- Product profitability analysis.

BENEFITS OF EXAMINING BIG-SPENDING CENTERS—Maximum-expenditure areas promise the greatest opportunity for:

COST SAVING—Say your analysis leads to a procedural change that cuts costs by 2 percent. The company obviously benefits more if it applies to a profit center spending $1 million rather than one spending a few thousand. And the expanded volume of transactions and procedures involved in handling and accounting for the larger expenditures offers greater opportunities for potential savings.

DISCOVERING IRREGULAR TRANSACTIONS—Illicit transactions are rarely buried in low-cost, low-volume areas, where cooked numbers tend to stand out. Deliberately select large-cost, heavy-volume centers for examination to increase your chances of uncovering possible fraud.

SPOTTING "CONTROL APATHY"—Enormous budgets can make line management careless with control. Consider this unfortunately real example: An internal auditor analyzing sales promotion expenses verified the purchase costs of a "cheap" giveaway intended to increase customer goodwill. But, checking to see how the marketing scheme had worked, he learned it had never been used. The sales manager had changed his mind and $10,000 worth of giveaways sat in a storeroom. The manager's attitude: "What's $10,000 against our $10 million budget?" An internal auditor can't expect to totally overcome this attitude, but persistent questioning will help.

If not apathetic, managers simply may be unaware that costs such as maintenance expenditures are controllable at all, and so make no specific control efforts. This is inadvertent waste, but unnecessary costs accumulate nonetheless. Your audit should spot such waste; your report should include corrective suggestions.

TWELVE SIGNS OF FAULTY CONTROL—Faulty controls open the door for waste, fraud, and higher costs. To identify problems, review previous audit reports, including your public accountant's, and do frequent performance and reporting breakdowns. Red flags are:

- Declining trend in return on investment.
- Deadlines for supplying information to higher management frequently missed.
- Line management unable to provide information requested.
- Erroneous information supplied to management.
- Information supplied in a form difficult to understand.
- High employee turnover.
- Employees' excessive walking, talking, telephoning, or absence from normal work stations.
- Clerical interruptions caused by excessive traffic.
- Wasted effort searching for material misplaced due to poor housekeeping, or poorly organized files.
- Awkward office layout causing additional time to perform routine tasks.
- Manual operations that could be mechanized.
- Poor morale.

If you spot one or more of these indicators, it's likely a full audit of the area will yield cost-saving results.

USE RATIO AND TREND ANALYSIS TO SPOT TROUBLE—Many different ratios are used by business and industry to help keep score of financial operating health. For example, the cash-to-sales figure, a capital utilization ratio, measures cash against volume transacted. Increases in this ratio over a period of time could indicate a company is keeping too much cash on hand to support a level of sales. Excess cash should be invested on a short-term basis.

Become familiar with the ratios that apply to your company's operations..., and apply them to successive periods to see what trends have developed. Look not only for glaring adverse trends, but for numbers that, though "okay" in the abstract, are below par for your specific industry. Industry figures are generally available from trade associations and from references like Robert Morris Associates' ANNUAL STATEMENT STUDIES. If you find a significant trend, consider it a direction sign for focusing your audit effort.

LOOK HARD AT YOUR PRODUCT LINE—The average company has at least some low-profit, marginal-profit, or money-losing products or services. Some may be worthwhile for nondollar reasons—for example, your company is seeking entry into a new field and has opted to gain visibility with a loss-leader—but they should be looked into. Spotting money drains that can be plugged—or moneymakers that merit further boosting–should be a major audit goal. Corporate management will make the final decisions, but your effort will help channel their energies in the most useful directions.

POINTER: By directing the internal audit effort to areas expected to produce the greatest yield, you maximize your contribution to your company. And that enhances your own stature in top management's eyes.[*]

KEEPING A WATCHFUL EYE ON INTERNAL ACCOUNTING CONTROL: A GENERAL REVIEW PROGRAM

Well-organized companies keep a constant check on accounting functions with internal accounting control systems. Systems vary with the size and complexity of the company, but all are after the same end result: To make sure assets are safe from unauthorized use, accounting records provide a reliable base for financial statement preparation, and accountability is maintained for all corporate assets. These days, that assurance is especially important to management because of the need to comply with the requirements of the Foreign Corrupt Practices Act.

Outside auditors provide some assurances that control systems are satisfactory, but their review is usually made annually. There's only one way for management to be satisfied that internal accounting controls are working properly during the year—the internal auditor.

MONITORING THE CONTROL SYSTEM—It's your job to design and direct a comprehensive review program aimed at evaluating the company's accounting control system. Of course, you'll review all the various facets of financial accounting: cash, receivables, inventories, fixed assets, etc. But you need to develop a general review program, too, to cover the OVERALL control system. Here's a general review program for a company with $10 to $25 million in sales (smaller companies may eliminate some of the questions):

[*]Reprinted by permission from the *Internal Auditing Alert*, Sample Issue 1982, Copyright © 1982, Warren, Gorham and Lamont Inc., 21 South St., Boston, Mass. All Rights Reserved.

- Is there an up-to-date organizational chart? Are there records that define in detail departmental and individual duties?
- Is the organization chart for the accounting department being followed? Do department employees rotate duties? Are any members of the department related to each other? Are any relatives of accounting department members employed elsewhere by the company?
- Is there a corporate accounting manual that describes the procedures to be followed in recording and summarizing accounting transactions?
- Is a chart of accounts in use? Does it describe the type of entries affecting each account?
- Are detailed accounting records available (e.g., accounts receivable, accounts payable)?
- Are accounting records kept in secure locations? Consider not only internal security and loss prevention, but also fire or flood damage.
- Is the accounting department headed by a competent individual, capable of supervising an accounting staff? Does the main office have controls on branch office accounting?
- Is the accounting department a separate entity, segregated from departments like credit, sales, manufacturing, and purchasing?
- How do operating budgets measure up against actual performance figures? Are material variances properly explained?
- Do current monthly statements include enough specific details to adequately supply management's information needs?
- Do journal entries include explanations or information to supplement and support them? Are all entries approved by an appropriate accounting officer?
- Who takes care of the company's insurance coverage needs? Is the coverage adequate to protect company assets? Consider especially: inventory levels, replacement value of fixed assets, business interruption insurance, additions to or deletions from fixed asset accounts.
- Are there any bank accounts in the name of the corporation not on the books of account?
- Are procedures for incoming mail adequate (e.g., to prevent against theft of incoming checks)?

NOTE: A general review might also address itself to additional areas, such as a company's cost system or product lines. The nature and extent of questions depend upon the particular enterprise.

AFTER THE EVALUATION Once your review is wrapped up, report

your findings to management. Include specific recommendations for improvement where you have spotted weak points.*

I/C FAILURE—AN EXAMPLE

Despite the best of efforts (or due to the lack thereof) fraud does occur. This example is adapted from the "Fraud Bulletin" (6/73) of the Bank Administration Institute.

X, an officer in a branch of a large commercial bank, was in charge of delinquent installment loan follow-up. Because of X's long experience in installment lending, X was frequently asked to assist in many other aspects of the installment lending operation. X was also authorized to approve cash transactions and record record changes.
X was able to:

1. Abstract customer insurance premium refunds.
2. Misappropriate loan and late charge payments.
3. Legitimate cashier's checks to customers for overpayments or refunds, on which the customers did not follow up on collecting, were deposited into X's personal accounts at the branch.

The fraud when finally uncovered involved over 1,000 entries and accounts.
Major factors that contributed to the fraud were:

1. A lax management attitude in allowing X to handle transactions from start to finish. As such, X was able to act as teller, bookkeeper, and officer. This is a direct violation of the concept of segregation of duties.
2. Apparently, endorsements on cashier's checks were not tested. Considering the volume of transactions, had this been done, even on a test basis, some of the forged endorsements on the legitimate cashier's checks would have been detected.
3. Had the activity in employee accounts been tested, the fraud may have been uncovered even sooner.

AUDIT PROGRAM

After completing your study of the balance sheet in Unit 10, you have a good listing of internal control points for a typical community bank. Listings like

* Reprinted by permission from the *Internal Auditing Alert*, Sample Issue 1982, Copyright © 1982, Warren, Gorham and Lamont Inc., 21 South St., Boston, Mass. All rights reserved.

these are part of what CPAs, internal auditors, and supervisory examiners use in their evaluation of I/C. Based on their I/C reviews, detailed audit programs are prepared. The scope, or extent, of these programs will depend on the auditor's judgment as to the effectiveness of the existing I/C. I am concluding this unit with a suggested internal audit program for a typical community bank. Indicated under each of the program areas would be:

1. The detailed steps to be performed.
2. Estimated frequency of examination.
3. Estimated length of each examination.
4. The areas which require confirmation requests.
5. Which area should be examined on a surprise basis.

You will note that the program is organized in balance sheet order. As in most audit programs, the income and expense accounts which are related to accounts in the balance sheet are tested in conjunction with the examination of those accounts.

SUGGESTED INTERNAL AUDIT PROGRAM

CASH

1. Periodic counts of teller cash funds should be made. It is suggested that tellers be counted quarterly and vault cash monthly.
2. An analysis of teller differences should be maintained with notations made to show attempts to locate uncleared items.

CASH ITEMS

Cash items accounts should be balanced and reviewed on a monthly basis for old or uncollectable items. This work should be cross referenced to work in overdrafts and reconciling items in the correspondent bank accounts to be sure that these cash items are not being bounced back from account to account.

DUE FROM BANKS

A review of all due from account reconciliations must be performed on a monthly basis. Dates of entries for correspondent and per bank should be compared for unnecessary delays indicating breakdowns in precedure. Old unentered items should be followed up on so that they do not become stale to the point of being uncollectable.

INVESTMENTS

All investments of the bank should be confirmed directly with the depository at least semi-annually. Analysis of yields should be maintained which would indicate any large fluctuations in income. Any such fluctuations should be followed up on. The bond ledger should be run and balanced approximately every other month.

REAL ESTATE LOANS

1. The balancing of the real estate loan trial balance should be reviewed for unusual items and proper posting of payments.
2. The escrow accounts and interest income on real estate loans should be tested on a monthly basis. Verification of the physical existence, by either telephone call or visit to the property, for new loans, on a test basis, is also suggested.
3. The weighted average interest rate on real estate loans should be computed and compared to the effective interest rate.

COMMERCIAL AND INSTALLMENT LOANS

Procedures in these areas would parallel those suggested for real estate loans. Due to the volatility and relatively high incidence of fraud in installment loans, a larger scope of telephone calls and visits for verification of existence is suggested.

OVERDRAFTS

Overdrafts should be reviewed on a weekly basis. Notations should be made on the collection efforts of old or large items.

FEDERAL FUNDS SOLD OR COMMERCIAL PAPER PURCHASED

Primary exposure in this area is income that is not being received. Monthly tests should be made to see that all income due the bank is being received.

FIXED ASSETS

A permanent record of all fixed asset additions should be maintained along with supporting invoices.

OTHER ASSETS

Other asset accounts should be reviewed for proper handling of transactions on a monthly basis. Where other asset accounts relate to another area, such as interest receivable and loans, work on these accounts should be covered when examining the major area.

DEMAND DEPOSITS

Review of the processing of demand deposits should be continuous. A balancing review should be made weekly, along with reviews of other demand deposits, to determine that:

1. The balances are properly stated.
2. All fee income is being recorded.
3. Old or misposted items do not exist.
4. Register copies of official checks agree with control accounts.

On a test basis, the endorsements of the payees on official checks should be verified, where possible, and the payees reviewed for propriety. Large checks cashed or cash back should be tested to see that proper officer approval was obtained. Sample tests should be made to see that signature cards on closed accounts are being promptly pulled from the active file. Any activity on dormant accounts should be tested for proper officer approval.

TIME DEPOSITS

Procedures and frequency should be roughly similar to that of the demand deposit area.

OTHER LIABILITIES

Other liability accounts should be reviewed for proper handling of transactions therein on a monthly basis. Where other liability accounts relate to other areas, such as loans or investments, work on these accounts should be covered in the other balance sheet area.

CAPITAL FUNDS

The bank should annually run the stock certificate book and balance the stockholders' ledger to the total outstanding stock in the bank. All entries or changes in the undivided profits account should be explained and dates of board approval shown.

SECURITY GAINS AND LOSSES

All entries in this account should be explained and dates of proper officer or board approval shown.

INTEREST EXPENSE ON SAVINGS DEPOSITS

At the end of every interest payment period, the total interest expense should be reviewed on an overall basis and interest paid on individual accounts recomputed on a test basis.

OCCUPANCY EXPENSES

These accounts should be reviewed on a monthly basis and unusual fluctuations and large entries investigated for propriety. Disbursements should be traced to documents of original entry on a test basis.

SAFE DEPOSIT BOX RENTAL INCOME

A periodic comparison to last year's rental income along with a comparison to the total possible rental income on a yearly basis should be made approximately once a year.

OTHER OPERATING INCOME

Approximately once a quarter the entries in this account should be reviewed. Effective testing of the inclusion of all income that is due the bank will be done during the work done on the applicable balance sheet accounts. For instance, if a cashier's check is to be sold with a one dollar fee charged, the inclusion of this fee should be traced to the entry in the related income account.

REVIEW PROJECT

In handling this material in the classroom, I have asked the class to break up into groups. Each group would be assigned a different area from the suggested internal audit program and asked to develop specific procedures to be performed for that area. The groups could then be asked to support the scope of their proposed examinations based on different sized banks or on banks of the same size having different levels of I/C.

The following outlines the duties and functions typically found under each of the functional areas in Exhibit 12-1. Those who perform the unit review project may want to try writing audit programs for functional areas as well as, or instead of, audit programs written around balance sheet classifications.

    I. Administrative Functions (in support of service functions)

        A. Plan of organization

        B. Policy and procedure formulation

        C. Internal auditing

EXHIBIT 12-1

Functions of a Typical Bank

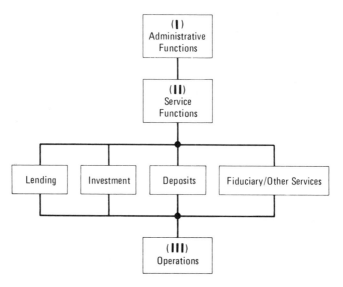

D. Branch/subsidiary bank administration

E. Information system:

1. Budgeting
2. Cost accounting
3. Operations analysis
4. Financial reporting
5. Regulatory reporting

F. Advertising and promotion

G. Salary and wage administration

H. Capital equipment acquisition/control

I. Tax planning

II. Service Functions

A. Lending (or extension of credit)—a bank's primary function

1. Review and authorization of credit risk
2. Loan disbursement and collection
3. Delinquent loan follow-up
4. Collateral valuation and control

B. Investment (managing liquidity through secondary utilization of funds)

    1. Management of:

        a. Investment securities

        b. Trading account securities

        c. Money market funds

    2. Duties include:

        a. Purchase and redemption of securities

        b. Valuation and safeguarding of securities

C. Deposits (managing a bank's primary source of liquidity)

    1. Areas include:

        a. Demand deposits

        b. Time deposits

    2. Duties include:

        a. Depositor transaction processing

        b. Computing and recording:

            • Interest on time deposits

            • Service fees on deposits

D. Fiduciary and other services (non-funds related services). The following are major examples listed alphabetically.

    1. Collection items

    2. Letters of credit

    3. Lock box service

    4. Mortgage loan servicing

    5. Safe deposit box rental

    6. Safekeeping

    7. Travelers checks/savings bonds, etc.

    8. Trust services

III. Operations (The operations area can be viewed as those functions related to processing and control of transactions generated in the service functions.) The major duties that would fall in this classification are:

A. Physical control over cash

B. Control over official checks

C. Proof operations

D. Maintenance of general ledger

E. Reconciliation of subsidiary ledgers to general ledger control accounts

13
DATA PROCESSING

There was nothing unusual about the man slouched in the back seat of a nondescript Ford sedan driving slowly through the streets of Washington....

Perching a pair of Ben Franklin specs on a bubble nose, he laid a briefcase across his lap and opened it. The underside of the lid held a visual display screen, and a keyboard console, bordered by two rows of colored lights, lay across the bottom. He typed out a combination of numbers and waited a brief moment while the signal was bounced by satellite to his corner office at the White House. There a computer, programmed by his aides, whirred into life and began relaying his workload for the day.

The incoming data arrived in code and was electronically deciphered in milliseconds by the battery-operated microprocessor on his lap, the final text reading out in green lower-case letters across the screen.

First came the correspondence, followed by a series of memos from his security council staff. Next came the daily reports from various governmental agencies, the Joint Chiefs of Staff and the director of Central Intelligence. He quickly digested them to memory before erasing their contents from the microprocessor's storage unit.

All except two.*

This quote is not science fiction. The technology for the briefcase computer is here! You will not have to be on the White House staff to have access to such a tool. In fact, if you work for a large corporation, you may already be using small computers.

OVERVIEW OF EXISTING BANK COMPUTER OPERATIONS

Since all banks currently use some form of electronic data processing, I will only survey the current state of the art here.

Off Line Processing

With off line processing, control totals for the general ledger control accounts are developed from summaries of the daily batches processed in proof. When these batches are computer processed, the detailed subsidiary ledgers are updated and the totals from the resulting subledger trial balances are compared to the general ledger control totals.

Following is an example from DDA to illustrate these procedures.

Monday, June 1
This is the first day of business for a new bank. Initial deposits to DDA accounts (all outclearing items) amount to $80,000. This was the only activity for DDA.

Tuesday, June 2
The June 1 detailed trial balance of DDA accounts, which the bank's service bureau prepared the previous night, is balanced to the $80,000 balance in the general ledger account. Tellers will use the June 1 trial balance for "look ups" and make notations thereon of today's DDA activity. At the close of business on June 2, there were net increases in DDA from outclearings of $30,000. This evening, these items, along with any inclearing cash letters, will be processed by the service bureau.

* From NIGHT PROBE! by Clive Cussler. New York: Bantam Books, Inc., 1981.

Wednesday, June 3
This morning, the June 2 detailed DDA trial balance is reconciled to the general ledger control account. The service bureau processed inclearings with a net of $12,000 against DDA, along with the outclearing June 2 credits, so the reconciled June 2 balance of the DDA trial balance and the general ledger control account should be $98,000 ($80,000 + $30,000 − $12,000). The reconciled June 2 DDA trial balance would be what the tellers would use for "look ups," etc. on June 3.

The process described would continue to repeat itself.

On Line Processing

With on line, or real time, processing, all teller-generated transactions are immediately updated in the subsidiary ledger records by terminals linked to a control computer. The processing of inclearing items would also be immediately updated in the same fashion. Here is the way the June 1-3 off line activity, discussed above, could be handled with on line processing.

Monday, June 1
The $80,000 outclearing batch is checked against the computer's $80,000 control total.

Tuesday, June 2
The tellers would make computer terminal inquiries on customer account balances. No "hard copy" of the DDA trial balance is required since the computer can access any DDA customer account on a random basis. (In data processing jargon, RAM means Random Access Memory.)

Wednesday, June 3
The $98,000 opening balance of DDA accounts is already in computer memory and the bank is ready for another busy day.

As you can see, on line processing is far easier and provides much better internal control. Not so long ago, on line processing was also very *expensive*, but that is a changing story with the technological advances that are giving us dirt cheap electronic communications and data handling systems.

THE FUTURE IN DATA PROCESSING

Banking is still very much a paper handling business with each Federal Reserve District handling a larger number of checks each year than the number of hamburgers McDonalds has sold since 1957.

Anyone familiar with data processing hardware (machines) knows that the electrical/mechanical process of reading MICR data is a *very slow* way to input computer data. This is all going to change as we begin to turn into a checkless, paperless society. I would highly recommend that you read what Toffler has to say about computers in *Future Shock* and his follow-up book, *The Third Wave*. Some of the changes are already here and some will soon be. Here are some examples:

- Automatic teller machines.
- Interface of cable TV and computer systems allowing customers to perform teller functions with the bank from their own homes or businesses.
- Massive data bases linked to microcomputer systems allowing electronic transfer of funds between accounts, anywhere. These transfers would be both bank- and customer-generated, thus eliminating the need for checks.

Try this not too futuristic scenario:

It is 5 o'clock in the evening of April 15th and you decide that you had better file your income taxes. After dinner, you sit down at your computer terminal and link into your confidential IRS file maintained at the National Computer Center. On January 3rd, your employer had already transmitted your earnings (Form W-2) data to your IRS file. Also, on January 4th, all banks and brokerage firms that you do business with had transmitted your other income data (Form 1099) into your IRS file so all you have to do now is interface your home accounting system, with your itemized deductions, into the IRS file.

You do this and your CRT (Cathode Ray Tube, i.e., TV tube) display says that you owe $100. The display is also prompting you either to accept this sad fact or to ask for a hard copy (paper) printout of the return computations to review.

You decide to edit the hard copy and find, much to your joy, that, somehow, you failed to get a major deduction into your home accounting software (computer program). You enter the change and have your IRS file updated accordingly. The CRT now says that you have a refund coming of $100.

You push the proper function key on your computer terminal and accept the refund. In 1/10,000 of a second, $100 is electronically transferred from the TT&L account at your local bank into your DDA account there. Your home accounting package is also updated to reflect the additional $100 in your DDA account. You are also happy to see, on the screen, that the IRS has accepted all of your return input and does not anticipate the need to request any sort of other input for audit verification. The session is closed when you acknowledge acceptance of your filed return and refund. This entire process took less than 15 minutes and you decide to enjoy the rest of your evening celebrating your refund.

MICROCOMPUTER APPLICATIONS IN BANKING

The technology for my little tax story is here and available to anyone who can afford a microcomputer. You could obtain a good one for about the cost of a good video cassette player and camera system. The following describes the four basic software packages that make microcomputers extremely desirable personal and business assets.

Word Processing Software

Banks, like most businesses, do a lot of typing. Word processing is, simply, nothing more than typing electronically. What's so great about typing on a computer? There are at least two great advantages.

1. The ability to edit and make changes without retyping entire pages.
2. The ability to store the data electronically which creates the possibility of the paperless office.

Ninety-eight percent of this text was prepared using a word processer (THE MAGIC WINDOW) with the same system described in Appendix A. The contents of this entire book could be stored on one small floppy disc. (Floppy discs look like 45 RPM records but are made of material akin to tape recorder tape. Thus, they are very flexible and so they are christened floppy discs. You may also see disc spelled disk.)

Exhibit 13-1 is an example of a draft of a memo. Any good typist (as you can see, I am not one) would retype the entire memo rather than cut, paste, and white-out in this case. Exhibit 13-2 is the corrected version of the memo (which does contain some relevant information). It took me, fumble fingers, about 45 seconds to make the indicated corrections and changes.

General Ledger Software

You are already aware that THE FIRST TYPICAL BANK is an example of a microcomputer general ledger application. Since the BPI package cannot accept individual entries over $1 million, large banks would use more powerful packages; but the basic operations of general ledger programs are no different than the operations of the BPI package. Exhibit 13-3 provides suggested review steps in deciding on accounting hardware and software.

Electronic Worksheets

There is a whole family of electronic worksheet programs available. The first and most widely used of these programs is VISICALC.[*] What can you do with VISICALC? With VISICALC, you can produce any type of worksheet that you could produce with paper and pencil on a columnar pad. The tremendous advantage of an electronic worksheet over the paper and pencil version is the ability to change selected data and have the computer update the balance of your computations *instantly*.

Exhibit 13-4 is an example of a budget forecast prepared for a school district. Take the time to check the math in Exhibit 13-4.

That took some time, didn't it? Now, take the Other Sources amount and change it to $100,000 for each year. This change will also require that you recompute the interest for years X2, X3, and X4. The interest is computed as 15% of the previous year's average fund balance. After making these two sets of changes, change all of the related totals and percentages.

Now that really took some time, didn't it! Exhibit 13-5 was done with VISICALC in about two minutes. Half of that time was in printing.

BUDGETING ELECTRONICALLY

Hopefully, you were impressed with Exhibits 13-4 and 13-5 and can see the applications of electronic worksheets in budgeting and forecasting for banks as well as for all businesses. In responsibility accounting, as noted in Unit 11, the manager of each profit and/or expense center could prepare forecasts for his or her own area of responsibility. As these forecasts percolated up the organization chart, the detailed forecasts could be combined at various levels. The final output would be a consolidated forecast for the entire organization like the one presented for the school district in Exhibits 13-4 and 13-5.

A frequent request by loan officers of loan customers is for projections of cash flow. Many customers may not be able to come up with such a report without getting an expensive accountant involved, and the customer may look elsewhere for his loan. A solution to this problem would be for the bank to have a standardized cash flow forecasting model on VISICALC. The loan officer could input the specific assumptions into the electronic worksheet while reviewing the details of the loan request with the customer. This would give both the banker and the customer a good common understanding of the proposed loan package, thus reducing future misunderstandings and providing a basis for subsequent revisions as the customer's needs change. This would also provide a good basis to compare actual versus expected results.

[*] VISICALC® is a trademark of Personal Software, Inc., VisiCorp.

EXHIBIT 13-1

Draft of Memo Produced on a Word Processor

TO: FELLOW FACULTY AND STAFF

FROM: Jim Patten

DRAFT

SUBJECT: Demonstration of Apple computer

Next Wednesday and Thursday (10-21&22) I will have my Apple II
computer on campus to demonstrate to you and several of my
accounting classes. This is the software that I will have on
board:

> THE MAGIC WINDOW-This is a word processor with which this
> memo was generated.

> BPI GENERAL LEDGER ACCOUNTING PACKAGE.
> > Will handle-
> > > 400 General Ledger Accounts
> > > 500 Accounts Receivable
> > > 300 Accounts Payable
> > > 100 Employee Earning Records
> > > Up to 10 Departmentalized Income Statements
> > > Balance Sheet Capable on Consolidating
> > > of Grouping Accounts

> VISICALC-This is said to be the one software package that
> justifies owning a microcomputer. I have spent
> only about five hours with VISICALC, and I have
> to agree with that statement!

> > Here is what I will have to show you---
> > An electronic grade book
> > A budgeting and forecasting model

Imagine in any teaching environment, where graphs or any type
of number shuffling is important, the ability to bring the data
alive on screen and to be able to back up the "moving"
presentation with hard copy for student review.

You are welcome to visit my Accounting 101 classes (my schedule
is posted on my office door) to see the BPI package
demonstrated. I will be here on both days from 8AM to 4PM and
will have the equipment available for you to see when I am free
of classes. I'm sure if you stop by the Division office those
days, someone can tell you where to find Patten's Apple.

> PS: If you are already a member of "THE THIRD WAVE" and own
> a micro, please feel free to bring in your own software,
> or just stop by to compare notes.

142

FAVORITE

EXHIBIT 13-2

Corrected Version of Exhibit 13-1

TO: FELLOW FACULTY AND STAFF

FROM: Jim Patten

SUBJECT: Demonstration of Apple Computer

Next Wednesday and Thursday (10-21&22) I will have my Apple II
computer on campus to demonstrate for you and several of my
accounting classes. This is the software that I will have on
board:

        THE MAGIC WINDOW-This is a word processor with which this
                    memo was generated.

    BFI GENERAL LEDGER ACCOUNTING PACKAGE.
            Will handle-
                    400 General Ledger Accounts
                    500 Accounts Receivable
                    200 Accounts Payable
                    100 Employee Earning Records
                    Up to 10 Departmentalized Income Statements
                    Balance Sheet Capable of Consolidating
                        or Grouping Accounts

    VISICALC-This is said to be the one software package that
                justifies owning a microcomputer. I have spent
                only about five hours with VISICALC, and I have
                to agree with that statement!

                Here is what I will have to show you---
                    An electronic grade book
                    A budgeting and forecasting model

Imagine in any teaching environment, where graphs or any type
of number shuffling is important, the ability to bring the data
alive on screen and to be able to back up the "moving"
presentation with hard copy for student review.

You are welcome to visit my Accounting 101 classes (my schedule
is posted on my office door) to see the BFI package
demonstrated. I will be here on both days from 8AM to 4PM and
will have the equipment available for you to see when I am free
of classes. I'm sure if you stop by the Division office those
days, someone can tell you where to find Patten's Apple.

    PS: If you are already a member of "THE THIRD WAVE" and own
        a micro, please feel free to bring in your own favorite
        software, or just stop by to compare notes.

EXHIBIT 13-3
Review of a Firm's Automated Accounting Requirements

A. DETERMINE THE OPERATING CYCLE

Merchandising Firm	Service Firm
Cash	Cash
Inventory	Costs of Providing Services
Accounts Receivable	Accounts Receivable
Cash	Cash

B. DETERMINE THE VOLUME AND NATURE OF TRANSACTIONS

- Number of checks written
- Nature and volume of cash receipts
- Number of customers
- Number of vendors
- Composition of inventory
  - Number of different types
  - Quantity of each type
  - Level of and need for inventory control
- Number of employees
  - Salaried
  - Hourly
  - Special union reporting?
- Number of locations
- Any special regulatory reporting or tax situations?

C. DETERMINE THE ADEQUACY OF THE EXISTING SYSTEM OF INTERNAL CONTROL

Automating a poor system of internal control will just perpetuate a bad situation—only faster.

D. OTHER CONSIDERATIONS

When considering automation of the accounting system, the potential benefit of a computer for applications such as word processing, engineering, or as a sales tool should be considered.

Exhibits 13-6 and 13-7 provide an example of such a cash flow projection/budget. The illustrations cover cash flow for the first two years, done by quarter, of a proposed school of airbrush arts. The projection assumes that only 50% of the maximum enrollment would be achieved during these two years. Study the design of the exhibits so that you can follow through in doing the related unit review project. (*Helpful Hint*: Note how the ending cash balance for year 1, $38,014 (Exhibit 13-6), ties into the beginning cash balance for year 2 in Exhibit 13-7.

Data Base Management Software

A data base is nothing more than information stored in some logical order. Data base software is able to retrieve the information contained within the data base and rearrange and/or summarize it in any manner.

The cleanest example of a data base is a mailing list. Here are some of the sorts and summaries that a data base system can do with a mailing list.

1. How many names are on the list?
2. Sort in alphabetical order by zip code.
3. Print out all names in zip codes XXX91 AND XXX92 for M through S.
4. Print out all addresses on Main Street in the towns of Springfield and Columbus.

Could you think of other sorts or summaries?

Exhibit 13-8 is a business example of a data base system. Look it over now.

If you are familiar with advertising (some large banking organizations have their own internal ad department) or can imagine the problems that these businesses must deal with, you can see that the data base format was laid out to capture most of these problems. Once the data for each job is entered in the data base, management can assess the status of each element of individual jobs or can summarize, say, deadline status on all jobs or jobs for a particular customer. The combination of sorts, inquiries, and summarizations on a good data base management system is limited only to the extent of the user's imagination. You will be asked to try your hand at this in the unit review projects.

EXHIBIT 13-4
School District Funds Flow Estimate

	FISCAL X1	FISCAL X2	FISCAL X3	FISCAL X4
BASE DATA:				
FTE PROJECTION	9000	8500	7500	7000
TUITION RATE	20	25	26	26
ASSESSED VAL M$	4200	4400	4600	4900
TAX RATE	15	16	17	17
SOURCE OF FUNDS				
TUITION	5940000	7012500	6435000	6006000
PROPERTY TAXES	6642000	7532800	8367400	8913100
STATE REIMB.	5397900	5829732	6296111	6799799
INTEREST	1090940	938245	1108069	1287647
OTHER SOURCES	1362300	1200000	1100000	1000000
TOTAL	20433140	22513277	23306579	24006546
USE OF FUNDS				
SALARIES & BEN	15000000	16800000	18816000	21073920
CONT. SERVICES	2800000	640000	700000	750000
MATERIALS & SUP	170000	209100	257193	316347
TRAVEL & MEET.	120000	150000	187500	234375
FIXED CHARGES	400000	432000	466560	503885
UTILITIES	1300000	1625000	2031250	2539063
CAPITAL OUTLAY	450000	486000	524880	566870
OTHER	50000	50000	50000	50000
TOTAL	20290000	20392100	23033383	26034460
NET FUNDS FLOW	143140	2121177	273196	-2027914
BEG. FUND BAL.	6183397	6326537	8447714	8720910
ENDING FUND BAL	6326537	8447714	8720910	6692997
% ANALYSIS:				
TUITION	0.29	0.31	0.28	0.25
PROPERTY TAXES	0.33	0.33	0.36	0.37
STATE REIMB.	0.26	0.26	0.27	0.28
INTEREST	0.05	0.04	0.05	0.05
OTHER SOURCES	0.07	0.05	0.05	0.04
	1.00	1.00	1.00	1.00
SALARIES & BEN	0.74	0.82	0.82	0.81
CONT. SERVICES	0.14	0.03	0.03	0.03
MATERIALS &SUP	0.01	0.01	0.01	0.01
TRAVEL & MEET.	0.01	0.01	0.01	0.01
FIXED CHARGES	0.02	0.02	0.02	0.02
UTILITIES	0.06	0.08	0.09	0.10
CAPITAL OUTLAY	0.02	0.02	0.02	0.02
OTHER	0.00	0.00	0.00	0.00
	1.00	1.00	1.00	1.00

EXHIBIT 13-5
School District Funds Flow Estimate—Revised

	FISCAL X1	FISCAL X2	FISCAL X3	FISCAL X4
BASE DATA:				
FTE PROJECTION	9000	8500	7500	7000
TUITION RATE	20	25	26	26
ASSESSED VAL M$	4200	4400	4600	4900
TAX RATE	15	16	17	17
SOURCE OF FUNDS				
TUITION	5940000	7012500	6435000	6006000
PROPERTY TAXES	6642000	7532800	8367400	8913100
STATE REIMB.	5397900	5829732	6296111	6799799
INTEREST	1090940	843573	829123	823180
OTHER SOURCES	100000	100000	100000	100000
TOTAL	19170840	21318605	22027634	22642079
USE OF FUNDS				
SALARIES & BEN	15000000	16800000	18816000	21073920
CONT. SERVICES	2800000	640000	700000	750000
MATERIALS & SUP	170000	209100	257193	316347
TRAVEL & MEET.	120000	150000	187500	234375
FIXED CHARGES	400000	432000	466560	503885
UTILITIES	1300000	1625000	2031250	2539063
CAPITAL OUTLAY	450000	486000	524880	566870
OTHER	50000	50000	50000	50000
TOTAL	20290000	20392100	23033383	26034460
NET FUNDS FLOW	-1119160	926505	-1005749	-3392381
BEG. FUND BAL.	6183397	5064237	5990742	4984993
ENDING FUND BAL	5064237	5990742	4984993	1592612
% ANALYSIS:				
TUITION	0.31	0.33	0.29	0.27
PROPERTY TAXES	0.35	0.35	0.38	0.39
STATE REIMB.	0.28	0.27	0.29	0.30
INTEREST	0.06	0.04	0.04	0.04
OTHER SOURCES	0.01	0.00	0.00	0.00
	1.00	1.00	1.00	1.00
SALARIES & BEN	0.74	0.82	0.82	0.81
CONT. SERVICES	0.14	0.03	0.03	0.03
MATERIALS &SUP	0.01	0.01	0.01	0.01
TRAVEL & MEET.	0.01	0.01	0.01	0.01
FIXED CHARGES	0.02	0.02	0.02	0.02
UTILITIES	0.06	0.08	0.09	0.10
CAPITAL OUTLAY	0.02	0.02	0.02	0.02
OTHER	0.00	0.00	0.00	0.00
	1.00	1.00	1.00	1.00

EXHIBIT 13-6
Cash Flow Projection/Budget—Year 1

SCHOOL OF AIRBRUSH ARTS
CASH FLOW PROJECTION/BUDGET

50% ASSUMPTION—FIRST YEAR
MAX CLASS SIZE—20 STUDENTS
AVG TUITION/STUDENT $255

	1ST QTR	2ND QTR	3RD QTR	4TH QTR	TOTAL
# CLASSES		2	12	12	26
MAX ENROLL	0	40	240	240	520
MAX TUITION	0	10200	61200	61200	132600

REVENUE:
.5

TUITION	0	5100	30600	30600	66300
OTHER					
TOTAL	0	5100	30600	30600	66300

EXPENDITURES:

ADMIN		900	500	500	1900
ADVERISING	2000	1000	1000	1000	5000
BOND & CERT	175				175
EQUIPMENT	3911				3911
INSURANCE	500				500
RENT		6000	6000	6000	18000
MISC ART SUP	200	100	100	100	500
PHOTO SUP	100	200	200	200	700
SALARIES		2400	2400	2400	7200
SPARE PARTS	200	100	100	100	500
STORE STOCK	100	300	300	300	1000
UTILITIES		1000	1000	1000	3000
OTHER					0
					0
TOTAL	7186	12000	11600	11600	42386
NET CASH FLOW	-7186	-6900	19000	19000	23914
BEG CASH	14100	6914	14	19014	14100
END CASH	6914	14	19014	38014	38014

EXHIBIT 13-7
Cash Flow Projection/Budget—Year 2

SCHOOL OF AIRBRUSH ARTS
CASH FLOW PROJECTION/BUDGET

50% ASSUMPTION—SECOND YEAR
MAX CLASS SIZE-20 STUDENTS
AVG TUITION/STUDENT $255

	1ST QTR	2ND QTR	3RD QTR	4TH QTR	TOTAL
# CLASSES		2	12	12	26
MAX ENROLL	0	40	240	240	520
MAX TUITION	0	10200	61200	61200	132600

REVENUE:

	1ST QTR	2ND QTR	3RD QTR	4TH QTR	TOTAL
.5					
TUITION	0	5100	30600	30600	66300
OTHER					
TOTAL	0	5100	30600	30600	66300

EXPENDITURES:

	1ST QTR	2ND QTR	3RD QTR	4TH QTR	TOTAL
ADMIN		900	500	500	1900
ADVERISING	2100	1300	1300	1300	6000
BOND & CERT	135				135
EQUIPMENT	200				200
INSURANCE	500				500
RENT	6000	6000	6000	6000	24000
MISC ART SUP	200	100	100	100	500
PHOTO SUP	100	200	200	200	700
SALARIES		2400	2400	2400	7200
SPARE PARTS	200	100	100	100	500
STORE STOCK	100	300	300	300	1000
UTILITIES		1000	1000	1000	3000
OTHER					0
					0
TOTAL	9535	12300	11900	11900	45635
NET CASH FLOW	-9535	-7200	18700	18700	20665
BEG CASH	38014	28479	21279	39979	38014
END CASH	28479	21279	39979	58679	58679

EXHIBIT 13-8
Sample Data Base File

```
            THE CREATIVE ADVERTISING AGENCY
                                        ! JOB #
                JOB COST AND BILLING CONTROL !     ----------
                                        !
                                        !
CUSTOMER:                               ! DATE PLACED
                                        !               ----
                                        !
                                        ! DEADLINE
                                        !               -------
                                        !
                                        ! DELIVERED
                                        !----------------------
PERSON TO CONTACT                       PHONE
-------------------------------------           --- --- ----
            ******D A T E S*******    $$$$$$C O S T S$$$$$
VENDOR:     PLACED   DUE  DELIVERED     ESTIMATED      ACTUAL
                                        $              $
---------------  ------  ---  ---------
                                        $              $
---------------  ------  ---  ---------
                                        $              $
---------------  ------  ---  ---------
                                        $              $
---------------  ------  ---  ---------
                                        $              $
---------------  ------  ---  ---------

                                        ---------      --------
                                        $              $
                                        =========      ========
TOTAL ESTIMATED BILLING                 $              $
                                        =========      ========

BILLING HISTORY:
   INVOICE #  DATE  AMOUNT
   ---------  ----  ------


COMMENTS:
```

150

REVIEW PROJECTS

A. Go back and review the facts in the unit relative to Exhibits 13-6 and 13-7. Now further assume that the salaries shown in the projections do not include any salary allowance for the owner, a sole proprietor. The owner of Airbrush wants to make a $25,000 loan from your bank to be paid back over the 24 month projection period.

INSTRUCTIONS: What would be your decision if you were the loan officer that had to decide on granting this loan? List the factors that you considered in your decision.

B. Prepare a listing of the information that you would like to be able to obtain out of a computerized data base management system for installment loans. Have fun and use your imagination with this project!

14

TAXATION OF BANKS

Let's begin this unit with a review of the aspects of corporate income taxes that have already been covered in the text.

INCOME TAX PROCEDURES

You should now refer back to the material under this same heading that appears in Unit 9.

P&L PRESENTATION OF INCOME TAXES

Now that you have refreshed your memory regarding procedures, look back into Unit 11 and review the material under P + L Presentation on Income Taxes.

Now that you have looked over the Unit 11 material on income taxes, read Note 6 to SAMPLE BANK's financial statements (Appendix C).

Let me hasten to point out that a full explanation of Note 6 is not easy even in graduate level accounting courses. What you will see here, in keeping with the theme of this text, are the fundamentals of corporate taxes.

DETERMINATION OF TAXABLE INCOME

One thing that you should understand from reading SAMPLE BANK's Note 6 is that I made the deliberate simplification (in Unit 11) of assuming that there were no differences between pretax book income and taxable income. I did this in Unit 11 to highlight the fact that taxable income is, in fact, the excess of revenues over expenses. Under the Internal Revenue Code, not all revenues are subject to taxation and not all expenses are deductible. These items are referred to as permanent differences between book and taxable income. To explain permanent differences, you can restate the 1978 numbers for SAMPLE BANK as shown in Exhibit 14-1.

EXHIBIT 14-1
Book Income Subject to Tax

Net income		1,435,000
Add back book tax provision		146,000
Pretax accounting income (also state taxable income)		1,581,000
FEDERAL ADJUSTMENTS:		
Deduct:		
State portion of book tax provision	36,000	
Nontaxable interest	1,306,000	1,342,000
Subtotal		239,000
Add:		
Nondeductible expenses		89,696
Book income subject to federal tax		328,696

In Exhibit 14-1, I am deviating from the numbers actually used in SAMPLE BANK in order to keep the basic concepts from being bogged down by technical complications.

The $1,306,000 (which does tie back to SAMPLE BANK) and the $89,696 (my assumption) are both examples of permanent differences. This all may seem a bit confusing at this point, but have patience, it should all become clear as you proceed.

EXHIBIT 14-2

Federal Income Tax Rates—Corporations

	TAXABLE INCOME	RATE
First	25,000	17%
Second	25,000	20%
Third	25,000	30%
Fourth	25,000	40%
Over 100,000		46%

In addition to the federal taxes shown in Exhibit 14-2, most states, also, assess a tax on corporate income. (State income taxes are deductible to arrive at federal taxable income. Large corporations tend to use the highest federal tax rate of 46% plus the state tax rate in budgeting for corporate taxes. Later on, for illustration, we will use a rate of 50%.

Let's assume that SAMPLE BANK's state has a flat 2.3% tax rate on corporate income. The computation of the book provision would be as shown in Exhibit 14-3.

EXHIBIT 14-3

Computation of Book Tax Provision

1. State income tax		36,000
Federal income tax:		
2. Tax on ordinary income	131,950	
3. Less investment tax credit	21,950	110,000
Book tax provision		146,000

1. The state tax is 2.3% times $1,581,000 (rounded). The $1,581,000 is the pretax accounting income. Although state and local interest is exempt from federal taxation, there is no such exemption from state taxation. The $89,696 in expenses, not deductible on the federal return, is assumed to be deductible on the state tax return.

2. This amount is based on applying the tax rates in Exhibit 14-2 to the $328,696 computed in Exhibit 14-1.

3. The investment tax credit is included, in this example, to show the effects of all types of credits on the tax liability. (See Schedule J of Form 1120 for the other tax credits.) They are handled as a direct reduction of the book income tax expense. As noted in Unit 4, the investment tax credit can amount to up to 10% (or more) of the cost of qualifying fixed assets purchases. SAMPLE BANK's funds statement indicates fixed assets purchases, in 1978, of $439,000 and we will assume that half of that amount qualifies for the 10% rate.

COMPUTATION OF THE TAX LIABILITY

The last four pages of this unit are a reproduction of Form 1120, the federal corporate income tax return. The Form 1120 is partially filled in from the tax data that I have developed based on SAMPLE BANK. The only other assumptions that you need to follow the 1120 form are:

1. Depreciation expense per the tax return exceeded the depreciation per books by $128,696.
2. Four estimated tax payments of $10,500 each were made during the year.

To help you follow through and understand the Form 1120 example, this would be the order in which the Form 1120 would be completed.

1. Schedule M-1 is the best starting point. In Schedule M-1, you can see that you know quite a bit about income taxes just by knowing how to get to net income per books. As a practical matter, learning corporate taxes is a matter of knowing what goes in between lines 1 and 10 on Schedule M-1.
2. Schedule M-2 is the IRS version of the capital statement.
3. Schedule L is just a balance sheet—again, IRS style.
4. Schedule J should be reviewed next. The numbers that I have filled in there should be self-explanatory.
5. Lines 30, 31, and 32 on page 1 of Form 1120 should trace back to Schedules M-1 and J.

DEFERRED INCOME TAX PAYABLE

Note 6 for SAMPLE BANK refers to a year-end balance of deferred income tax of $1,102,000. Where did all that money come from? How will this liability be paid? This is one of the thorniest accounts in all of GAAP and, particularly, in banking. The answers to the two questions are easy in theory but very difficult in practice. In practice, tax rates do change as well as other factors (refer to the discussion of Provision for Loan Losses and Taxes at the end of this unit). Here, I will stick to the theory.

CREATION AND REDUCTION OF DEFERRED TAXES PAYABLE

The explanation of a "deferred tax" situation is best illustrated by the example of depreciable assets. Let's say an asset has a cost of $10 million which, for GAAP, must be written off over 10 years on a straight-line basis. The Internal Revenue Code, however, will allow a 5-year straight-line write-off. Let's further assume that income, before tax and before the depreciation deduction, is $3 million each year over the asset's 10-year life. We will, also, use our handy tax rate of 50%. I have prepared Exhibit 14-4 based on these assumptions. Take some time to look it over.

EXHIBIT 14-4
Deferred Taxes Illustrated

COLUMN>>	(1)	(2)	(3)	(4)	(5)	(6)	(7)	(8)	(9)
YEAR									
1	3	2	1	1	.5	2	1	1.5	.5
2	3	2	1	1	.5	2	1	1.5	.5
3	3	2	1	1	.5	2	1	1.5	.5
4	3	2	1	1	.5	2	1	1.5	.5
5	3	2	1	1	.5	2	1	1.5	.5
6	3		1	3	1.5	2	1	.5	(.5)
7	3		1	3	1.5	2	1	.5	(.5)
8	3		1	3	1.5	2	1	.5	(.5)
9	3		1	3	1.5	2	1	.5	(.5)
10	3		1	3	1.5	2	1	.5	(.5)
TOTALS	30	10	10	20	10.0	20	10	10.0	-0-

Column explanations:

(1) Book income before depreciation and taxes.

(2) Tax depreciation deduction.

(3) Depreciation per GAAP.

(4) Taxable income (column 1 − 2).

(5) Tax liability (50% of column 4).

(6) Pretax accounting income (column 1 − 3)

(7) Book tax provision per GAAP (50% of column 6). This column would also be GAAP net income since a 50% tax rate is used.

(8) Net income if deferred tax was not recognized (column 6 − 5).

(9) Deferred tax payable increase or (decrease). This amount can be computed by finding the difference between columns 5 and 7, or by multiplying the annual timing difference (columns 2 − 3) times the 50% tax rate.

GAAP tells us that income tax expense, or book tax provision, should be based on the pretax book income that is subject to tax and that depreciation should be based on the useful lives of the fixed assets. Therefore, under GAAP, net income would be $1 million each year (column 7, Exhibit 14-4).

Good tax planning says take every deduction that you can as soon as possible. Thus, you would go with the five-year write-off and have a Schedule M-1 item every year for 10 years.

Looking at the totals for the 10 years in Exhibit 14-4, you can see that, in the long run, the amount of net income would be the same with or without recognizing the deferred portion of the annual tax (see totals for columns 7 and 8). If you did not recognize the deferred portion of the annual tax and reported only the income tax paid as your income tax expense each year, net income would be the amounts shown in column 8. GAAP would say that the net income was overstated (by 50%) for years 1 through 5 and understated (by 50%) in years 6 through 10.

To arrive at proper GAAP net income (column 7 in Exhibit 14-4), the following entries would be made:

XX-XX-XX
8900 PROVISION FOR INCOME TAXES   .5
       XXXX Appropriate "CASH" account   .5
       Effect of entries to record payment
       of taxes in years 1-5 (amount paid
       per column 5).

XX-XX-XX
8900 PROVISION FOR INCOME TAXES   .5
       29XX Deferred income tax payable   .5
       Entry to record recognition of
       deferred taxes payable in years 1-5
       (column 9).

XX-XX-XX
8900 PROVISION FOR INCOME TAXES   1.5
       XXXX Appropriate "CASH" account   1.5
       Effect of entries to record payment
       of taxes in years 6-10 (amount paid
       per column 5).

XX-XX-XX
29XX Deferred income tax payable   .5
       8900 PROVISION FOR INCOME TAXES   .5
       Entry to record reduction in
       deferred taxes payable in years
       6-10 (column 9).

The net effect of these two sets of transactions is to give a balance of 1 each year in account 8900.

SUMMARY

Let's start summarizing with Exhibit 14-5.

EXHIBIT 14-5
Book Tax Provision vs. Tax Liability

	FEDERAL	STATE	TOTAL
Book tax provision (Exhibit 14-3)	110,000	36,000	146,000
Tax liability	50,800	36,000	86,800
Difference	59,200	-0-	59,200

There is no difference between state income taxes per books and return. The federal tax liability is the total federal tax bill for the year. That's Line 10 of Schedule J in your sample Form 1120.

The question now is, What accounts for the $59,200 difference? The answer lies in Schedule M-1 of Form 1120. The only Schedule M-1 item that is treated differently, between the books and the tax return in our example, is the $128,696 in tax depreciation in excess of book depreciation. Using the explanation in the detail for Exhibit 14-4, we see that this amount creates a deferred tax liability of $59,200 (46% x $128,696). Exhibit 14-5 is restated in Exhibit 14-6.

EXHIBIT 14-6
Footnote Detail of Income Taxes

YEAR ENDED DECEMBER 31	CURRENTLY PAYABLE		FEDERAL DEFERRED	TOTAL
	FEDERAL	STATE		
1978	50,800	36,000	59,200	146,000

Now look back again to Note 6 for SAMPLE BANK (Appendix C). The lead in to Note 6 and Exhibit 14-6 should look very similar. As noted within the unit, I changed and simplified the details of SAMPLE BANK's actual timing differences to better explain the basic tax mechanics and theories.

CASH VS. ACCRUAL BASIS

Banks with footings (total assets) in excess of $25 million must maintain their books on an accrual basis of accounting. For income tax reporting, however, all banks may elect either the cash or the accrual basis of accounting, regardless of how the books are maintained. In the SAMPLE BANK Form 1120 example, I have assumed that the accrual basis is used for both tax and books to keep the explanation more straightforward.

In practice, most banks report income taxes on a cash basis. This is due to the fact that cash basis taxable income is usually lower than accrual basis income. Again, in tax planning, you use every legal method allowed to minimize the amount of income taxes paid.

When a bank uses accrual accounting for financial reporting and the cash basis for income tax reporting, there are, of course, differences between the book and cash basis incomes. These are all timing differences and are handled in the same manner as the timing differences due to variations between tax and book depreciation, as discussed earlier in this unit. Just as in the case of book and tax depreciation, cash and accrual basis incomes will be the same in the long run.

PROVISION FOR LOAN LOSSES AND TAXES

In Unit 5, I discussed the theory and entries for recording loan losses. I also noted there that the IRS allows banks to compute loan losses on a percentage basis, rather than on an experience basis as called for by GAAP. Obviously, the two methods will produce different results. The resulting differences are handled as timing differences, since it is assumed that these differences will follow a pattern like that shown in Exhibit 14-4. The real practical problem is, Will the timing differences, due to loan losses, ever disappear as they do in the case of timing differences from depreciation?

Since tax and GAAP are to be the same after 1987, under current tax law, one wonders how the timing differences will be eliminated. This issue is currently unresolved and may remain so for some time. I will leave this topic, making you aware that it is an issue that may influence future bank GAAP and the way in which we analyze bank financial statements, which is the topic of Unit 15.

REVIEW QUESTIONS

The following questions are based on the SAMPLE BANK tax situation discussed in this unit.

1. What would be the 12-31-78 balance in account 8900 before making any adjusting entries for taxes unpaid? (*Hint*—See Project 2, Unit 9.)

2. What would be the 12-31-78 adjusting entry to record the book provision for taxes. The debit side of your entry should properly allocate taxes to the components of the pretax income to which the taxes relate. (*Hint*—See Unit 11.)

U.S. Corporation Income Tax Return

OMB No. 1545-0123

For calendar year 1981 or other tax year beginning ...., 1981, ending ...., 19 ......

▶For Paperwork Reduction Act Notice, see page 1 of the instructions

19XX

Check if a—	Use IRS label. Otherwise please print or type.	Name SAMPLE BANK	D. Employer identification number
A. Consolidated return ☐		Number and street	E. Date incorporated
B. Personal Holding Co. ☐			
C. Business Code No. (See page 9 of Instructions)		City or town, State, and ZIP code	F. Total assets (see Specific Instructions) $

Gross Income

1 (a) Gross receipts or sales $ .... (b) Less returns and allowances $ .... Balance ▶	1(c)	
2 Cost of goods sold (Schedule A) and/or operations (attach schedule)	2	
3 Gross profit (subtract line 2 from line 1(c))	3	
4 Dividends (Schedule C)	4	
5 Interest on obligations of the United States and U.S. instrumentalities	5	
6 Other interest	6	
7 Gross rents	7	
8 Gross royalties	8	
9 (a) Capital gain net income (attach separate Schedule D)	9(a)	
(b) Net gain or (loss) from Form 4797, line 11(a), Part II (attach Form 4797)	9(b)	
10 Other income (see instructions—attach schedule)	10	
11 TOTAL income—Add lines 3 through 10	11	

Deductions

12 Compensation of officers (Schedule E)	12	
13 (a) Salaries and wages .... 13(b) Less WIN and jobs credit(s) .... Balance ▶	13(c)	
14 Repairs (see instructions)	14	
15 Bad debts (Schedule F if reserve method is used)	15	
16 Rents	16	
17 Taxes	17	
18 Interest	18	
19 Contributions (not over 5% of line 30 adjusted per instructions)	19	
20 Amortization (attach schedule)	20	
21 Depreciation from Form 4562 (attach Form 4562) ...., less depreciation claimed in Schedule A and elsewhere on return ...., Balance ▶	21	
22 Depletion	22	
23 Advertising	23	
24 Pension, profit-sharing, etc. plans (see instructions)	24	
25 Employee benefit programs (see instructions)	25	
26 Other deductions (attach schedule)	26	
27 TOTAL deductions—Add lines 12 through 26	27	
28 Taxable income before net operating loss deduction and special deductions (subtract line 27 from line 11) .	28	
29 Less: (a) Net operating loss deduction (see instructions—attach schedule) . . 29(a)		
(b) Special deductions (Schedule C) . . . . 29(b)	29	
30 Taxable income (subtract line 29 from line 28)	30	200,000

Tax

31 TOTAL TAX (Schedule J)	31	50,800
32 Credits: (a) Overpayment from 1980 allowed as a credit		
(b) 1981 estimated tax payments 42,000		
(c) Less refund of 1981 estimated tax applied for on Form 4466 . (...............)		
(d) Tax deposited: Form 7004 .... Form 7005 (attach) .... Total ▶		
(e) Credit from regulated investment companies (attach Form 2439)		
(f) Federal tax on special fuels and oils (attach Form 4136 or 4136–T)	32	42,000
33 TAX DUE (subtract line 32 from line 31). See instruction C3 for depositary method of payment . (Check ▶ ☐ if Form 2220 is attached. See instruction D.) ▶ $...............	33	8,800
34 OVERPAYMENT (subtract line 31 from line 32)	34	
35 Enter amount of line 34 you want: Credited to 1982 estimated tax ▶ .... Refunded ▶	35	

Please Sign Here

Under penalties of perjury, I declare that I have examined this return, including accompanying schedules and statements, and to the best of my knowledge and belief, it is true, correct, and complete. Declaration of preparer (other than taxpayer) is based on all information of which preparer has any knowledge.

▶ .... Signature of officer Date ▶ Title ....

Paid Preparer's Use Only

Preparer's signature ▶		Date	Check if self-employed ▶ ☐	Preparer's social security no.
Firm's name (or yours, if self-employed) and address ▶			E.I. No. ▶
			ZIP code ▶

Schedule L Balance Sheets	Beginning of tax year		End of tax year	
ASSETS	(A)	(B)	(C)	(D)
1 Cash				
2 Trade notes and accounts receivable				
(a) Less allowance for bad debts				
3 Inventories				
4 Gov't obligations: (a) U.S. and instrumentalities .				
(b) State, subdivisions thereof, etc.				
5 Other current assets (attach schedule)				
6 Loans to stockholders				
7 Mortgage and real estate loans				
8 Other investments (attach schedule)				
9 Buildings and other depreciable assets				
(a) Less accumulated depreciation				
10 Depletable assets				
(a) Less accumulated depletion				
11 Land (net of any amortization)				
12 Intangible assets (amortizable only)				
(a) Less accumulated amortization				
13 Other assets (attach schedule)				
14 Total assets		103,804,000		105,205,000
LIABILITIES AND STOCKHOLDERS' EQUITY				
15 Accounts payable				
16 Mtges, notes, bonds payable in less than 1 year . .				
17 Other current liabilities (attach schedule) . . .				
18 Loans from stockholders				
19 Mtges, notes, bonds payable in 1 year or more . .				
20 Other liabilities (attach schedule)				
21 Captial stock: (a) Preferred stock				
(b) Common stock				
22 Paid-in or capital surplus				
23 Retained earnings—Appropriated (attach sch.) . .				
24 Retained earnings—Unappropriated		2,914,000		4,028,000
25 Less cost of treasury stock		( )		( )
26 Total liabilities and stockholders' equity		103,804,000		105,205,000

Schedule M–1 Reconciliation of Income Per Books With Income Per Return			
1 Net income per books	1,435,000	**7** Income recorded on books this year not in-cluded in this return (itemize)	
2 Federal income tax	110,000		
3 Excess of capital losses over capital gains		(a) Tax-exempt interest $.1.306.000	
4 Income subject to tax not recorded on books this year			
(itemize) _____		_____	
_____		_____	1,306,000
_____		**8** Deductions in this tax return not charged	
5 Expenses recorded on books this year not deducted in		against book income this year (itemize)	
this return (itemize)		(a) Depreciation . . . $128696	
(a) Depreciation . . . . . $_____		(b) Contributions carryover . $_____	
(b) Contributions carryover . . $_____		_____	
Non-deductible expenses		_____	128,696
_____	89,696	**9** Total of lines 7 and 8	1,434,696
6 Total of lines 1 through 5 . .	1,634,696	**10** Income (line 28, page 1)—line 6 less 9 . .	200,000

Schedule M–2 Analysis of Unappropriated Retained Earnings Per Books (line 24 above)			
1 Balance at beginning of year	2,914,000	**5** Distributions: (a) Cash	321,000
2 Net income per books	1,435,000	(b) Stock	
3 Other increases (itemize) _____		(c) Property	
_____		**6** Other decreases (itemize) _____	
_____		_____	
_____		**7** Total of lines 5 and 6	321,000
4 Total of lines 1, 2, and 3	4,349,000	**8** Balance at end of year (line 4 less 7) . . .	4,028,000

✿ U.S. GOVERNMENT PRINTING OFFICE: 1981-343-117 E.I. 43-0787287

Form 1120   **Schedule A**   Cost of Goods Sold (See Instructions for Schedule A)   Page **2**

1 Inventory at beginning of year	
2 Merchandise bought for manufacture or sale	
3 Salaries and wages	
4 Other costs (attach schedule)	
5 Total—Add lines 1 through 4 . . . . . NOT APPLICABLE TO BANKS	
6 Inventory at end of year	
7 Cost of goods sold—Subtract line 6 from line 5. Enter here and on line 2, page 1	

8 **(a)** Check all methods used for valuing closing inventory: *(i)* ☐ Cost *(ii)* ☐ Lower of cost or market as described in Regulations section 1.471–4 (see instructions) *(iii)* ☐ Writedown of "subnormal" goods as described in Regulations section 1.471–2(c) (see instructions)

    (b) Did you use any other method of inventory valuation not described above? . . . .   ☐ Yes   ☐ No

    If "Yes," specify method used and attach explanation ▶ ----------------------------

    (c) Check if the LIFO inventory method was adopted this tax year for any goods (If checked, attach Form 970.) . . . . . . ☐

    (d) If the LIFO inventory method was used for this tax year, enter percentage (or amounts) of closing inventory computed under LIFO . . . .

    (e) If you are engaged in manufacturing, did you value your inventory using the full absorption method (Regulations section 1.471–11)? . . . .   ☐ Yes   ☐ No

    (f) Was there any substantial change in determining quantities, cost, or valuations between opening and closing inventory? . . .   ☐ Yes   ☐ No

    If "Yes," attach explanation.

Schedule C   Dividends and Special Deductions (See instructions for Schedule C)

	(A) Dividends received	(B) %	(C) Special deductions: multiply (A) × (B)
1 Domestic corporations subject to 85% deduction		85	
2 Certain preferred stock of public utilities		59.13	
3 Foreign corporations subject to 85% deduction		85	
4 Wholly-owned foreign subsidiaries subject to 100% deduction (section 245(b)) .		100	
5 Total—Add lines 1 through 4. See instructions for limitation			
6 Affiliated groups subject to the 100% deduction (section 243(a)(3))		100	
7 Other dividends from foreign corporations not included in lines 3 and 4			
8 Income from controlled foreign corporations under subpart F (attach Forms 3646) .			
9 Foreign dividend gross-up (section 78)			
10 DISC or former DISC not included in line 1 (section 246(d))			
11 Other dividends			
12 Deduction for dividends paid on certain preferred stock of public utilities (see instructions)			
13 Total dividends—Add lines 1 through 11. Enter here and on line 4, page 1 ▶			
14 Total deductions—Add lines 5 through 12. Enter here and on line 29(b), page 1 ━━━━━━▶			

Schedule E   Compensation of Officers (See instruction for line 12)

1. Name of officer	2. Social security number	3. Time devoted to business	Percent of corporation stock owned		6. Amount of compensation	7. Expense account allowances
			4. Common	5. Preferred		

Total compensation of officers—Enter here and on line 12, page 1 . . . .

Schedule F   Bad Debts—Reserve Method (See instruction for line 15)

1. Year	2. Trade notes and accounts receivable outstanding at end of year	3. Sales on account	Amount added to reserve		6. Amount charged against reserve	7. Reserve for bad debts at end of year
			4. Current year's provision	5. Recoveries		
1976						
1977						
1978						
1979						
1980						
1981						

Schedule J   Tax Computation (See instructions for Schedule J on pages 7 and 8)

Note: *Fiscal year corporations, see instructions on pages 10 and 11. Omit line 1, complete line 2(a) and, if applicable, line 2(b), and enter on line 3, the amount from line 44, Part III, of the fiscal year worksheet provided on page 11 of the instructions.*

1 Taxable income (line 30, page 1)   200,000

2 (a) Are you a member of a controlled group? . . . . ☐ Yes ☒ No

  (b) If "Yes," see instructions and enter your portion of the $25,000 amount in each taxable income bracket:

    (i) $................ (ii) $................ (iii) $................ (iv) $................

3 Income tax (see instructions to figure the tax; enter this tax or alternative tax from Schedule D, whichever is less). Check if from Schedule D ▶ ☐   72,750

4 (a) Foreign tax credit (attach Form 1118) . . . .

  (b) Investment credit (attach Form 3468)   21950

  (c) Work incentive (WIN) credit (attach Form 4874) . . . . . .

  (d) Jobs credit (attach Form 5884) . . . .

  (e) Other credits (see instructions—attach forms and schedule) . . . . . .

5 Total—Add lines 4(a) through 4(e)   21,950

6 Subtract line 5 from line 3   50,800

7 Personal holding company tax (attach Schedule PH (Form 1120)) . . . .

8 Tax from recomputing prior-year investment credit (attach Form 4255) . . . .

9 Minimum tax on tax preference items (see instructions—attach Form 4626) . . . .

10 Total tax—Add lines 6 through 9. Enter here and on line 31, page 1   50,800

Additional Information (See page 8 of instructions)

G Did you claim a deduction for expenses connected with:

(1) Entertainment facility (boat, resort, ranch, etc.)? . . . .

(2) Living accommodations (except employees on business)? . .

(3) Employees attending conventions or meetings outside the North American area? (See section 274(h)) . . . . .

(4) Employees' families at conventions or meetings? . . . .

If "Yes," were any of these conventions or meetings outside the North American area? (See section 274(h)) . . . . .

(5) Employee or family vacations not reported on Form W-2? . .

H (1) Did you at the end of the tax year own, directly or indirectly, 50% or more of the voting stock of a domestic corporation? (For rules of attribution, see section 267(c).) . . . . .

If "Yes," attach a schedule showing: (a) name, address, and identifying number; (b) percentage owned; (c) taxable income or (loss) (e.g., if a Form 1120: from Form 1120, line 28, page 1) of such corporation for the tax year ending with or within your tax year; (d) highest amount owed by you to such corporation during the year; and (e) highest amount owed to you by such corporation during the year.

(2) Did any individual, partnership, corporation, estate or trust at the end of the tax year own, directly or indirectly, 50% or more of your voting stock? (For rules of attribution, see section 267(c).) If "Yes," complete (a) through (e). . . . . .

(a) Attach a schedule showing name, address, and identifying number.

(b) Enter percentage owned ▶

(c) Was the owner of such voting stock a person other than a U.S. person? (See instructions) . . . .

If "Yes," enter owner's country ▶

(d) Enter highest amount owed by you to such owner during the year ▶

(e) Enter highest amount owed to you by such owner during the year ▶

(Note: For purposes of H(1) and H(2), "highest amount owed" includes loans and accounts receivable/payable.)

I If you were a member of a controlled group subject to the provisions of section 1561, check the type of relationship:

(1) ☐ parent-subsidiary   (2) ☐ brother-sister

(3) ☐ combination of (1) and (2) (See section 1563.)

J Refer to page 9 of instructions and state the principal:

Business activity

Product or service

K Were you a U.S. shareholder of any controlled foreign corporation? (See sections 951 and 957.) If "Yes," attach Form 3646 for each such corporation . . . .

L At any time during the tax year, did you have an interest in or a signature or other authority over a bank account, securities account, or other financial account in a foreign country (see instructions)? . . . .

M Were you the grantor of, or transferor to, a foreign trust which existed during the current tax year, whether or not you have any beneficial interest in it? . . . .

If "Yes," you may have to file Forms 3520, 3520-A or 926.

N During this tax year, did you pay dividends (other than stock dividends and distributions in exchange for stock) in excess of your current and accumulated earnings and profits? (See sections 301 and 316) . . . .

If "Yes," file Form 5452. If this is a consolidated return, answer here for parent corporation and on Form 851, Affiliations Schedule, for each subsidiary.

O During this tax year was any part of your tax accounting records maintained on a computerized system? . . . .

15
ANALYSIS OF
BANK PERFORMANCE

OVERALL VIEW

Users of financial statements are primarily concerned with the two major aspects of solvency and profitability. *Solvency* is the ability of a company to pay its current obligations. *Profitability* is a measure of the excess of revenues over expenses. All companies can be classified in terms of profitability and solvency according to the chart in Exhibit 15-1.

EXHIBIT 15-1

Solvency/Profitability Classification Chart

TYPE	SOLVENCY	PROFITABILITY
#1	+	+
#2	−	+
#3	+	−
#4	−	−

+ = Solvent or profitable

− = Insolvent or unprofitable

A primary concern for financial institutions is solvency. All financial institution regulatory agencies constantly monitor the level of solvency and can, and do, take action to avoid loss of depositors' funds in financial institutions that are approaching insolvency. (Witness the forced merger by regulatory agencies of financial institutions to protect depositors.) In general terms, you could say that financial institutions must fall into either the #1 or #3 type classifications in Exhibit 15-1.

Bankers, in dealing with loan customers, see all types of companies. The automobile industry, currently, would fit into the #3 type, with Chrysler hovering back and forth between type #3 and type #4.

Type #2 companies can make good loan customers since continued profitability should overcome a temporarily insolvent situation. A loan to a customer like this could establish a very good relationship between the bank and the customer, especially if the customer turns into a solid #1 type firm.

Type #1 is, clearly, the most desirable situation. In fact, of the four types, only #1 is long term. The other three types are in situations of flux. For instance, #2 type firms could go to either #1 type or #4 type while #3 type firms could go to #1 or #4 types. Type #4 companies must go to one of the other three types or to type #5, which would be out-of-business.

FINE TUNING

Obviously, there are wide ranges within each of the four broad classifications presented in Exhibit 15-1. Investors just don't tell their stock brokers to purchase only #1 type companies' stock for their portfolios. Nor does a bank set out to be just a #1 type bank. What investors want stock in and management wants to be is number one of the type #1s!

An interesting phenomenon is that there is little agreement about the nature of a top #1 type company. What is number one from an investor's viewpoint will depend upon his or her willingness to accept risk. For a high risk taker, investments in #2 type firms with good profit growth potential may be very attractive. Such firms, if they are going up the ladder to #1 types, are typically highly leveraged and, as I pointed out in Unit 10, leverage can be very profitable.

Management's willingness to accept risk in running the business will determine where the firm falls in the mix of profitability and solvency. Financial institutions that desire a high degree of profitability tend to do so at the risk of low solvency and much scrutiny by regulators. Banks that maintain extremely solvent balance sheets, generally, are not high profit performers.

THE FUNDS STATEMENT

The only component of the financial statements that I have not covered thus far is the funds statement. I placed the funds statement in this unit since it is a prime tool for judging both profitability and solvency. My concern is more that you appreciate what you can glean from the funds statement and less that you know how to, mechanically, assemble it, although I do give you some practice at it in the unit review projects.

Today, many financial analysts skim over the rest of the financial statements and go right into the funds statement. Take time now to review the funds statements for both TYPICAL NONBANK and SAMPLE BANK in Appendix C.

SAMPLE BANK's funds statement is in a self-balancing format while TYPICAL NONBANK's (TNB) funds statement balances to the changes in funds. My personal preference is the TNB format since it focuses on what the funds statement is all about—the change in funds.

Funds can be defined as either the change in cash or the change in working capital. TNB's funds statement is prepared based on the working capital definition of funds. Working capital is the difference between current assets and liabilities. Since the concept of working capital is not applicable in bank financial statements, cash and due from banks is the funds concept used in bank financial statements. Exhibit 15-2 is a summarization of SAMPLE BANK's 1978 funds statement focusing on the change in funds.

EXHIBIT 15-2

Sample Bank (Appendix C) Funds Statement

FUNDS PROVIDED FROM:

Operations	$1,758,000	
Increase in deposits	2,852,000	
Reduction in investments	7,108,000	$11,718,000

FUNDS APPLIED TO:

Purchase of fixed assets	$ 439,000	
Dividends paid or declared	321,000	
Increases in:		
Fed funds sold	2,100,000	
Loans, net	4,874,000	
Investment in		
leveraged leases, net	784,000	
Other assets	614,000	
Decreases in:		
Fed funds purchased	2,279,000	
Other liabilities	234,000	$11,645,000

INCREASE IN CASH AND DUE FROM BANKS		$ 73,000

Another reason that I prefer the format of the funds statement in Exhibit 15-2 is that it stresses the components of the operating cycle, which are discussed in earlier units. The primary source of funds for any firm is from operations. The spread between the interest margin less operating expenses is the source of funds from operations for banks. (*Note:* Noncash expenses like depreciation must be added back to net income to arrive at this amount.) Banks must carefully monitor changes in deposits in order to determine how much in funds is available for lending and investment activities. The primary nonoperating uses of funds are the payment of dividends and the purchase of fixed assets.

The reason financial analysts consider the funds statement so vital is that it portrays all of the items noted above. SAMPLE BANK appears to be a healthy organization with adequate profitability and funds flow. TYPICAL NONBANK appears to have had a healthy profit and increase in funds. However, 80% of its funds provided were from debt. If you read the footnote, you will see that that debt is part of a $1 million loan package with a relatively short payoff period. The future annual funds outflow to service this debt will more than exceed its funds provided from operations in 19X1. An analyst would, certainly, want to know if the future funds inflow from the sale of the new product line will be sufficient to keep TYPICAL NONBANK solvent.

RATIO ANALYSIS

There are many different percentage, or ratio, comparisons that can be made in banking. The Bank Administration Institute, in its annual *Index of Bank Performance*, lists over 50 ratios. Six of the most significant of these ratios have been selected for discussion. Exhibit 15-3 shows a segmented reporting of these ratios for BAI member banks along with SAMPLE BANK's results. Here are the six formulas:

(1)   RETURN ON ASSETS $= \dfrac{\text{NET INCOME}}{\text{AVERAGE ASSETS}}$

(2)   RETURN ON EQUITY $= \dfrac{\text{NET INCOME}}{\text{AVERAGE STOCKHOLDERS' EQUITY}}$

(3)   YIELD ON EARNING ASSETS $= \dfrac{\text{INTEREST INCOME}}{\text{AVERAGE EARNING ASSETS}}$

Note: The interest income in this formula has to be tax effected.

You know from Unit 14 that SAMPLE BANK's interest income included $1,306,000 of tax-free interest. You also know, from Unit 14, that SAMPLE BANK's effective tax rate was almost 50%. (I used 50% in Exhibit 15-3.) Had the $1,306,000 been subject to tax, the net income of the bank would have been $653,000 less (50% of $1,306,000). Since the $7,011,000 of interest income reported by SAMPLE BANK includes both taxable and nontaxable interest, it is an apple and orange number for the formula. You would either have to reduce the taxable interest by the tax thereon or gross up the nontaxable interest to the pretax basis of the taxable interest. The latter approach is the one used so, therefore, $1,306,000 is added to SAMPLE BANK's reported interest income so that all the dollars in this formula are on a tax equivalent basis.

$$(4) \quad \text{YIELD TO BREAK EVEN} = \frac{\text{OPERATING EXPENSE (net of service \& fee income)}}{\text{AVERAGE EARNING ASSETS}}$$

$$(5) \quad \text{NET INTEREST MARGIN} = \frac{\text{NET INTEREST INCOME}}{\text{INTEREST INCOME}}$$

The interest amounts are also on a tax equivalent basis as in formula 3.

$$(6)$$
$$\text{OPERATING EXPENSE TO OPERATING INCOME} = \frac{\text{OPERATING EXPENSE}}{\text{OPERATING INCOME}}$$

ANALYSIS ON DATA FROM THE FORMULAS

You can see from Exhibit 15-3 that SAMPLE BANK stacks up well against the industry results, except in interest margin where it falls in the lower 25%.

It is earning a return of 1.4% on its total assets which represents a 15.2% return to its stockholders. (This is the effect of leverage explained in Unit 10.) The interest earned (on a pretax basis) represents an overall 8.7% return on its earning assets. In order to break even, the earning assets need to earn at least 5.9%. SAMPLE BANK is able to retain 51.2% of its interest earned. The bank's operating expenses represent 80.8% of its operating income.

Having read this unit, you should have some insight into financial statement analysis. An even better way to learn is by doing the unit review projects.

PRICE/EARNINGS RATIO

I will conclude this unit with a discussion of this important ratio, which is commonly referred to as the PE ratio. The PE formula is as follows:

$$PE = \frac{\text{MARKET VALUE OF STOCK}}{\text{EARNINGS PER SHARE}}$$

For most large corporations whose stock is publicly traded, the PE ratio is a major factor influencing the market value of their common stock. All publicly held corporations subject to SEC regulations must publish their earnings per share (EPS) on a quarterly basis. I discussed the computation of EPS in Unit 10. Now would be a good time to review that material.

Investors use the PE formula to solve, not for the PE ratio itself but, rather, for what the market value of the stock should be. Does this sound confusing? Let's try to clarify this statement by using SAMPLE BANK's EPS data (Appendix C) to explain.

Assume, first of all, that the $9.57 and $8.87 EPS numbers are EPS numbers for two consecutive quarters as follows:

QUARTER ENDING	EPS
6-30-X1	8.87
9-30-X1	9.57

Further assume that the stock has been trading in the market at around $89 between 6-30-X1 and 9-30-X1. The 9-30-X1 EPS number is released to the public on about 10-15-X1.

Now, here is the catch in the PE ratio. The stock market already knows about what the PE ratio should be for the stock within various industries and companies. Let's use this example—the market says the PE ratio for steel industry companies should be 3. This means that if a typical firm in the steel industry has an EPS of $5, investors would be willing to pay around $15 for the stock. If the stock is actually trading at below $15 per share when the $5 EPS is reported, the price of the stock will tend to increase to $15, since the market feels that the stock is underpriced at less than $15 and, therefore, a good buy. On the other hand, just the opposite effect should take place if the stock is trading at over $15 per share.

How does the market determine what the PE ratio should be? If you could answer this question you would be a billionaire. The factors that influence the determination of the PE ratio, and changes thereof, are as diverse as the factors that influence banks' prime lending rates. No one knows all of the factors, in either case, or how combinations of known factors will influence the final results. You really have to accept the PE ratio as a given. Let's assume that the PE ratio for SAMPLE BANK is considered to be 10. Based on the $8.87, 6-30-X1 EPS, the current trading price of $89 is about the right price. What will happen to the market value on 10-15-X1 when the 9-30-X1 EPS of $9.57 is reported?

If the PE ratio continues to remain at 10, the price of the stock will tend to increase to around $95.70. If a firm's PE ratio remains relatively constant, a firm can increase the market value of its stock by increasing EPS. How does a firm increase EPS? The answer, of course, is by good management and profit performance, which are factors that a firm can control.

REVIEW PROJECTS

A. Prepare a funds statement for THE FIRST TYPICAL BANK in Appendix F. Use Exhibit 15-2 as a guide for your working paper. Remember that 1984 is FIRST TYPICAL BANK's first year of business, so all of the beginning balances for the balance sheet were zero.

B. Verify the computation of the six ratios shown for SAMPLE BANK in Exhibit 15-3.

C. Assume that the EPS for SAMPLE BANK was $7.00 for the quarter ended 12-31-X1. What would be the indicated market value of the stock, assuming that the PE ratio went from 10 to 12?

EXHIBIT 15-3
Key Banking Ratios

INDUSTRY RESULTS:

PERCENTILE	(1)	(2)	(3)	(4)	(5)	(6)
UPPER 10%	1.5*	18.0	9.2	5.2	66.1	72.9
UPPER 25%	1.2	15.1*	8.7*	5.7	61.8	78.9*
MEDIAN	.9	12.0	8.3	6.3*	56.0	84.6
LOWER 25%	.6	8.3	7.8	7.1	50.8*	90.1
LOWER 10%	.3	2.9	7.5	8.0	47.0	96.7
SAMPLE BANK	1.4	15.2	8.7	5.9	51.2	80.8

Key:

(1) Return on assets

(2) Return on equity

(3) Tax equivalent yield on earning assets

(4) Yield to break even

(5) Net interest margin

(6) Total operating expense as a percent of operating income

* Indicates SAMPLE BANK is in the percentile.

A
THE CHART OF ACCOUNTS

USE AND DESIGN OF "THE CHART"

As students of accounting you realize that the general ledger is the accountant's tool for summarizing the financial activities of an enterprise. The Chart of Accounts is the road map, if you would, for the general ledger. It contains the assigned account number, classification, and title of every account that appears in the general leger.

The Chart of Accounts that you find here is used throughout the text. It is based along the basic guideline of a publication of the Bank Administration Institute, *A Financial Information System for Community Banks*.

The chart should help you fit the accounts into the basic framework of the accounting formula. You should use it as a "laundry list" so you can keep track of the accounts that have been introduced and be able to say, "OK, account 5000 was initially used in Unit 4, and completed in detail in Unit 8."

The chart and the various journal entry and related financial statement examples were generated with an Apple microcomputer using software by BPI Systems Inc. Since I did not wish to overhaul the software, I stayed within the numbering system of the BPI package. (Perhaps this could be useful at your bank?) So, realizing that this is not perhaps the most superior breakdown, here is the numbering scheme. (Remember that the system we used here costs under $4,000. Have you ever priced a customized system?)

NUMBERS

	FROM	TO
CASH & DUE FROM	1000	1999
INVESTMENTS	1200	1399
LOANS	1400	1499
FIXED ASSETS	1500	1599
OTHER ASSETS	1600	1999
DEPOSITS	2000	2499
OTHER LIABILITIES	2500	2999
EQUITY ACCOUNTS:		
Capital—Permanent Accounts	3000	3999
Temporary Income & Expense Accounts	4000	8999

TRIAL BALANCE
AS OF   01/01/77

ACCOUNT NUMBER	TYPE	ACCOUNT NAME	BALANCE
1000	ASSETS	CURRENCY & COIN	0.00
1021	ASSETS	REDEEMED SAVINGS BONDS	0.00
1023	ASSETS	UNPOSTED DEBITS	0.00
1024	ASSETS	TRANSIT ITEMS	0.00
1099	ASSETS	OTHER ITEMS IN COLL	0.00
1101	ASSETS	DUE FROM BANK A---Z	0.00
1200	ASSETS	RESERVE ACCT (FED/ST)	0.00
1301	ASSETS	INVESTMENT SEC-FACE	0.00
1302	ASSETS	UNAMORTIZED PREMIUM-INV	0.00
1303	ASSETS	UNAMORTIZED DISCOUNT-INV	0.00
1398	ASSETS	FEDERAL FUNDS SOLD	0.00
1399	ASSETS	SEC PUR/RESELL AGREE	0.00
1401	ASSETS	COMMERCIAL LOANS	0.00
1402	ASSETS	PART SOLD-COM'L LNS	0.00
1403	ASSETS	UNEARNED DISCOUNT-COM'L LNS	0.00
1404	ASSETS	PART PURCHASED-COM'L LNS	0.00
1421	ASSETS	INSTALLMENT LOANS	0.00
1423	ASSETS	UNEARNED DISCOUNT-INST LNS	0.00
1440	ASSETS	REAL ESTATE LOANS	0.00
1461	ASSETS	CREDIT CARD LOANS	0.00
1464	ASSETS	IMMEDIATE CR COLL ITEMS	0.00
1465	ASSETS	OVERDRAFTS	0.00
1490	ASSETS	RES FOR POSS LN LOSSES	0.00
1501	ASSETS	BANK BLDG & IMPR'S-COST	0.00
1502	ASSETS	ACCUM DEPR-BLDG	0.00
1521	ASSETS	FUR & FIX-COST	0.00
1522	ASSETS	ACCUM DEPR-F&F	0.00
1541	ASSETS	LAND	0.00
1551	ASSETS	LEASEHOLD IMPROVEMENTS	0.00
1552	ASSETS	ACCUM AMORTIZATION-LH IMPR	0.00
1801	ASSETS	REAL ESTATE OWED (NET)	0.00
1840	ASSETS	REPOSSESSIONS	0.00
1850	ASSETS	CASH ITEMS-NOT IN COLL	0.00
1901	ASSETS	INT REC-INVESTMENTS	0.00
1921	ASSETS	INT REC-FED FUNDS SOLD	0.00
1922	ASSETS	INT REC-SEC PUR/RESELL	0.00
1931	ASSETS	INT (& FEES) REC-LOANS	0.00
1951	ASSETS	PREPAID INSURANCE	0.00
1952	ASSETS	PREPAID FDIC ASSESSMENT	0.00
1957	ASSETS	PREPAID RENT	0.00
1979	ASSETS	OTHER PREPAID EXPENSES	0.00
2010	LIABILITIES	DDA-INDIVIDUALS/COS	0.00
2031	LIABILITIES	US TT&L ACCOUNT	0.00
2039	LIABILITIES	OTHER US DDA	0.00
2040	LIABILITIES	DDA-STATE & LOCAL GOVT	0.00
2061	LIABILITIES	OFFICIAL CHECKS (ALL TYPES)	0.00
2081	LIABILITIES	UNPOSTED CREDITS	0.00
2084	LIABILITIES	UNDISBURSED LOAN PROCEEDS	0.00
2101	LIABILITIES	DUE TO BANK A---Z	0.00
2201	LIABILITIES	SAVINGS & TIME DEPOSITS	0.00
2410	LIABILITIES	FEDERAL FUNDS PURCHASED	0.00

TRIAL BALANCE
AS OF 01/01/77

ACCOUNT NUMBER	TYPE	ACCOUNT NAME	BALANCE
2420	LIABILITIES	SEC SOLD-REPUR AGREE	0.00
2600	LIABILITIES	MORTGAGE DEBT	0.00
2610	LIABILITIES	OTHER LIAB FOR BORROWED MONEY	0.00
2620	LIABILITIES	BORROWINGS FROM FED RES BK	0.00
2820	LIABILITIES	DIVIDENDS PAYABLE	0.00
2841	LIABILITIES	INT PAY-SAV & TIME DEPOSITS	0.00
2931	LIABILITIES	INT PAY-FED FUNDS PUR	0.00
2932	LIABILITIES	INT PAY-SEC SOLD/REPUR AGR	0.00
2935	LIABILITIES	INT PAY ON BORROWED MONEY	0.00
2941	LIABILITIES	INCOME TAXES PAYABLE-FEDERAL	0.00
2951	LIABILITIES	INCOME TAXES PAYABLE-STATE	0.00
2976	LIABILITIES	REAL ESTATE TAXES PAYABLE	0.00
2978	LIABILITIES	OTHER TAXES PAYABLE	0.00
2980	LIABILITIES	ACCOUNTS PAYABLE	0.00
2990	LIABILITIES	OTHER ACCRUED LIABILITIES	0.00
2999	LIABILITIES	SUBORDINATED DEBT	0.00
3100	CAPITAL	PREFERRED STOCK	0.00
3200	CAPITAL	COMMON STOCK	0.00
3300	CAPITAL	SURPLUS	0.00
3400	CAPITAL	UNDIVIDED PROFITS	0.00
3500	CAPITAL	CURRENT YEAR EARNINGS	0.00
4010	INCOME	INT INCOME-INVESTMENTS	0.00
4020	INCOME	INT & FEES ON LOANS	0.00
5000	EXPENSES	INT EXP-DEP & DEBT	0.00
6010	EXPENSES	SALARIES & WAGES	0.00
6020	EXPENSES	PAYROLL TAXES	0.00
6030	EXPENSES	GROUP INSURANCE	0.00
6040	EXPENSES	OTHER EMPLOYEE BENEFITS	0.00
6100	EXPENSES	OCCUPANCY EXPENSES	0.00
6200	EXPENSES	DEPRECIATION EXPENSE	0.00
6210	EXPENSES	AMORTIZATION-LH IMPR'S	0.00
6300	EXPENSES	FURNITURE & EQUIP EXPENSES	0.00
6900	EXPENSES	OTHER OPERATING EXPENSES	0.00
8000	INCOME	DDA SERVICE CHARGES	0.00
8010	INCOME	OTHER S/C ON DEPOSITS	0.00
8020	INCOME	OTHER S/C & FEES	0.00
8030	INCOME	OTHER MISC INCOME	0.00
8400	INCOME	SECURITY G/L-(NET)	0.00
8800	EXPENSES	OTHER MISC EXPENSE	0.00
8900	EXPENSES	PROVISION FOR INCOME TAXES	0.00
9999	INCOME	INCOME TRANSFER	0.00

	TOTAL		0.00

Now that you have looked over the Chart of Accounts (you have, haven't you?), you should have at least one question. What is account 9999? Well, this is an account generated by the software that accomplishes the feat of adding up (the net, of course) of all of the income and expense accounts to automatically determine the net income or loss (Heaven forbid), and then transfer this amount into the balance sheet account that we have selected to accumulate the current year profits. In our case this is account 3500.

Why all of the abbreviations? First of all, we have tried to stick to very commom abbreviations (G/L = Gain or Loss). So the sooner you begin to recognize the abbr's., the more familiar you will be with the jargon involved, both in the classroom and on the job. Many times this is 80% of the battle. Second, we have tried to keep the account titles to a reasonable length so they will not be too drastically truncated when printed in journals and other listings. You see the system we have used here holds to the theory than any report larger than letter size is a waste of paper.

Another point—Ignore the AS OF date 1-1-77 on the Trial Balance, or what we are calling The Chart of Accounts. This is a default date that always appears whenever all of the account balances are zero. (*Default*—That's a data processing term meaning: Unless you do something, this is what is going to happen.)

You will become more familiar with the mechanics of the package as you go through this text. Don't worry though, I am not out to teach you data processing. You should be able to follow the system through its various steps with no data processing skills. Of course, if you do happen to have a microcomputer available, such as the Apple II or one of its competitors, the task of using this text, either as a learner or as an instructor, could be enhanced.

B

THE CALL REPORT

In this Appendix I have reproduced the basic forms of the Call Report. Below is the Introduction from the general instructions of the Call Report package.

Introduction

Every National bank is required to file a Consolidated Report of Condition (Including Domestic Subsidiaries) as of the end of each calendar quarter and must submit, semi-annually, as of June 30th and December 31st, a Consolidated Report of Income (Including Domestic and Foreign Subsidiaries). Additionally, banks with total resources exceeding $300 million as of the prior year end are required to file Consolidated Reports of Income quarterly. Banks engaging in foreign operations will also submit quarterly "Consolidated Reports of Condition (Including Domestic and Foreign Subsidiaries)." All banks will prepare the Report of Income on a fully consolidated foreign and domestic basis. These reports shall be prepared in accordance with the following instructions. For the treatment of particular problems that may not be covered by these instructions, inquiries may be addressed to the Comptroller of the Currency, The Administrator of National Banks, Washington, D. C. 20219.

The bank's books on the date of the Report of Condition should reflect a fair presentation of the bank's condition.

BALANCE SHEET at the close of business on •_____

Statement of Resources and Liabilities

		month	day	year

Thousands of dollars

		Sch.	Item	Col.		THOUSANDS	Hnds	Cts	

ASSETS

		Sch.	Item	Col.		THOUSANDS	Hnds	Cts	
1.	Cash and due from banks	C	7				XXX	XX	1
2.	U.S. Treasury securities	B	1	E			XXX	XX	2
3.	Obligations of other U.S. Gov't. agencies and corps	B	2	E			XXX	XX	3
4.	Obligations of States and political subdivisions	B	3	E			XXX	XX	4
5.	Other bonds, notes, and debentures	B	4	E			XXX	XX	5
6.	Federal Reserve stock and corporate stock						XXX	XX	6
7.	Trading account securities						XXX	XX	7
8.	Federal funds sold and securities purchased under agreements to resell	D	4				XXX	XX	8
9. a.	Loans, Total (excluding unearned income)	A	10		XXX XX				9a
b.	Less: Reserve for possible loan losses				XXX XX				b
c.	Loans, Net						XXX	XX	c
10.	Direct lease financing						XXX	XX	10
11.	Bank premises, furniture and fixtures, and other assets representing bank premises						XXX	XX	11
12.	Real estate owned other than bank premises						XXX	XX	12
13.	Investments in unconsolidated subsidiaries and associated companies						XXX	XX	13
14.	Customers' liability to this bank on acceptances outstanding						XXX	XX	14
15.	Other assets	G	7				XXX	XX	15
16.	TOTAL ASSETS (sum of items 1 thru 15)						XXX	XX	16

LIABILITIES

		Sch.	Item	Col.		THOUSANDS	Hnds	Cts	
17.	Demand deposits of individuals, prtnshps., and corps.	F	1f	A			XXX	XX	17
18.	Time and savings deposits of individuals, prtnshps., and corps.	F	1f	B+C			XXX	XX	18
19.	Deposits of United States Government	F	2	A+B+C			XXX	XX	19
20.	Deposits of States and political subdivisions	F	3	A+B+C			XXX	XX	20
21.	Deposits of foreign govts. and official institutions	F	4	A+B+C			XXX	XX	21
22.	Deposits of commercial banks	F	5+6	A+B+C			XXX	XX	22
23.	Certified and officers' checks	F	7	A			XXX	XX	23
24.	TOTAL DEPOSITS (sum of items 17 thru 23)						XXX	XX	24
a.	Total demand deposits	F	8	A	XXX XX				a
b.	Total time and savings deposits	F	8	B+C	XXX XX				b
25.	Federal funds purchased and securities sold under agreements to repurchase	E	4				XXX	XX	25
26.	Liabilities for borrowed money						XXX	XX	26
27.	Mortgage indebtedness						XXX	XX	27
28.	Acceptances executed by or for account of this bank and outstanding						XXX	XX	28
29.	Other liabilities	H	9				XXX	XX	29
30.	TOTAL LIABILITIES (excluding subordinated notes and debentures)						XXX	XX	30
31.	Subordinated notes and debentures						XXX	XX	31

EQUITY CAPITAL

					THOUSANDS	Hnds	Cts	
32.	Preferred stock a. No. shares outstanding _____ (par value)					XXX	XX	32
33.	Common stock a. No. shares authorized _____							
	b. No. shares outstanding _____ (par value)					XXX	XX	33
34.	Surplus					XXX	XX	34
35.	Undivided profits					XXX	XX	35
36.	Reserve for contingencies and other capital reserves					XXX	XX	36
37.	TOTAL EQUITY CAPITAL (sum of items 32 thru 36)					XXX	XX	37
38.	TOTAL LIABILITIES AND EQUITY CAPITAL (sum of items 30, 31, and 37)					XXX	XX	38

MEMORANDA

			THOUSANDS	Hnds	Cts	
1.	Average for 15 or 30 calendar days ending with call date:					
a.	Cash and due from banks (corresponds to Item 1 above)			XXX	XX	1a
b.	Fed. funds sold and securities purchased under agreements to resell (corresponds to Item 8 above)			XXX	XX	b
c.	Total loans (corresponds to subitem 9a above)			XXX	XX	c
d.	Time deposits of $100,000 or more (corresponds to memoranda subitems 3a plus 3b below)			XXX	XX	d
e.	Total deposits (corresponds to Item 24 above)			XXX	XX	e
f.	Fed. funds purchased and securities sold under agreements to repurchase (corr. to Item 25 above)			XXX	XX	f
g.	Liabilities for borrowed money (corresponds to Item 26 above)			XXX	XX	g
2.	Standby letters of credit outstanding			XXX	XX	2
3.	Time deposits of $100,000 or more:					
a.	Time certificates of deposit in denominations of $100,000 or more			XXX	XX	3a
b.	Other time deposits in amounts of $100,000 or more			XXX	XX	b

178

SCHEDULE A—LOANS
(Including rediscounts and overdrafts)

	Thousands of dollars		
	THOUSANDS	Hnds.	Cts

1. Real estate loans (include only loans secured primarily by real estate:
   a. Construction and land development . . . . | | XXX | XX | 1a
   b. Secured by farmland (including farm residential and other improvements) . . . . | | XXX | XX | b
   c. Secured by 1-4 family residential properties:
      (1) Insured by FHA or guaranteed by VA . . . . | | XXX | XX | c1
      (2) Conventional . . . . | | XXX | XX | c2
   d. Secured by multi-family (5 or more) residential properties:
      (1) Insured by FHA . . . . | | XXX | XX | d1
      (2) Conventional . . . . | | XXX | XX | d2
   e. Secured by nonfarm nonresidential properties . . . . | | XXX | XX | e
2. Loans to financial institutions:
   a. To real estate investment trusts and mortgage companies . . . . | | XXX | XX | 2a
   b. To domestic commercial banks . . . . | | XXX | XX | b
   c. To banks in foreign countries . . . . | | XXX | XX | c
   d. To other depository institutions (Mutual Savings Banks, Savings and Loan
      Associations, Credit Unions) . . . . | | XXX | XX | d
   e. To other financial institutions . . . . | | XXX | XX | e
3. Loans for purchasing or carrying securities (secured or unsecured):
   a. To brokers and dealers in securities . . . . | | XXX | XX | 3a
   b. Other loans for purchasing or carrying securities . . . . | | XXX | XX | b
4. Loans to farmers (except loans secured primarily by real estate; include loans for households
   and personal expenditures) . . . . | | XXX | XX | 4
5. Commercial and industrial loans (except those secured primarily by real estate) . . . . | | XXX | XX | 5
6. Loans to individuals for household, family, and other personal expenditures
   (include purchased paper):
   a. To purchase private passenger automobiles on instalment basis . . . . | | XXX | XX | 6a
   b. Credit cards and related plans:
      (1) Retail (charge account) credit card plans . . . . | | XXX | XX | b1
      (2) Check credit and revolving credit plans . . . . | | XXX | XX | b2
   c. To purchase other retail consumer goods on instalment basis:
      (1) Mobile homes (exclude travel trailers) . . . . | | XXX | XX | c1
      (2) Other retail consumer goods (exclude credit cards and related plans) . . . . | | XXX | XX | c2
   d. Instalment loans to repair and modernize residential property . . . . | | XXX | XX | d
   e. Other instalment loans for household, family, and other personal expenditures . . . . | | XXX | XX | e
   f. Single-payment loans for household, family, and other personal expenditures . . . . | | XXX | XX | f
7. All other loans . . . . | | XXX | XX | 7
8. Total loans, Gross (sum of Items 1 thru 7) . . . . | | XXX | XX | 8
9. Less: Unearned income on loans . . . . | | XXX | XX | 9
10. Total loans (excluding unearned income) (must equal Asset Subitem 9a) . . . . | | XXX | XX | 10

179

SCHEDULE B—SECURITIES—DISTRIBUTION BY REMAINING MATURITY (Book Value)

Investment Securities (Items correspond to Asset, items 2, 3, 4, and 5)	A. 1 year and less	B. Over 1 thru 5 years	C. Over 5 thru 10 years	D. Over 10 years	E. Total
					Thousands of dollars
1. U.S. Treasury securities	XXX XX	XXX XX	XXX XX	XXX XX	XXX XX 1
2. Obligations of other U.S. Government agencies and corporations	XXX XX	XXX XX	XXX XX	XXX XX	XXX XX 2
3. Obligations of States and political subdivisions	XXX XX	XXX XX	XXX XX	XXX XX	XXX XX 3
4. Other bonds, notes, and debentures	XXX XX	XXX XX	XXX XX	XXX XX	XXX XX 4
5. Total	XXX XX	XXX XX	XXX XX	XXX XX	XXX XX 5

SCHEDULE C—CASH AND DUE FROM BANKS

Thousands of dollars

	THOUSANDS	Hnds	Cts	
1. Cash items in process of collection and unposted debits (unposted debits from Schd. I)		XXX	XX	1
2. Demand balances with banks in the United States		XXX	XX	2
3. Other balances with banks in the United States		XXX	XX	3
a. Including interest bearing balances .... XXX XX				a
4. Balances with banks in foreign countries		XXX	XX	4
a. Including interest bearing balances .... XXX XX				a
5. Currency and coin		XXX	XX	5
6. Reserve with Federal Reserve Bank		XXX	XX	6
7. Total (must equal Asset, Item 1)		XXX	XX	7

SCHEDULE D—FEDERAL FUNDS SOLD AND SECURITIES PURCHASED UNDER AGREEMENTS TO RESELL

Thousands of dollars

	THOUSANDS	Hnds	Cts
1. With domestic commercial banks		XXX	XX
2. With brokers and dealers in securities and funds		XXX	XX
3. With others		XXX	XX
4. Total (must equal Asset, Item 8)		XXX	XX

SCHEDULE E—FEDERAL FUNDS PURCHASED AND SECURITIES SOLD UNDER AGREEMENTS TO REPURCHASE

Thousands of dollars

	THOUSANDS	Hnds	Cts
1. With domestic commercial banks		XXX	XX
2. With brokers and dealers in securities and funds		XXX	XX
3. With others		XXX	XX
4. Total (must equal Liability, Item 25)		XXX	XX

SCHEDULE F—DEPOSITS

Thousands of dollars

Deposits	A. Demand	B. Savings	C. Time	
1. Deposits of individuals, partnerships, corporations:				
a. Individuals and nonprofit organizations		XXX XX		1a
b. Corporations and other profit organizations		XXX XX		b
c. Total (sum of 1a and 1b)	XXX XX	XXX XX	XXX XX	c
d. Mutual savings banks	XXX XX	XXX XX	XXX XX	d
e. Deposits accumulated for payment of personal loans			XXX XX	e
f. Total (sum of 1c, 1d and 1e) (Col. A must equal Liability, Item 17 and Cols. B and C must equal Liability, Item 18)	XXX XX	XXX XX	XXX XX	f
2. Deposits of United States Government	XXX XX	XXX XX	XXX XX	2
3. Deposits of States and political subdivisions	XXX XX	XXX XX	XXX XX	3
4. Deposits of foreign governments and official institutions, central banks, and international institutions	XXX XX	XXX XX	XXX XX	4
5. Deposits of commercial banks in the United States	XXX XX	XXX XX	XXX XX	5
6. Deposits of banks in foreign countries (including balances of foreign branches of other American banks)	XXX XX	XXX XX	XXX XX	6
7. Certified and officers' checks, travelers' checks, letters of credit (must equal Liability, Item 23)	XXX XX			7
8. Total deposits	XXX XX	XXX XX	XXX XX	8

SCHEDULE G—OTHER ASSETS

Thousands of dollars

	THOUSANDS	Hnds	Cts
1. Securities borrowed		XXX	XX
2. Due from foreign branches, Net		XXX	XX
3. Income earned or accrued but not collected		XXX	XX
4. Prepaid expenses		XXX	XX
5. Cash items not in process of collection		XXX	XX
6. All other (itemize): a. Balances with savings and loan associations		XXX	XX

(Itemize amounts over 25% of Item 7 below)

. . . .
. . . .
. . . .
. . . .

	THOUSANDS	Hnds	Cts
. . . .		XXX	XX
7. Total (must equal Asset, Item 15)		XXX	XX

SCHEDULE H—OTHER LIABILITIES

Thousands of dollars

	THOUSANDS	Hnds	Cts
1. Securities borrowed		XXX	XX
2. Due to foreign branches. Net		XXX	XX
3. Dividends declared but not yet payable		XXX	XX
4. Expenses accrued and unpaid		XXX	XX
5. Amounts in transit to banks . . .		XXX	XX
6. Minority interest in consolidated subsidiaries . . .		XXX	XX
7. Deferred income taxes: a. IRS bad debt reserve		XXX	XX
b. Other		XXX	XX

8. All other (Itemize amounts over 25% of Item 9 below)

. . . .
. . . .
. . . .

	THOUSANDS	Hnds	Cts
. . . .		XXX	XX
9. Total (must equal Liability, Item 29)		XXX	XX

SCHEDULE I—OTHER DATA FOR DEPOSIT INSURANCE ASSESSMENTS

Thousands of dollars

	THOUSANDS	Hnds	Cts	
1. Unposted debits (see instructions):				
a. Actual amount of all unposted debits or single factor ____% of item 24		XXX	XX	1a
or: b. Separate amount of unposted debits or separate factors:				
1. Actual amount for demand deposits or ____% of subitem 24a		XXX	XX	b1
2. Actual amount for time and savings deposits or ____% of subitem 24b		XXX	XX	b2
2. Unposted credits (see instructions):				
a. Actual amount of all unposted credits or single factor ____% of item 24		XXX	XX	2a
or: b. Separate amount of unposted credits or separate factors:				
1. Actual amount for demand deposits or____% of subitem 24a		XXX	XX	b1
2. Actual amount for time and savings deposits or ____% of subitem 24b		XXX	XX	b2
3. Uninvested trust funds (cash) held in bank's own trust department not included in Item 24		XXX	XX	3

The balance of this Appendix consists of the Income Statement and supporting schedules for the Call Report.

SECTION A—SOURCES AND DISPOSITION OF INCOME (Indicate losses in parentheses)

	Thousands of dollars		
	THOUSANDS	Hnds	Cts
1. Operating income:			
a. Interest and fees on loans		XXX	XX	1a
b. Interest on balances with banks		XXX	XX	b
c. Income on Federal funds sold and securities purchased under agreements to resell in domestic offices		XXX	XX	c
d. Interest on U.S. Treasury securities		XXX	XX	d
e. Interest on obligations of other U.S. Government agencies and corporations		XXX	XX	e
f. Interest on obligations of States and political subdivisions of the U.S.		XXX	XX	f
g. Interest on other bonds, notes, and debentures		XXX	XX	g
h. Dividends on stock		XXX	XX	h
i. Income from direct lease financing		XXX	XX	i
j. Income from fiduciary activities		XXX	XX	j
k. Service charges on deposit accounts in domestic offices		XXX	XX	k
l. Other service charges, commissions, and fees		XXX	XX	l
m. Other income (Section D, Item 4)		XXX	XX	m
n. Total operating income (sum of Items 1a thru 1m)		XXX	XX	n
2. Operating expenses:			
a. Salaries and employee benefits		XXX	XX	2a
b. Interest on time certificates of deposit of $100,000 or more issued by domestic offices		XXX	XX	b
c. Interest on deposits in foreign offices		XXX	XX	c
d. Interest on other deposits		XXX	XX	d
e. Expense of Federal funds purchased and securities sold under agreements to repurchase in domestic offices		XXX	XX	e
f. Interest on borrowed money		XXX	XX	f
g. Interest on subordinated notes and debentures		XXX	XX	g
h. 1. Occupancy expense of bank premises, Gross .... XXX XX				h1
2. Less: Rental income .... XXX XX				h2
3. Occupancy expense of bank premises, Net		XXX	XX	h3
i. Furniture and equipment expense		XXX	XX	i
j. Provision for possible loan losses (or actual net loan losses) (Section C, Item 4)		XXX	XX	j
k. Other expenses (Section E, Item 3)		XXX	XX	k
l. Total operating expenses (sum of Items 2a thru 2k)		XXX	XX	l
3. Income before income taxes and securities gains or losses (Item 1n minus 2l)		XXX	XX	3
4. Applicable income taxes (domestic and foreign)		XXX	XX	4
5. Income before securities gains or losses (Item 3 minus 4)		XXX	XX	5
6. a. Securities gains (losses), Gross .... XXX XX				6a
b. Applicable income taxes (domestic and foreign) .... XXX XX				b
c. Securities gains (losses), Net		XXX	XX	c
7. Net income (Item 5 plus or minus 6c)		XXX	XX	7
OR			
7. Income before extraordinary items		XXX	XX	7
8. Extraordinary items, Net of tax effect (Section F, Item 2c)		XXX	XX	8
9. Net income (Item 7 plus or minus 8)		XXX	XX	9

SECTION B—CHANGES IN EQUITY CAPITAL

(Indicate decreases and losses in parentheses)	A. Preferred stock (Par value)	B. Common stock (Par value)	C. Surplus	D. Undivided profits and capital reserves	E. Total equity capital	
					Thousands of dollars	
1. Balance beginning of period	XXX XX	XXX XX	XXX XX	XXX XX	XXX XX	1
2. Net income (loss)				XXX XX	XXX XX	2
3. Sale, conversion, acquisition or retirement of capital	XXX XX	XXX XX	XXX XX	XXX XX	XXX XX	3
4. Changes incident to mergers and absorptions	XXX XX	XXX XX	XXX XX	XXX XX	XXX XX	4
5. Cash dividends declared on common stock				( )XXX XX	( )XXX XX	5
6. Cash dividends declared on preferred stock				( )XXX XX	( )XXX XX	6
7. Stock dividends issued	XXX XX	XXX XX	XXX XX	XXX XX	XXX XX	7
8. Other increases (decreases) (itemize):	XXX XX	XXX XX	XXX XX	XXX XX	XXX XX	8
. . . .						
. . . .						
. . . .						
9. Balance end of period	XXX XX	XXX XX	XXX XX	XXX XX	XXX XX	9

SECTION C—RESERVE FOR POSSIBLE LOAN LOSSES (Valuation Reserve) Thousands of dollars

	THOUSANDS	Hnds	Cts	
1. Balance beginning of period		XXX	XX	1
2. Recoveries credited to reserve		XXX	XX	2
3. Changes incident to mergers and absorptions		XXX	XX	3
4. Provision for possible loan losses		XXX	XX	4
5. Losses charged to reserve . . . . (	)	XXX	XX	5
6. Balance end of period		XXX	XX	6

185

SECTION D—OTHER OPERATING INCOME

Other income

1. Trading account income,
   Net . . . . | | XXX | XX |
2. Equity in net income (loss) of unconsolidated subsidiaries and associated companies . . . . | | XXX | XX |
3. All other: (itemize amounts over 25% of item 4 below) . . . .
   . . . .
   . . . .
   . . . .
   . . . .
   . . . . | | XXX | XX |
4. Total (must equal Section A, Item 1m) . . . . | | XXX | XX |

SECTION E—OTHER OPERATING EXPENSES

Other expenses

1. Minority interest in consolidated subsidiaries . . . . | | XXX | XX |
2. All other: (itemize amounts over 25% of item 3 below) . . . .
   . . . .
   . . . .
   . . . .
   . . . .
   . . . . | | XXX | XX |
3. Total (must equal Section A, Item 2k) . . . . | | XXX | XX |

SECTION F—MEMORANDA

Thousands of dollars

	THOUSANDS	Hnds.	Cts	
1. Provision for income taxes for current period:				
a. Provision for Federal income taxes		XXX	XX	1a
b. Provision for State and local income taxes		XXX	XX	b
c. Provision for foreign income taxes		XXX	XX	c
d. Total (must equal Section A, Items 4 and 6b and Section F, Item 2b)		XXX	XX	d
2. Extraordinary items (itemize):				
a.		XXX	XX	2a
b. Less: Applicable income taxes (domestic and foreign)		XXX	XX	b
c. Extraordinary items, Net (must equal Section A, Item 8)		XXX	XX	c
3. Number of employees on payroll at end of period				3
a. Number of full time equivalent employees on payroll at end of period				3a
4. Number of subsidiaries consolidated				4

5. List all mergers, consolidations and purchases during reporting period: . . . .

Name and location	Date	
. . . .		5
. . . .		
. . . .		

C
FINANCIAL STATEMENTS

Included in this appendix are financial statements for:

TYPICAL NONBANK, INC.

and

SAMPLE BANK

TYPICAL is provided to allow the users of the text to compare the contrasts and similarities between bank and nonbank entity financial statements. For example, TYPICAL shows the routine balance sheet distinction between current and noncurrent assets and liabilities. The current and noncurrent classifications are, of course, not applicable in banking.

The SAMPLE BANK statements are reproduced from the illustrated bank financial statements from the "Proposed Audit Guide—Audit of Banks," of the

American Institute of Certified Public Accountants. I have avoided the use of references to specific years within the text, except in the case of the bond illustration in Unit 4 and in the case of SAMPLE BANK. I felt that specific year references were helpful to the text users in the case of bonds having a 10-year life. In SAMPLE BANK's case, the user will no doubt utilize the AICPA material, so leaving SAMPLE BANK "untouched," as it were, gives the user a direct link between this important reference and the text.

TYPICAL NONBANK INC

19X1 Financial Statements

Balance Sheet
Income Statement
Retained Earnings Statement
Funds Statement
Notes to the Financial Statements

TYPICAL NONBANK INC
balance sheet
as of December 31, 19X1

ASSETS

CURRENT ASSETS
    CASH $ 30,397
    ACCOUNTS RECEIVABLE-Net   467,725
    INVENTORIES   322,148 $ 820,270

FIXED ASSETS
    COST $753,527
    ACCUMULATED DEPRECIATION   83,957 $ 669,570

OTHER ASSETS $ 182,988

                                        $1,672,828

LIABILITIES

CURRENT LIABILITIES
    ACCOUNTS PAYABLE $337,020
    INSTALLMENT NOTES PAYABLE   20,181
    CURRENT PORTION OF DEBT   48,070
    ACCRUED LIABILITIES   8,298
    TAXES WITHHELD   922 $ 414,491

LONG-TERM LIABILITIES
    LONG-TERM DEBT $1,000,000
    LESS CURRENT PORTION   48,070 $ 951,930

        TOTAL LIABILITIES $1,366,421

STOCKHOLDER'S EQUITY

PAID IN CAPITAL
    COMMON STOCK -1000 no par shares
        authorized and issued $ 1,000

RETAINED EARNINGS $305,407 $ 306,407

                                          $1,672,828

The accompanying notes are an integral part of this statement.

TYPICAL NONBANK INC
income statement
for the year ended Dec 31, 19X1

SALES		$1,976,620
COST OF PRODUCT SOLD		
Beginning Inventory		$ 96,362
Product Purchases	$1,091,716	
Direct Labor	160,046	
Other Costs	354,025	
Product Costs For The Year	1,605,787	
Cost Of Product Available For Sale	1,702,149	
Less: Ending Inventory	322,148	1,380,001
GROSS PROFIT ON SALES		596,619
OPERATING EXPENSES		421,324
OPERATING INCOME		175,295
NON-OPERATING INCOME		591
INCOME BEFORE TAX		175,886
PROVISION FOR INCOME TAX		726
Net Income		$ 175,160

The accompanying notes are an integral part of this statement.

TYPICAL NONBANK INC
retained earnings statement
for the year ended Dec 31,19X1

Retained Earnings:

BALANCE January 1	$130,247
ADD:	
NET INCOME FOR THE YEAR	175,160

BALANCE December 31	$305,407
	=======

The accompanying notes are an integral part of this statement.

TYPICAL NONBANK INC
funds statement
for the year ended Dec 31,19X1

Funds Provided
FROM OPERATIONS:
Net income for the year	$ 175,160
Add—Depreciation on fixed assets which lowered net income but had no effect on working capital	45,048
Total from operations	220,208
Proceeds from bank loan	886,667
TOTAL FUNDS PROVIDED	$1,106,875

Funds Applied
Cash advanced to affiliate	$ 172,988
Purchase of fixed assets	600,580
Increase in current portion of debt	48,070
Debt repayment	36,666
TOTAL FUNDS APPLIED	$ 858,304
INCREASE IN WORKING CAPITAL	$ 248,571

Changes in working capital
Increase (Decrease) in current assets:
Cash	$ (2,005)
Accounts Receivable	315,257
Inventory	225,786
Prepaid Expenses	(3,000)
	$ 536,038

(Increase) Decrease in current liabilities:
Accounts Payable	$ (238,745)
Installment Notes Payable	424
Current Portion Of Debt	(48,070)
Taxes Withheld	1,415
Accrued Liailities	(2,491)
	$ (287,467)
INCREASE IN WORKING CAPITAL	$ 248,571

The accompanying notes are an integral part of this statement.

NOTE A - ACCOUNTING POLICIES

INVENTORIES

Inventories are stated at lower of cost or market value. As described in note B, cost was determined by the first-in, first-out method.

TANGIBLE FIXED ASSETS

Tangible fixed assets are stated at cost. Depreciation is computed using the straight-line method for financial reporting purposes with lives ranging from three to seven years.

For income tax purposes, recovery of capital costs for tangible fixed assets is made using the Accelerated Cost Recovery System for 19X1 additions ($600,580) over five years.

Expenditures for major renewals and betterments which extend the useful lives of property and equipment are capitalized. Expenditures for maintenance and repairs are charged to expense as incurred.

FEDERAL INCOME TAX

Certain items of expense are recognized for income tax purposes in different periods from those in which such items are recognized for financial reporting purposes. These include depreciation as mentioned above. Deferred income taxes are provided for the tax effects of these timing differences.

The 19X1 provision for taxes only reflects state income tax since the amount of investment tax credit eliminates any federal income taxes for the current year.

INVESTMENT TAX CREDITS

Investment tax credits reduce income tax expense for the period
in which the related assets are placed into service.

NOTE B - INVENTORIES

At December 31, inventories consisted mainly of raw material and
work in process, since the company tends to run production based
on orders rather than build a finished goods inventory.
Inventories are stated at lower of cost or market. Cost is
determined by the first-in, first-out method.

NOTE C - TANGIBLE FIXED ASSETS

Tangible fixed assets are stated at cost. Depreciation is
computed using the straight-line method for financial purposes
and amounted to $45048 in 19X1. The estimated useful lives
of the assets range between three to seven years .

For income tax purposes recovery of capital costs for tangible
fixed assets is made using accelerated methods of cost recovery
over statutory periods.

The cost of assets sold, retired, or otherwise disposed of and
the related allowance for depreciation are eliminated from the
accounts, and any resulting gain or loss is included in oper-
tions.

NOTE D - LONG-TERM DEBT AND OTHER OBLIGATIONS

LONG-TERM DEBT

In 19X0, the company obtained a one million dollar Small
Business Administration backed loan package.

The SBA portion of the loan is $600,000 payable over seven
years. The purpose of the loan was to finance the equipment for
the company's new product line. The bulk of the equipment, which
collateralizes the SBA portion of the loan, was acquired in
19X1. The SBA loan rate will float quarterly at 2.75% over
Chicago prime. The principal is to be repaid over 84 months
(starting 2/X2) under the following schedule.

# OF MO'S	PMT/MO	TOTAL PMT'S
12	$ 4,370	$ 52,440
12	5,075	60,900
12	5,890	70,680
12	6,835	82,020
12	7,935	95,220
12	9,210	110,520
12	10,685	128,220
TOTALS 84		$600,000

The remaining $400,000 of this loan package is a renewable line
of credit.

LONG-TERM LEASES

The Company leases certain buildings and equipment under
long-term leases. Most of the Company's leases are capital
leases for a period of five to seven years.

Future obligations over the primary terms of the Company's
long-term leases as of December 31, 19X1, are:

19X2	19X3	19X4	19X5	19X6	Beyond
$158,270	$94,950	$63,350	$63,350	$57,600	$57,600

NOTE E - RELATED PARTY TRANSACTIONS

Included on the balance sheet under other assets is $182,988
which repesents advances to ABC SALES INC. As shown on the
funds statement, all but $10,000 of this amount was advanced
during 19X1. Both corporations are owned by the same sole
shareholder.

SAMPLE BANK

Comparative Financial Statements
1978-1977

The Accountant's Report
Balance Sheets
Statement of Income
Statement of Changes in Stockholders' Equity
Statement of Changes in Financial Position
Notes to Financial Statements

Note: SAMPLE BANK is from "Proposed Audit Guide–Audit of Banks," The Banking Committee, AICPA, 1980.

ILLUSTRATIVE BANK FINANCIAL STATEMENTS

To the Board of Directors

Sample Bank

Sampletown, U.S.A.

We have examined the accompanying balance sheets of
Sample Bank as of December 31, 1978 and 1977 and the related
statements of income, changes in stockholders' equity and
changes in financial position for the years then ended. Our
examinations were made in accordance with generally accepted
auditing standards and, accordingly, included such tests of
the accounting records and such other auditing procedures as
we considered necessary in the circumstances.

In our opinion, the financial statements referred to
above present fairly the financial position of Sample Bank at
December 31, 1978 and 1977, and the results of its operations
and changes in its financial position for the years then
ended, in conformity with generally accepted accounting
principles applied on a consistent basis.

Officetown, U.S.A.

January 24, 1979

SAMPLE BANK

BALANCE SHEETS

December 31, 1978 and 1977

ASSETS	1978	1977
Cash and due from banks	$ 5,498,000	$ 5,425,000
Interest-bearing deposits in banks	1,000,000	1,000,000
Investment account securities (Note 2):		
U.S. Treasury securities	11,023,000	14,674,000
Obligations of other U.S. government agencies and corporations	2,493,000	4,690,000
Obligations of states and political subdivisions	23,279,000	23,364,000
Other securities	900,000	800,000
Trading account securities	4,640,000	5,915,000
Federal funds sold and securities purchased under reverse repurchase agreements	2,100,000	---
Loans, net of unearned discount and allowance for loan losses (Note 3)	48,586,000	43,772,000
Investment in leveraged leases, net (Note 4)	1,897,000	1,113,000
Office buildings, equipment and leasehold improvements, net (Note 5)	2,144,000	1,878,000
Customers' acceptance liability	237,000	379,000
Other assets	1,408,000	794,000
	$105,205,000	$103,804,000

LIABILITIES		
Deposits:		
Demand deposits	$ 24,534,000	$ 24,061,000
Savings deposits	32,135,000	31,449,000
Other time deposits	33,074,000	31,381,000
	89,743,000	86,891,000
Federal funds purchased and securities sold under repurchase agreements	2,279,000	4,558,000
Acceptances outstanding	237,000	379,000
Accrued interest and other liabilities	1,918,000	2,062,000
Subordinated debentures (Note 7)	1,000,000	1,000,000
	95,177,000	94,890,000

Commitments and contingent liabilities (Note 9)

STOCKHOLDERS' EQUITY		
Capital stock, common, par value $10; authorized and outstanding 150,000 shares	1,500,000	1,500,000
Surplus	4,500,000	4,500,000
Retained Earnings (Note 11)	4,028,000	2,914,000
	10,028,000	8,914,000
	$105,205,000	$103,804,000

The accompanying notes are an integral part of these financial statements.

SAMPLE BANK

STATEMENTS OF INCOME

for the years ended December 31, 1978 and 1977

	1978	1977
Interest Income		
Interest and fees on loans	$ 4,359,000	$ 4,027,000
Interest on investment account securities:		
U.S. Treasury securities	741,000	836,000
Obligations of other U.S. government agencies and corporations	186,000	268,000
Obligations of states and political subdivisions	1,248,000	1,256,000
Other securities	58,000	42,000
Interest on trading account securities	221,000	241,000
Interest on federal funds sold and securities purchased under reverse repurchase agreements	132,000	105,000
Interest on deposits in banks	66,000	72,000
	7,011,000	6,847,000
Interest Expense		
Interest on deposits	3,946,000	3,840,000
Interest on federal funds purchased and securities sold under repurchase agreements	33,000	78,000
Interest on subordinated debentures (Note 7)	80,000	80,000
	4,059,000	3,998,000
Net Interest Income	2,952,000	2,849,000
Provision for loan losses (Note 3)	60,000	68,000
Net interest income after provision for loan losses	2,892,000	2,781,000
Other Income		
Trust department income	187,000	166,000
Service fees	106,000	103,000
Trading account profits and commissions	174,000	67,000
Other	74,000	77,000
	541,000	413,000
Other Expenses		
Salaries and wages	727,000	718,000
Pensions and other employee benefits (Note 8)	153,000	130,000
Occupancy expenses, net of revenue 1978, $52,000; 1977, $47,000	356,000	304,000
Furniture and equipment expenses	92,000	62,000
Other operating expenses	655,000	586,000
	1,983,000	3,194,000
Income before income taxes and net securities gains (losses)	1,450,000	1,394,000
Applicable income taxes (Note 6)	80,000	48,000
Income before net securities gains (losses)	1,370,000	1,346,000
Securities gains (losses), net of related taxes (benefits) 1978, $66,000; 1977, $(15,000)	65,000	(15,000)
Net Income	$ 1,435,000	$ 1,331,000
Per share of common stock:		
Income before net securities gains (losses)	$ 9.13	$ 8.97
Net Income	$ 9.57	$ 8.87

The accompanying notes are an integral part of these financial statements.

SAMPLE BANK

STATEMENTS OF CHANGES IN STOCKHOLDERS' EQUITY

for the years ended December 31, 1978 and 1977

	Total	Capital Stock	Surplus	Retained Earnings
Balance, December 31, 1976	$ 7,904,000	$1,500,000	$4,500,000	$1,904,000
Net Income	1,331,000	---	---	1,331,000
Cash dividends declared	(321,000)	---	---	(321,000)
Balance, December 31, 1977-	8,914,000	1,500,000	4,500,000	2,914,000
Net Income	1,435,000	---	---	1,435,000
Cash dividends declared	(321,000)	---	---	(321,000)
Balance, December 31, 1978 (Note 11)	$10,028,000	$1,500,000	$4,500,000	$4,028,000

The accompanying notes are an integral part of these financial statements.

SAMPLE BANK

STATEMENTS OF CHANGES IN FINANCIAL POSITION

for the years ended December 31, 1978 and 1977

	1978	1977
FINANCIAL RESOURCES PROVIDED		
Operations		
Net income	$ 1,435,000	$ 1,331,000
Items not requiring an outlay of resources during the year:		
Depreciation and amortization	173,000	162,000
Deferred income taxes	90,000	113,000
Provision for loan losses	60,000	68,000
Total resources provided by operations	1,758,000	1,674,000
Increase in deposits	2,852,000	2,386,000
Reduction in:		
Investment account securities	5,833,000	63,000
Trading account securities	1,275,000	128,000
	11,718,000	4,251,000
FINANCIAL RESOURCES APPLIED		
Purchase of fixed assets	$ 439,000	$ 78,000
Dividends paid or declared	321,000	321,000
Increase in:		
Cash and due from banks	73,000	34,000
Federal funds sold and securities purchased under reverse repurchase agreements	2,100,000	---
Loans, net	4,874,000	325,000
Investment in leveraged leases, net	784,000	---
Other assets	614,000	101,000
Reduction in:		
Federal funds purchased and securities sold under repurchase agreements	2,279,000	3,252,000
Accrued interest and other liabilities	234,000	140,000
	$11,718,000	$ 4,251,000

The accompanying notes are an integral part of these financial statements.

NOTES TO FINANCIAL STATEMENTS

Note 1. Significant Accounting Policies

- Investment account securities:

  Investment account securities are stated at cost adjusted
  for amortization of premiums and accretion of discounts,
  which are recognized as adjustments to interest income.
  Gains or losses on disposition are computed by the
  specific identification method.

- Trading account securities:

  Trading account securities are carried at market value.
  Valuation and sales gains and losses are included in
  other income.

- Loans and allowance for loan losses:

  Loans are stated at face value, net of unearned discount
  and the allowance for loan losses. Unearned discount on
  installment loans is recognized as income over the terms
  of the loans by the sum-of-the-months-digits method.
  Interest on other loans is credited to operations based
  on the principal amount outstanding.

  Lease financing transactions included with loans consist
  of both direct financial and leveraged leases. Unearned
  income is amortized by a method that results in an
  approximate level rate of return when related to the
  unrecovered lease investment.

The allowance for loan losses is established through a provision for loan losses charged to expenses. The allowance represents an amount which, in management's judgment will be adequate to absorb probable losses on existing loans that may become uncollectible. Management's judgment in determining the adequacy of the allowance is based on evaluations of the collectibility of loans. These evaluations take into consideration such factors as changes in the nature and volume of the loan portfolio, current economic conditions that may affect the borrowers' ability to pay, overall portfolio quality, and review of specific problem loans.

Loans are placed on nonaccrual status when management believes that the borrower's financial condition, after giving consideration to economic and business conditions and collection efforts, is such that collection of interest is doubtful. Loans are charged against the allowance for loan losses when management believes that the collectibility of the principal is unlikely.

Depreciation:

Office equipment, buildings, and leasehold improvements are stated at cost less accumulated depreciation computed principally on the straight line method over the estimated useful lives of the assets. Leasehold improvements are depreciated on the declining balance method over the shorter of estimated useful lives of the improvements or terms of the related leases.

- Pension plan:

  The Bank has a noncontributory pension plan covering substantially all employees. The Bank's policy is to fund pension costs accrued. Prior service costs are being amortized over a period of thirty years.

- Income taxes:

  Provisions for deferred income taxes are made as a result of timing differences between financial and taxable income. These differences relate principally to depreciation of fixed assets, accretion of discounts on investment account securities, provisions for loan losses, and differences in method of recognizing income from leases. Investment tax credits resulting from purchases of equipment for the Bank's use are accounted for under the flow-through method as a reduction of income tax expense in the period the assets are placed in service. Investment tax credits on lease equipment are recognized over a period of time related to the recovery of the lease investment that gives rise to the credits.

- Earnings per share:

  Earnings per share are based on the weighted average number of shares outstanding.

Note 2. Investment Account Securities

Carrying value and approximate market value of investment account securities are summarized as follows:

	December 31, 1978	
	Carrying Value	Estimated Market Value
U.S. Treasury securities	$11,023,000	$10,801,000
Securities of other U.S. government agencies and corporations	2,493,000	2,392,000
Obligations of states and political subdivisions	23,279,000	23,056,000
Other securities	900,000	837,000
	$37,695,000	$37,086,000

	December 31, 1977	
	Carrying Value	Estimated Market Value
U.S. Treasury securities	$14,674,000	$14,858,000
Securities of other U.S. government agencies and corporations	4,690,000	4,740,000
Obligations of states and political subdivisions	23,364,000	23,442,000
Other securities	800,000	727,000
	$43,528,000	$43,767,000

Investment account securities with a carrying value of $6,892,000 and $13,524,000 at December 31, 1978 and 1977, respectively, were pledged to secure public deposits, securities sold under agreements to repurchase, and for other purposes as required by law.

Note 3. Loans

Major classifications of loans are summarized as follows:

	December 31,	
	1978	1977
Commercial	$14,634,000	$11,823,000
Real estate construction	4,200,000	4,223,000
Real estate mortgage	10,346,000	10,482,000
Installment	24,119,000	21,002,000
	53,229,000	47,530,000
Less: unearned discount	(1,986,000)	(1,822,000)
	51,313,000	45,708,000
Allowance for loan losses	(830,000)	(823,000)
Loans, net	$50,483,000	$44,885,000

Loans on which the accrual of interest has been discontinued or reduced amounted to $73,000 and $96,000 at December 31, 1978 and 1977, respectively. If these loans had been current throughout their terms, interest income would have approximated $7,100 and $9,600 for 1978 and 1977, respectively. Interest income, which is recorded only as received, amounted to $300 and $700 for 1978 and 1977, respectively.

Changes in the allowance for loan losses were as follows:

	Year ended December 31,	
	1978	1977
Balance, beginning of year	$ 823,000	$ 819,000
Provision charged to operations	60,000	68,000
Loans charged off	(80,000)	(103,000)
Recoveries	27,000	39,000
Balance, end of year	$ 830,000	$ 823,000

Note 4. Investment in Leveraged Leases

Leveraged leases of equipment to customers composed of the following:

	December 31,	
	1978	1977
Gross rents	$ 4,248,000	$ 2,760,000
Nonrecourse debt	1,219,000	785,000
Net rentals receivable	3,029,000	1,975,000
Estimated residual value	222,000	115,000
Less: unearned income	(1,354,000)	(977,000)
Investment in leveraged leases	$ 1,897,000	$ 1,113,000

Note 5. Office buildings, equipment and leasehold improvements

Major classifications of fixed assets are summarized as follows:

	December 31,	
	1978	1977
Land	$ 535,000	$ 526,000
Buildings	1,417,000	1,144,000
Furniture	691,000	596,000
Leasehold improvements	112,000	125,000
	2,755,000	2,391,000
Less: accumulated depreciation	(611,000)	(513,000)
	$ 2,144,000	$ 1,878,000

Note 6. Income Taxes

The total income taxes in the statements of income are as follows:

Year ended December 31,	Currently Payable		Deferred	Total
	Federal	State		
1978	$ 20,000	$ 36,000	$ 90,000	$146,000
1977	(105,000)	25,000	113,000	33,000

Accumulated deferred income taxes of $1,102,000 and
$1,012,000 at December 31, 1978 and 1977, respectively, are
included in accrued interest and other liabilities.

The items that caused timing differences resulting in
deferred income taxes were as follows:

	Year Ended December 31,	
	1978	1977
Income on leases recognized on the finance method for books but recognized on the operating method for income tax purposes (Note 3)	$ 73,000	$ 22,000
Excess of provision for loan losses over deduction for federal income tax purposes	(3,000)	(2,000)
Accretion of discount on investment account securities	6,000	78,000
Accelerated depreciation	10,000	10,000
Other, including investment tax credits	4,000	5,000
	$ 90,000	$113,000

Interest income totaling $1,306,000 and $1,298,000 for
1978 and 1977, respectively, is exempt from federal income
taxes; accordingly, the tax provision is less than that
obtained by using the statutory federal corporate income tax
rate.

Note 7. Subordinated Debentures

Subordinated debentures consist of 8% notes due
June 1, 1981. The notes may be prepaid, in whole or in part,
at a premium of 1.833% to May 1, 1979 and at reducing
premiums thereafter. The terms also place restrictions on
incurrence of debt, mergers, and payment of cash dividends.

211

As of December 31, 1978, none of these restrictions result in any effective limitation of the manner in which the Bank is currently operating.

Note 8. Pension Plan

The Bank has a noncontributory pension plan covering substantially all of its employees. The total pension expense of 1978 and 1977 was $39,000 and $27,000 respectively, which includes, as to certain defined benefit plans, amortization of past service cost over 30 years. The company makes annual contributions to the plans equal to the amounts accrued for pension expense. A comparison of accumulated plan benefits and plan net assets for the Bank's defined benefit plans is presented below:

	January 1,	
	1978	1977
Actuarial present value of accumulated plan benefits:		
Vested	$1,500,000	$1,350,000
Nonvested	2,800,000	2,650,000
	$4,300,000	$4,000,000
Net assets available for benefits	$2,050,000	$1,900,000

The weighted average assumed rate of return used in determining the actuarial present value of accumulated plan benefits was 6 percent for both 1978 and 1977.

Note 9. Commitments, Contingent Liabilities,
and Rental Expense

The Bank leases three branch offices under noncancellable
agreements, which expire between December 31, 1982 and
November 30, 1987 and require various minimum annual rentals.

One of the leases also requires payment of the property
taxes and insurance on the property.

The total minimum rental commitment at December 31, 1978
under the leases mentioned in the first paragraph is $548,000
which is due as follows:

Due in the year ending December 31, 1979	$ 85,000
1980	85,000
1981	85,000
1982	85,000
1983	60,000
Due in the remaining term of the leases	148,000
	$548,000

The total rental expense amounted to $85,000 and $55,000 for
1978 and 1977, respectively.

In the normal course of business, the Bank makes various
commitments and incurs certain contingent liabilities, which
are not reflected in the accompanying financial statements.
These commitments and contingent liabilities include various
guarantees, commitments to extend credit, and standby letters
of credit. At December 31, 1978 commitments under standby
letters of credit aggregated $150,000. The Bank does not
anticipate any material losses as a result of these
transactions.

Various legal proceedings are pending against the Bank. Management believes that the aggregate liability, if any, resulting from them will not be material.

Note 10. Related Party Transactions

At December 31, 1978, certain officers, directors or companies in which they have 10 percent or more beneficial ownership were indebted to the Bank in the aggregate amount of $600,000.

Note 11. Retained Earnings

Banking regulations limit the amount of dividends that may be paid without prior approval of the Bank's regulatory agency. Retained earnings available for dividends were $2,000,000 at December 31, 1978.

D
GLOSSARY

As in the Bibliography in Appendix G, I have selected banking terms and jargon geared to the needs of the users of this text. I have chosen to make this a "working" glossary by asking the users to look up terms rather than attempt to explain all of the terms within the units.

As an aid in understanding the unit material, I have indicated, after each term, the unit number to which the term is primarily related.

ACCOMMODATING BANK (3)   A correspondent bank that receives or provides funds as a service to its correspondent banks.

ACCOUNTING ENTRY TICKET (2)   Ticket used as a posting medium in place of columnar journals as books of original entry.

ACCOUNTS PAYABLE (9)   A current liability representing the amount owed by an individual or a business to a creditor for merchandise or services purchased on open account or short-term credit.

ACCOUNTS RECEIVABLE (6)   Money owed a business enterprise for merchandise bought on open account (i.e., without the giving of a note or other evidence of debt).

ACCRUAL ACCOUNTING (2)   The method of recording expenses and earnings as they occur, regardless of the date of payment or collection.

ACTIVITY CHARGE (7)   A service charge imposed on checking account depositors by banks for check or deposit activity, where the average balances maintained are not enough to compensate for the cost of handling the items.

ADVICES (3)   Connotes several types of forms used in the banking field.   Generally speaking, an advice is a form of letter that relates or acknowledges certain activity or result with regard to depositor's relations with a bank. Examples are credit advice, debit advice, advice of payment, advice of execution, etc.

ALLOWANCE FOR LOAN LOSSES (5)   A valuation allowance established and maintained by estimated charges against operating income to provide a balance for absorbing possible losses deemed to be inherent in a bank's loan portfolio.

ALTERED CHECK (7)   A check on which the date, payee, or amount has been changed or erased. A bank is responsible for paying a check as it is originally drawn. Consequently, it may refuse to pay a check that has been altered.

ABA NUMBER (7)   A numerical coding system originated by the American Bankers Association to easily identify banks and to aid in sorting checks for their proper final destination. Each bank has a different number.

AMERICAN BANKERS ASSOCIATION (1)   The national organization of banking, organized to "promote the general welfare and usefulness of banks and financial institutions." Generally called ABA.

AMERICAN INSTITUTE OF BANKING (1)   The educational section of the American Bankers Association organized to provide educational opportunity in banking for bank people. Usually called AIB.

AMORTIZATION (4)   The gradual reduction of a debt by means of equal periodic payments sufficient to meet current interest and liquidate the debt at maturity.

ASSET (2)   Anything owned by an individual or business that has commercial or exchange value.

AUDIT FUNCTION (12)   Periodic or continuous verification of the bank's assets and liabilities performed by the auditor who is appointed by the board of directors. Among the assets and liabilities more regularly verified are cash, loans, collateral for loans, and savings and checking accounts.

AVAILABILITY DATE (7)   The date on which checks payable at out-of-town banks are considered collected and converted into cash. This is determined by the geographical location of the drawee bank, in relation to time and distance from the sending bank.

BAD DEBTS (5)   The amounts due on open accounts or loans that have been proved to be uncollectable.

BALANCE SHEET (1)   An itemized statement that lists the total assets and the total liabilities of a given business to portray its net worth at a given moment of time.

BALANCING (3)   The ultimate act of bringing two sets of related figures into agreement. As in proof work, the total of deposits being in agreement with the totals of all items making up the deposits. This is "balance" in banking parlance. All work in banks must be in balance, all debits equaling all credits.

BANK ADMINISTRATION INSTITUTE (1)   A bank trade association devoted to the professional advancement in the fields of bank audit, control, operations, personnel, and automation. It is active in research, technical areas, and education. Commonly called BAI.

BANK EXAMINER (12)   A representative of a federal or state supervisory agency, who examines the banks under his jurisdiction with respect to their financial condition, management, and policies.

BANK HOLDING COMPANY (1)   A company controlling one or more banks or bank holding companies. Bank holding companies are subject to Federal Reserve regulations and are permitted to engage in activities closely related to banking.

BANK STATEMENT (7)   A statement of a customer's account which the bank gives him monthly for his information. It shows all deposits made and all checks paid during the period and the balance. It is accompanied by the customer's canceled checks.

BATCH (3)   A group of deposits or incoming clearings assembled for proving purposes. A batch may consist of from, say, 100 to 2,500 items. The term *block* is sometimes used.

BEARER (7)   Person in possession of a check, note, or other instrument. "The person in possession of a bill or note which is payable to bearer."

BLOTTER (3)   A proof sheet summarizing a day's transactions, usually by department or branch. Postings are made from the blotter to the general and subsidiary ledgers.

BOND (4)   An interest-bearing certificate of debt, usually issued in series by which the issuer (a government or corporation) obligates itself to pay the principal amount and interest at a specified time, usually five years or more after date of issue. Although they are essentially debt instruments, bonds may be distinguished from promissory notes or other evidences of debt because of their formal execution under seal and certification by a bank or trust company that they are authorized by the board of directors of a corporation or other governing body.

BOOKKEEPING DEPARTMENT (2)   A department of a bank where the records of all depositors' checking accounts are posted and kept. In the large banks there may be found several bookkeeping departments, such as commercial, corporation, special checking, general ledger, bank ledger, foreign, etc.

BRANCH BANK (1)   A bank operating one or more branch offices controlled by the main office.

CALL (1)   A demand by bank supervisory agencies requiring submission of a report ("Call Report") on the bank's financial condition.

CANCELED CHECKS (7)   A check that has been paid and charged to the depositor's account, then perforated with the date of the payment and the drawee bank's name or clearinghouse number. These checks are retained in the files of the bank until a statement of the depositor's account is sent to him, at which time the canceled checks are submitted for his acceptance and approval.

CAPITAL (10)   The amount subscribed and paid by stockholders to permit a bank to function as such. Capital requirements of banks, both national and state, are governed by the size of the community in which they are chartered to operate. Supervisory authorities determine the amount of capital necessary for a bank to start operations in a given locality. In all cases, capital must be fully paid in cash before a bank is allowed to open for business.

CAPITAL NOTE (9)   Debt security issued by a bank that, by its terms, is subordinate in the event of liquidation to all other liabilities of the bank. In liquidation, a capital note is senior to the stockholder equity accounts.

CAPITAL SURPLUS (10)   Surplus usually created either by issuance of bank capital stock at a premium or by transfers from retained earnings.

CASH (3)   An all-embracing term associated with any business transaction involving the handling of currency (paper money) and specie (metal coins). The accounting terms *cash on hand* and *cash in banks* express the availability of money in the statements of businesses. A deposit ticket contains places to record "cash" deposited as distinguished from "checks" deposited. To "cash a check" means to convert a check into money.

CASHIER (1)   An officer of the bank who is charged with the custody of the bank's assets and whose signature is necessary on official documents. He may not delegate this authority so, in large banks where his duties are too numerous, assistant cashiers are appointed by the board of directors to perform specific duties.

CASHIER'S CHECK (7)   A bank's own check drawn upon itself and signed by the cashier or other authorized official. It is used to pay bank obligations and to disburse loan proceeds to borrowers, and is sold to customers for domestic remittances.

CASH ITEM (3)   Maturing coupons and bonds, petty cash vouchers, returned checks, due bills, and other similar items temporarily held pending liquidation.

CASH LETTER (3)   A list of items that are to be credited immediately to the account of a depositor (usually a bank or a large corporation). The items covered by such a letter may be charged back to the depositor's account if not paid.

CASH ON HAND (3)   Funds in the possession of tellers and a reserve fund kept in the vault.

CERTIFICATE OF DEPOSIT (CD) (8)   A receipt payable to the depositor for funds deposited with a bank. CDs are transferable and may be endorsed to other parties and negotiated like a check or other negotiable instrument. CDs may be payable on demand (demand CD) or at some specified date (time CD). Demand CDs generally bear no interest and time CDs bear interest at a simple interest rate. In addition, time CDs may contain a repayment notification clause (generally not less than 30 days).

CERTIFIED CHECK (7)   A check, drawn by a depositor against his own account, is stamped "certified" and signed by an authorized officer of the bank, indicating on its face that it is good. Checks are only certified against collected funds and for the maker of the check.

CHAIN BANK (1)   One of a group of banks owned and controlled by a group of individuals who, as joint directors, officers, or individual owners, take an active part in formulating policy and managing the banks in the chain.

CHARTER (10)   A document issued by a national or state supervisory agency granting a bank the right to do business. The terms and conditions under which the bank may operate are enumerated in the charter. As a general rule, state charters permit more latitude in the banking field than do national charters.

CHECK (7)   A written order signed by a depositor to the bank to pay a stipulated sum of money on demand to the person whose name appears on the face of the check or to his order. A check should be made payable to the order of a specific person or payee. If it is made to bearer or to cash, any holder may endorse it and demand payment.

CLEARINGS (7)   Checks and other items deposited for exchange among member banks of a clearinghouse. The total daily clearings are published in newspapers and other periodicals as an index of business activity.

CLEARINGHOUSE (7)   A place where representatives of member banks in the same locality meet each day at an agreed time to exchange checks, drafts, and similar items drawn on each other and to settle the resulting balances.

CLEARINGHOUSE ASSOCIATION (7)   A cooperative organization owned and operated by local banks who elect its officers and subsidize its operating expenses.

CLUB ACCOUNT (8)   A savings plan whereby the depositor makes periodic, usually weekly, payments. Coupon books frequently are issued to the depositor and a coupon generally accompanies each payment.

COLLATERAL (5)   Specific property that a borrower pledges as security for the repayment of a loan. The borrower agrees that the lender shall have the right to sell the collateral for the purpose of liquidating the debt if the borrower fails to repay the loan at maturity or otherwise defaults under the terms of the loan agreement.

COLLECTION DEPARTMENT (3)   The department handling checks, drafts, coupons, and other items received from depositors with instructions to credit their accounts after final payment is received.

COLLECTION ITEM (3)   An item received for collection and credit to a depositor's account after final payment.

COLLECTION LETTER (3)   The letter accompanying items to be handled for collection and credit after payment. Collection letters usually contain instructions for delivery of documents, protest, wire advices, and so forth.

COMPENSATING BALANCE (5)   A deposit balance maintained by a customer pursuant to lines of credit, borrowings, or agreements for other services.

COMPLETED TRANSACTION METHOD (4)   Recognition of securities gains and losses when realized.

COMPOUNDED (8)   In financial institutions, this term commonly relates to the frequency with which the interest is computed and added to the principal to arrive at a new actual balance. In the case of savings accounts, the terms interest compounded daily, monthly, quarterly, semiannually, or annually are used to inform depositors of increased earnings due to the frequency of compounding.

COMPTROLLER OF THE CURRENCY (1)   An appointed official in the United States Treasury Department who is responsible for the chartering, supervision, and liquidation of national banks.

CORPORATE TRUST (10)   A trust authorizing a bank to act as agent for a corporation. The bank may serve as registrar, transfer agent, and coupon and bond paying agent.

CORRESPONDENT BANK (3)   A bank serving as a depository for another bank. The correspondent bank accepts all deposits in the form of cash letters and collects items for its bank depositor. The depository bank will generally render all banking services to its correspondent in the depository bank's region.

COUNTERFEIT MONEY (3)   Spurious currency and specie coins that have been made to appear genuine. The act of creating counterfeit money is a felony under law and the conspirators of making and distributing counterfeit money are subject to long prison terms and heavy fines.

COUPON (4)   One of a series of promissory notes of consecutive maturities attached to a bond or other debt certificate representing interest and intended to be detached and presented for payment on or after their respective due dates.

CREDIT (5)   A term associated with the ability of a "legal entity" to borrow from a lender. The extension of credit is based upon the lender's faith and confidence in the borrower's promise to repay the funds borrowed from the lender. Usually this faith and confidence is based upon the lender's knowledge of the borrower's past performance in repaying debts, his financial history, his assets, standard of living, and manner of conducting business.

CREDIT DEPARTMENT (5)   The department responsible for obtaining, assembling, and retaining credit information on a bank's customers. Credit applications for loans generally are presented to this department by a loan officer. The credit department then gathers all available information on the customer and prepares it for the confidential use of the loan officer, who evaluates the creditworthiness of the customer. Also, this department obtains information and answers credit inquiries for correspondent banks.

CREDIT RATING (5)   The amount, type, and terms of credit, if any, which the credit department estimates can be extended to a loan applicant.

CREDIT RISK (5) The degree of risk, calculated by the credit department, that is connected with a particular request for credit.

CUSTOMERS' ACCEPTANCE LIABILITY (9) Customer liability on outstanding drafts and bills of exchange that have been accepted by a bank. This acceptance by the bank is referred to as a *banker's acceptance.*

DEALER RESERVE (5) A portion of the proceeds of the discounted installment sales contract retained by the bank to achieve limited protection against credit losses. Credit losses chargeable against these reserves are covered by the agreement entered into with the dealer.

DEBIT (2) Any amount in dollars and cents that, when posted, will increase the balance of an asset (resources) or expense account. All asset and expense accounts normally have debit balances and all liability, capital, and income accounts normally have credit balances. *Examples:* Checks drawn on the bank account of depositors are debits because they decrease a liability account balance when posted. Deposits are credits because they increase a liability account balance when posted. New loans are debits because they increase an asset account balance while paid-off loans are credits since they decrease an asset account balance when posted.

DEFERRED POSTING (3) A term used to describe a method of posting transactions. The two types of deferred posting methods are: (1) Partially deferred posting plan—the previous day's counter checks intersorted with the current day's inclearings and mail items, and posted in one run. (The previous day's counter work is delayed.) (2) Fully deferred posting plan—the previous day's inclearings and mail and the previous day's counter work are intersorted and posted in one run on the current day. (All checks posted one day after coming into the bank's possession–fully deferred.)

DEFICIT (2) The excess of liabilities over assets (negative net worth).

DEMAND DEPOSIT (7) Deposit funds subject to withdrawal on demand of depositor.

DEPOSIT (3) A deposit is an amount of "funds" consisting of cash (currency and specie), and/or checks, drafts, cash items, etc., that may be converted into cash upon collection. The deposit is given to the bank for the purpose of establishing and maintaining a credit balance with the bank. The depositor becomes a general creditor of the bank as evidenced by the depositor's account balance.

DEPOSITOR (7) An individual person, partnership, business proprietorship, corporation, organization, or association is termed a depositor when funds have been placed in a bank in the name of that legal entity.

DIRECT PAPER (5)   Installment loans originating from bank customers.

DIRECT SETTLEMENT (3)   Direct exchange by banks of checks, drafts, and similar items drawn on each bank. This practice generally is used in communities having a limited number of banks and, therefore, no need for a clearinghouse per se.

DIRECTORS' EXAMINATION (12)   Periodic examination of banks by their directors or a committee of the directors.

DISCOUNT (5)   1. The amount of interest withheld when a note or draft is purchased. 2. A note on which the interest is paid. 3. The process of making a loan by requiring a note larger by the agreed interest charge than the amount paid to the borrower or credited to his account (sometimes referred to as an add-on discount). A discount is distinguished from a loan by the fact that interest on a loan is collected at the time the note is paid or at regular intervals during the term of the loan, as in the case of a demand loan. 4. The process by which a Federal Reserve or other bank discounts for a member or customer bank the notes, drafts, or acceptances which the member bank already has discounted for its customers.

DORMANT ACCOUNT (8)   An account that has shown no activity initiated by the depositor over a long period of time. In many banks, dormant accounts are segregated from active accounts for control purposes. The bank is required to publish the names of all dormant account depositors for a specified period of time, after which the funds are transferred to the state for disposition.

DRAFT (BILL OF EXCHANGE) (7)   A signed written order addressed by one person (the drawer) to another person (the drawee) directing the latter to pay a specified sum of money to the order of a third person (the payee).

DRAWEE (7)   The bank is known as the drawee when it is paying a check. Any party, such as a bank, from whom the payment of a check or other instrument is expected.

DRAWER (7)   The person or business who writes a check or draft upon another legal entity, such as the (drawee) bank.

DUE FROM ACCOUNT (3)   Asset control account used to record transactions initiated by the bank placing deposits in other banks.

DUE TO ACCOUNT (3)   Liability control account used to record transactions originating in a depository institution for deposits held for other banks.

EDP (ELECTRONIC DATA PROCESSING) (13)   This is an all-inclusive term and is liberally interpreted to mean the overall science of converting data by electronic means to any desired form.

EMBEZZLEMENT (12)   The fraudulent appropriation "to one's own use" of the money or property entrusted to his care.

ENCODING (3)   Enscribing or imprinting MICR (magnetic ink character recognition) characters (e.g., customer's account number) on checks, deposits, and other documents to be processed by a computer.

ENDORSEMENT (7)   When a party writes a legal signature upon the back of an instrument, this constitutes an endorsement. An endorsement is required on a negotiable instrument in order to transfer and pass a title to another party, who becomes a holder in due course.

EQUITY (2)   This is the ownership right or the risk interest in property. It can also be described as the monetary value of a property or business which exceeds the claims and/or liens against it by others.

ESCHEAT (8)   The reversion of property, such as the property of a decedent with no heirs and unclaimed or abandoned property, to the state.

ESCROW (5)   Delivery of a deed to a third person who releases it to the grantee upon the fulfillment of certain specified conditions. Also commonly used to designate accounts credited with the periodic deposits of mortgagors for the payment of real estate taxes and insurance premiums by the bank on behalf of the mortgagor.

EXCHANGE (7)   The settlement of items drawn on other banks through a clearinghouse or by "direct settlement" between banks.

EXCESS RESERVES (1)   A term used to designate the amount of funds held in reserve in excess of the legal minimum requirements, whether funds are on deposit in the Federal Reserve Bank, in a bank approved as a depository, or in the cash reserve carried within its own vaults.

FACE VALUE (4)   The par value, the monetary value, or the principal value of an instrument is known as its face value. It is upon the face value that interest is computed on interest- bearing obligations, such as notes, bonds, mortgages, etc.

FAIR VALUE (5)   The amount one can reasonably expect to receive in a current (but not forced) sale from a willing buyer. It is measured by market value when an active market exists. If no active current market exists for the assets acquired but exists for similar assets, the selling price in the market for similar assets may be helpful in estimating the fair value of the assets acquired. If no market price is available, a forecast of expected cash flows may aid in estimating the fair value of assets transferred, provided the expected cash flows are discounted at a rate commensurate with the risk involved.

FEDERAL DEPOSIT INSURANCE CORPORATION (FDIC) (1)   A governmental corporation that insures the deposits of Federal Reserve System member banks and nonmember banks electing to join the FDIC. Deposits are insured up to a specified amount. In return for this protection, each bank pays an assessment based on total deposits.

FEDERAL FUNDS (4) A loan by a bank (or borrowings by a bank) to decrease (or increase) its reserve account with a Federal Reserve Bank.

FEDERAL HOME LOAN MORTGAGE CORPORATION (FHLMC) (1) The corporation was chartered by an act of Congress in July 1970, for the purpose of assisting in the development and maintenance of a secondary market in conventional residential mortgages. The corporation purchases mortgages from financial institutions, the accounts of which are insured by an agency of the U.S. government. The corporation is often referred to as "Freddie Mac."

FEDERAL RESERVE BOARD (FRB) (1) A board of seven members, appointed by the President of the United States and confirmed by the U.S. Senate, responsible for supervising, coordinating, and formulating monetary policy. The FRB has regulatory power over member banks.

FEDERAL RESERVE SYSTEM (1) The central banking system of the United States, created by an act of Congress (Federal Reserve Act) in 1913. The system includes national and state member banks and 12 Federal Reserve Banks and their branches.

FIFO (FIRST IN FIRST OUT) (8) This term denotes a method of computing interest and the effect withdrawals have on earnings for the period. The FIFO method is using the oldest money on deposit for withdrawals during the interest period. It was originally designed to discourage withdrawals by demanding the maximum penalty.

FLOAT (7) A term used to describe the amount of funds in the process of collection represented by checks in the possession of one bank but drawn on other banks, either local or out-of-town. The true available balance of a depositor's account is generally computed by deducting the float from the ledger balance as shown on the bank's books.

FORGERY (7) The alteration of any document or instrument with the intent to defraud or prejudice any individual constitutes forgery, which is a statutory crime punishable by imprisonment. The most common concept of forgery is a false signature placed on an instrument. However, raising the amount, altering the payee, changing the number, or writing a true signature to an instrument known to be false, or changing an entry in a deposit passbook constitutes forgery.

GENERAL LEDGER (2) The most important record in the bank. Every transaction that takes place in the bank during the business day is reflected through various departmental subsidiary records to the general ledger, where the totals of these subsidiary records are posted to the general ledger. Some entries are posted directly to the general ledger but for like entries in large volume, some subsidiary record is created within a department so that the total of all like entries may be sent to the general ledger as a single posting medium.

GENERAL LEDGER DEBIT AND CREDIT TICKETS (2) Transaction slips used by banks in place of columnar journals as books of original entry.

GOVERNMENT NATIONAL MORTGAGE ASSOCIATION (GNMA) (4) A wholly owned corporate instrumentality of the United States government that purchases, services, and sells mortgages insured or guaranteed by the Federal Housing Administration (FHA) and the Veterans Administration (VA) and that may perform other secondary market functions to support the home mortgage market. The association is often referred to as "Ginny Mae."

GROUP BANK (1) An affiliate of a holding company that controls a substantial part of the stock of one or more other banks.

HOLDOVERS (3) Items that are unprocessed at the end of the day. These unprocessed transactions include rejected items that are generally disposed of in the following day's business. They include checks drawn on other banks, items lacking endorsement, checks subject to "stop payment" orders, and items which, if charged, would create an unauthorized overdraft.

IDENTIFICATION (7) The procedure by which a person attempts to ascertain the true identity of another. A bank does this through documents, contacts with other banks, and other means. THERE IS NO FOOL-PROOF IDENTIFICATION.

INDIRECT PAPER (5) Installment loans originating from dealer customers.

INSTALLMENT LOAN (5) A note repayable in installments (usually in level monthly amounts) with maturities depending on the nature of the loan.

INSUFFICIENT FUNDS (7) A term used to express the fact that a depositor's balance is inadequate for the bank to pay a check drawn against the account.

INSURED BANK (1) A bank that is a member of the Federal Deposit Insurance Corporation.

INTEREST (4) The price paid for the use of a borrowed commodity, especially money, is called interest. It has also been termed the "rental payment" for money borrowed.

INTEREST COLLECTED BUT NOT EARNED (UNEARNED INTEREST) (5) Interest that has been collected in advance of the contract to be performed or consideration to be met.

INTEREST EARNED BUT NOT COLLECTED (INTEREST RECEIVABLE) (5) Interest on loans and investment securities not collected in advance.

JOURNAL (2) A record of original entry. This record may be written in pen and ink at the time a transaction is made, or may be created either in original printing or carbonized as the posting of the entry is made by machine. The journal is a chronological record of the transactions as they transpire or a chronological record of the posting media posted after a "fine sort" has been made.

KITE (7) A term used in banking circles to describe the malpractice of individuals in taking advantage of the time element of check collections by the bank. The individual either has a cohort in a distant city or another account in another city himself. He deposits a check drawn on a bank in a distant city and then draws from this uncollected balance while the check is in the process of collection. He uses both bank accounts to his advantage to draw against "nonexistent" true balances.

LEDGER (2) A record of final entry in bookkeeping. A ledger account is posted with every transaction affecting this particular account.

LETTER OF CREDIT (7) A formal document in letter form addressed to and authorizing the beneficiary (for example, exporter) to draw a draft to a stated amount of money against the accepting bank.

LIABILITIES (2) In banking parlance, the liabilities are funds a bank owes. By far the largest item on the liability side of a bank's financial statement is the deposits. The current indebtedness of a bank to those other than depositors is usually small in total and represents current obligations that are to be paid on a certain future date, such as federal and real estate taxes.

LIABILITY LEDGER (5) A subsidiary ledger containing all obligations of an individual borrower.

LIFO (LAST IN FIRST OUT) (8) This term denotes a method of determining the effect of withdrawals on savings account interest computations. Withdrawals are made from the money that was deposited last. The withdrawal penalty under this plan is loss of interest on the last money deposited from the date of deposit to the date of withdrawal.

LINE OF CREDIT (5) A term applied to the maximum amount of credit that a bank will extend to a particular borrower (usually a business concern) over a stated period, subject to the borrower's meeting certain conditions, such as maintaining a specified cash balance on deposit at the bank.

LIQUIDITY (3) A term used to describe the solvency of a business and which has special reference to the degree of readiness in which assets can be converted into cash without loss.

LOAN (5)   A business transaction between two "legal entities" whereby one party, known as the lender, agrees to "rent" funds to the second party, known as the borrower. The funds may be rented with or without a fee. This fee is called interest or discount in banking circles. Banks are the principal lenders of funds for commercial purposes. Loans may be demand or time loans, depending upon the agreement as to maturity. They may also be secured or unsecured.

LOAN CLASSIFICATIONS USED BY SUPERVISORY AGENCIES (5)   *SUBSTANDARD:* A classification assigned to those loans inadequately protected by the current sound worth and paying capacity of the obligor, or by pledged collateral, if any. *DOUBTFUL:* A classification assigned to loans that have all the weaknesses inherent in an asset classified substandard and their collection or liquidation in full is highly questionable. *LOSS:* A classification assigned to those loans considered uncollectible and of such little value that their continuance as an active asset of the bank is not warranted. Loss classification does not mean that an asset has absolutely no recovery or salvage value. *OLEM:* Other loans especially mentioned—Loans that are currently "protected" but that exhibit potentially unwarranted credit risks.

LOCAL ITEMS (3)   A term used to describe items drawn on other banks in the same city as the bank holding possession of them. In some localities, they are also known as "city items" and are distinguished from "country collections" which are items drawn on banks outside the city.

MAIL DEPOSIT (7)   A deposit received by the bank from a depositor through the mail rather than over the counter. Many banks are using this means to reduce lobby activity.

MAKER (7)   The person who signs and delivers (executes) a check, note, or other promise to pay. The terms *drawer* and *maker* are interchangeable.

MEMORANDUM ACCOUNT (5)   An account used to control customers' assets or future commitments. This type of account is not reflected in the bank's balance sheet or statement of income. Types of memoranda accounts include unused commitments for letters of credit, collection items, items kept for safekeeping, future foreign exchange contracts, guarantees, and unused balances under lines of credit.

MICR (MAGNETIC INK CHARACTER RECOGNITION) (3)   The magnetic ink digits printed on bank checks and other documents in proof.

MICROFILM (3)   Microfilm is widely used in banks. A complete record of checks leaving the bank is recorded in its original state for future reference. Statements for all depositors are photographed before being sent to the customer. The checks enclosed in the statements are usually photographed on the day of posting. The problem of storing bulky records is thus eliminated.

MONEY ORDER (7)   A bank check sold by a bank to a customer for a fee. Amount may not exceed a certain amount.

MONTHLY PAYMENT LOAN (5)   A consumer or mortgage loan requiring a payment each month. Typically, these loans are made to consumers but are also made to industry for the purchase of capital equipment.

MORTGAGE (5)   An instrument of conveyance (generally of real estate) from a borrower, called a mortgagor, to the lender, called the mortgagee. The mortgage is only a "conditional" conveyance, in that the property remains with the use and occupancy of the mortgagor as long as the mortgagor lives up to the conditions of the mortgage.

MORTGAGE PARTICIPATION CERTIFICATE (PC) (4)   A certificate representing an undivided interest in specified residential conventional mortgages underwritten and owned by the FHLMC. The FHLMC unconditionally guarantees the payment of principal and interest.

NEGOTIABLE INSTRUMENT (4)   The Uniform Negotiable Instruments Act states: An instrument, to be "negotiable," must conform to the following requirements: (1) It must be in writing and signed by the maker or drawer; (2) It must contain an unconditional promise or order to pay a certain sum in money; (3) It must be payable on demand, or at a fixed or determinable future time; (4) It must be payable to order or to bearer; (5) Where the instrument is addressed to a drawee, he must be named or otherwise indicated therein with reasonable certainty. If instruments, such as checks, drafts, bills of exchange, acceptances, promissory notes, etc., meet the above requirements, they may be transferred by delivery to another person in good faith for a consideration.

NET OCCUPANCY EXPENSE OR NET OCCUPANCY INCOME (11) The difference between gross occupancy expense and rental income. This amount does not include expenses of other real estate owned; these expenses are generally included with other operating expenses.

NIGHT DEPOSITORY (7)   A small vault located on the inside of a bank but accessible to the street side of the bank building. This convenience is used by depositors and merchants who do not wish to hold money over until the next banking day. The vault is opened by two bank employees and the contents recorded. They are then processed and credited to the customer's account.

NOTE (5)   An instrument, such as a promissory note, which is the recognized legal evidence of a debt. It is an instrument signed by the maker, called the borrower, promising to pay a certain sum of money on a specified date at a certain place of business, to a certain business, individual, or bank, called the lender. It should meet all requirements of the Uniform Negotiable Instruments Act.

N.S.F. (7)   The abbreviation for "Not Sufficient Funds."

OBLIGATION (5)   The legal responsibility and duty of the debtor (the obligor) to pay a debt when due and the legal right of the creditor (the obligee) to enforce payment in the event of default.

OFFICIAL CHECK (7)   A check drawn by a bank on itself and signed by an authorized officer.

ON US CHECKS (3)   Those checks drawn on deposit accounts of the bank receiving them.

OVERDRAFT (5)   When a depositor draws a check for more than the balance on deposit in his account with a bank, he is said to be "overdrawn." The bank can either return the check, marked "NSF," to the bank from which it came or to the depositor who presented it for payment, or the bank may elect to render the customer a service and pay the check. When the bank pays the check, it creates an overdraft in the depositor's account. Some banks exact heavy service charges for checks returned for Insufficient Funds. Interest is often charged on overdrawn accounts.

PASSBOOK (8)   A document containing a complete record of a customer's account, showing deposits and withdrawals as well as the interest credited at regular periods. A bank may require that the passbook be presented for proper entry of transactions.

PASS-THROUGH CERTIFICATE (4)   A certificate guaranteed by GNMA representing shares in pools of mortgages insured by the FHA, VA, or Farmers Home Administration. The pools include mortgages with the same interest rate and same approximate maturity. The payback to investors includes both interest and principal, both guaranteed by GNMA. There are minimum trading unit amounts.

PAYEE (7)   The person whose name appears after the words "Pay to the Order of" on the face of a check. The person to whom funds are being paid.

POST (2)   Strictly speaking, this term describes the recording onto detailed subsidiary records (ledgers) amounts that have been originally recorded in chronological records of original entry (a blotter or journal). In the more general sense, considering the simplification developed through modern mechanization, the term *post* is used to describe the recording of transactions to individual ledger accounts and subsidiary records.

POSTDATED CHECK (7)   A check that is dated for a future date. Such checks cannot be paid by a bank upon presentation for payment and must be returned as a postdated check. If good, the check will be paid if presented on or after the date shown on it.

PRINCIPAL (5)   The face value or par value of an instrument which becomes the obligation of the maker or drawee to pay to a holder in due course. It is upon the principal amount that interest may be charged although, in some instances, the obligation is on the principal only. This is termed "non-interest-bearing" principal.

PROOF (5)   See Proof Department.

PROOF DEPARTMENT (3)   A department of a bank that is charged with the duties of sorting, distributing, and proving all transactions arising from the commercial operations of the bank. The proof function involves the creation of adequate records of all transactions, showing the proper distribution of all items going to other departments for further processing and proof of the correctness of all transactions passing through the bank. The records created by the proof department are of vital importance since examination of these records may be made months after a transaction occurs, in order to substantiate the accuracy of deposits made by customers and the legal fact that deposits were made by certain individual depositors. Proof is generally effected when an amount agrees with another amount within the same batch (i.e., total debits equal total credits).

RAISED CHECK (7)   A check on which the amount has been fraudulently increased.

RECONCILE (3)   A process of accounting for the difference in two records by properly accounting for each outstanding item which, if posted, would bring the two records into agreement. In large banks, a reconcilement department is set up to reconcile the daily statements from the Federal Reserve Bank with the "due from Federal Reserve Bank" account. All accounts in the "Due from Banks" ledger are also reconciled so that all outstanding checks and drafts that have been drawn by the bank may be properly accounted for. A section of the auditing department in banks is often set up to help depositors reconcile their bank statements with their passbooks and check stubs so that they may know what checks are outstanding.

REDEMPTION (4)   The liquidation of an indebtedness whether on maturity or prior to maturity, such as the retirement of a bond issue prior to its maturity date.

REQUIRED RESERVE (1)   The amount set aside out of a bank's deposits for the purpose of maintaining the confidence of the depositors in the ability of the bank to pay in cash. Banking law specifies the minimum reserves against demand and and time deposits and the place of deposit of the required reserve.

RESERVES (1)   Reserves are typically general or specific reserves. General reserves include the legal reserves, federal insurance reserve, reserve for contingencies, and reserve for bad debts when this reserve is classified in the equity section of the balance sheet. Such general reserves are considered appropriated (restricted) retained earnings. Specific reserves represent either (a) valuations against asset accounts (for example, allowance for losses) or (b) liabilities.

RESERVE REQUIREMENTS (1) The percentage of its customers' deposits each member of the Federal Reserve System is required by law to maintain in reserves on deposit with the Federal Reserve Bank in the member bank's district.

RETAINED EARNINGS (10) Undistributed earnings available for dividends.

RETURN ITEM (7) An item (for example, a check) returned unpaid by a designated payor bank.

RULE OF 78s (5) Use of the sum-of-the-digits method for amortization.

SAFEKEEPING (7) The use of a bank's vault facilities by a customer to store valuable assets, such as securities, jewelry, and art, for which the customer pays a fee, usually on an annual basis.

SAVINGS ACCOUNT (8) An account that is deposited in a bank usually in small amounts periodically over a long period of time and not subject to check. Savings accounts are also known as "time deposits." Savings accounts are usually interest-bearing and some banks also levy a service charge for excess withdrawal activity in an account.

SECURED LOAN (5) A loan that is secured by marketable securities or other marketable valuables. Secured loans may be either time or demand loans.

SERVICE CHARGE (7) A fee charged by a bank against a depositor for services rendered in the bookkeeping of the depositor's account.

SHORT SALE (4) A sale of securities that the seller does not own at the time of sale. The short sale must be covered by the seller through the subsequent acquisition and delivery of the securities sold short.

SIGHT DRAFT (7) A draft that is payable on presentation to the drawee.

SIGNATURE CARD (7) A card signed by each depositor and customer of the bank. The signature card is, technically, a contract between the bank and its customer in that it recites the obligations of both in their relationship with each other. The principal use of the signature card is that of identification of the depositor. Signature cards are made out in at least two sets, one for the signature file department, where all signatures are kept for ready reference, and the other for the file at the teller's window, where the depositor will most frequently transact business.

SINGLE ENTRY TICKET (3)   A medium for recording contra entries to cash transactions.

STALE CHECK (7)   A check that has been held an unreasonably long time after issue before being presented for payment. The bank usually refuses payment after six months.

STATEMENT OF CONDITION (1)   See Balance Sheet.

STOP PAYMENT (7)   An order (or request) by a depositor to his bank that it refuse payment of an item specified by him. A stop payment notice is prepared and signed by the depositor giving a complete description of the item to be stopped. If this check is presented for payment, it is the responsibility of the bank to refuse payment and to return it to the holder. The holder must then seek his payment from the maker.

SURPLUS (10)   Includes capital surplus and discretionary transfers from retained earnings.

SUSPENSE ACCOUNTS (3)   Accounts used to record items that will be held subject to clarification and transfer to the appropriate account.

TAX-EQUIVALENT REPORTING (11)   A practice of raising interest income on tax-exempt items (often securities) to a fully taxable basis with a corresponding increase in the provision for income taxes.

TELLER (3)   An employee of a bank who is assigned the duty of waiting on depositors and customers of the bank. The teller's principal responsibilities are to handle cash for the depositor and the bank and to serve the depositor or the customer as far as his duties will permit. The teller is the "personal" contact between the customer and the bank.

TIME DEPOSIT (8)   Savings, time certificates of deposit, commercial and public fund time deposits, and Christmas club and other club accounts. These may bear interest and may include escrow accounts.

TRANSFER TICKET (3)   Since no cash for items may be passed to another teller, these tickets are used in place of the cash. The amount of the ticket is then listed on the teller sheet in the proper place. These tickets are also used when buying or selling money.

TRANSIT ITEMS (3)   Cash items for credit to customers' accounts and payable outside the town or city of the bank receiving them.

TRUST (12)   An arrangement by which an individual or a corporation as trustee holds title to property for the benefit of one or more persons, usually under the terms of a will or other written agreement.

UNCOLLECTED FUNDS (7) A term used to describe that portion of a customer's deposit which has not been collected because the items deposited are en route to the drawee bank for payment. Checks drawn against uncollected funds are returned by banks where they are presented. These checks will not be paid by a bank until it knows that the funds are fully collected. The total uncollected funds for all depositors is the float total for a bank.

UNDIVIDED PROFITS (10) See Retained Earnings.

UNIT BANK (1) A bank that operates only in one location.

UNPOSTED DEBITS (3) Checks not charged against customers' demand deposit accounts until the following business day.

VAULT (3) A large room or rooms in a bank where the cash on hand is stored. A section of the vault is also set apart for "safe-deposit boxes." The vault is constructed so as to be impregnable to theft or damage by fire or water. Banks take pride in the construction of their vaults and the time lock doors which protect the most liquid of all assets.

VAULT CASH (3) That portion of the cash on hand that generally is not required for immediate use and is left in the bank vault as an intermediate reserve.

WITHDRAWAL (8) The manner in which funds on deposit in savings accounts may be paid out by the bank. The depositor must present his passbook and sign a withdrawal slip before the bank can pay out the funds against the deposit account. The signature on the withdrawal slip should always agree with the signature on file in the bank to insure that the right person is receiving the withdrawn funds.

WRITE-OFFS (5) An instrument that has been determined to be uncollectable since there are no known visible assets available with which to liquidate the obligation.

E
ANSWERS—
UNIT REVIEW QUESTIONS

UNIT 1

    1. C

    2. B

    3. D

    4. D

    5. D

    6. E

    7. A

    8. A

    9. C

10. 1. The state of the local and national economy.

     2. Key employee health and morale.

     3. Management ability

These are only three suggested items; there are many more.

UNIT 2

1. True—Likewise the normal balance of a liability account would be a credit.

2. False—The correct answer would be that liabilities must have increased by $538,000.

3. True—Although closing procedures can be performed more than once during a year, they must be done at the end of the year, since the data in the temporary accounts is not accumulated for more than 12 months.

4. True—You saw a simplified version of the balance sheet and the profit and loss statement. Remember the other three? If not, look back into Unit 1.

5.

JE#	NONEARNING ASSETS	+	EARNING ASSETS =	LIABIL- ITIES	+ PERMANENT +	(REVENUE	−	EXPENSE)
1	+10,000				+10,000			
2	+120,000			+120,000				
3	−7,000			−7,000				
4	+9,000			+10,800				−1,800
5>	+4,000							
5>	−4,000							
6			+22,000	+22,000				
7			+50,000	+50,000				
8	+3,000			+3,000				
9	−93,000			−93,000				
10	+6,000					+6,000		
11			+500			+500		
12	+2,000					+2,000		
13			−50			−50		
14	−10							−10
15				+2,000				−2,000
16				+600				−600
	+49,990		+72,450 =	+108,400	+10,000 +	(+8,450		−4,410)

UNIT 3

1. Simply following the instructions to this project should give you your solution.

2. See Appendix F.

UNIT 4

See Appendix F.

UNIT 5

See Appendix F.

UNIT 6

1. See Exhibit E-1. When you have completed the worksheet, compare the totals to the balance sheet for THE FIRST TYPICAL BANK in Appendix F. Observe how total assets agree between the worksheet and the balance sheet in Appendix F. The worksheet more closely parallels the proper GAAP for balance sheet presentations as shown in SAMPLE BANK in Appendix C. Make a note to perform similar comparisons when you complete the related projects in Units 9, 10, 11, and 15.
2. See Appendix F.

UNIT 7

1. The following internal control points are from responses to this project prepared by the students who took the course during the development of this text. How did your list compare to theirs?
   - Are official checks approved and signed by an officer?
   - Are limits set on check cashing and/or cash back?
   - Is there a limit on personal money orders?
   - Are stop payment suspects okayed by two employees?
   - Is there a three day uncollected funds period?
   - Is officer approval required on uncollected funds payouts?
   - Are uncollected balances reviewed by management?
   - Is certification of checks on uncollected funds prohibited?
   - Are tellers prohibited from preparing or altering deposit or withdrawal tickets?
   - Are there sufficient controls to identify and control dormant accounts?

- Are significant balance and closed account reports reviewed by management?
- Is return mail controlled by management?
- Are overdrafts and returned checks controlled by management?
- Is there rotation of duties relative to controlling overdrafts?
- Does the EDP system assure identification and reporting of all over-drawn accounts?
- Is the TT&L account properly controlled and reconciled?
- Are official checks reconciled at least weekly?
- Are unissued official checks under adequate control? (Dual control?)
- Do stop payments of official checks require officer approval?
- Is there adequate segregation of duties relative to official checks?
- Are signatures and endorsements on official checks reviewed?
- Are DDA trial balances reconciled to the general ledger control account(s)?
- Are balances checked for all checks cashed?
- Also, how about signatures?
- Are tellers prohibited access to dormant account records?
- Are "no-mail" accounts prohibited?
- Are they adequately controlled?
- Are resolutions on file for all corporate accounts?
- Does the bank's internal control program call for random confirmation of account balances?
- Are customer "balancing" problems and inquiries properly followed up on?
- Are employee accounts segregated and under dual review and control?
- Do employees have their personal account transactions processed through another employee?
- Are tests made on proper application of service charges?
- Are all closed accounts reported to the board?

2. See Appendix F.

UNIT 8

1. As in the answer to Unit 7, Project 1, this list was prepared by the students.
   - Is there a limit on withdrawals?
   - Are CD interest penalties reviewed by two employees?
   - Are all accounts under numerical control?
   - Are unissued passbooks and CDs under dual control?
   - Are CDs reconciled weekly?
   - Are accruals of interest properly computed and reviewed?
   - Are random tests made of interest paid?
   - Is officer approval required on withdrawals from dormant accounts?
   - Are tellers prohibited from opening new accounts?
   - Are special precautions given to "nonpersonalized" withdrawal tickets?
   - Are no-passbook withdrawals prohibited?
   - If no, are they adequately controlled? (How?)
   - Are signatures verified on all withdrawals?
   - Are tellers prohibited from overriding holds on accounts?
   - Are balances checked on all withdrawals?
   - Are withdrawal tickets canceled daily?
   - Are savings trial balances properly reconciled to the appropriate general ledger control account(s)?
   - Does the bank confirm account balances on a random basis?
2. See Appendix F.

UNIT 9

1. See Exhibit E-2.
2. See Appendix F.

UNIT 10

Questions

1. a. 190,000

b. 300,000

2. a. 3400 UNDIVIDED PROFITS 600,000

        2820 DIVIDENDS PAYABLE   600,000

b. No entry needed

c. 2820 DIVIDENDS PAYABLE 600,000

        XXXX Appropriate "CASH" account   600,000

3. a. $4,500,000 (15,000 shares x $30)

b. No effect on any of these totals

4. $3 million—

Assets	=	Liabilities	+	Paid in Capital	+	Retained Earnings
+ 10	=	+ 8		-0-		(3-1)

5. $1 million—

				Treasury Stock and		
Assets	=	Liabilities	+	Paid in Capital	+	Retained Earnings
+ 10	=	+ 8		+ 2.5 − .5		(1-1)

6. 15XX FIXED ASSETS 1,500,000

        3200 COMMON STOCK   500,000

        3300 SURPLUS   1,000,000

7. $98—

$$\text{Equity/Share} = \frac{(\text{Total Shareholders' Equity} - \text{Par Value of Preferred})}{\text{Number of Shares of Common Stock Outstanding}}$$

OR

$$\$98 = \frac{(10,300,000 - 500,000)}{100,000}$$

8. EPS = $14.50—

$$\text{EPS} = \frac{(\text{Net Income} - \text{Preferred Dividends})}{\text{Number of Shares of Common Stock Outstanding}}$$

OR

$$\$14.50 = \frac{(1,500,000 - 50,000)}{100,000}$$

9. a. XXXX   Appropriate "CASH" account   200,000
         3XXX TREASURY STOCK—AT COST   150,000
         3300 SURPLUS   50,000
  b. Total assets and shareholders' equity would increase by $200,000— no effect on net income.

10. In thousands of dollars:

	TOTAL	PREFERRED STOCK	COMMON STOCK	SURPLUS	RETAINED EARNINGS	TREASURY STOCK
Beg balance	10300	500	1100	4000	5000	(300)
Net income	1500				1500	
Sale of stock	4500		1000	3500		
Cash dividends:						
Preferred	(50)				(50)	
Common	(690)				(690)	
Sale of treasury stock	200			50		150
End balance	15760	500	2100	7550	5760	(150)

Projects

1. See Appendix F.
2. See Exhibit E-3.

UNIT 11

See Exhibit E-4.

UNIT 12

Since this is an open-ended project, no answer is provided here. The bibliography (Appendix G) does provide some good references.

UNIT 13

1. It would be doubtful if you could grant this loan request. Before making any loan payments or paying income and self-employment taxes, the owner would generate cash flow of $44,579 ($58,679 – $14,100). The principal repayment on the loan would reduce the cash flow even further, leaving the customer with less than $10,000 cash each year. Unless the customer could demonstrate an ability to adequately cover his or her personal expenses, interest, and taxes over the term of the loan, you would probably deny the loan.

2. The length of your list should be proportional to the length of time that you spent on this project. I have provided only a brief listing to give you an idea of some of the more important data that you would like to pull out.

   a. Projection of cash flow from payments on existing installment loans

   b. Aging of delinquent loans

   c. Loan concentration sorts by:
- Geographic area
- Type of collateral
- Type of customer

   d. Loans sorted by granting officers

If you currently work in a bank, request to see the types of installment loan reporting package there and compare it to your list.

UNIT 14

1. The balance would be $31,500 or (3 x $10,500), assuming that the estimated tax payments were made according to the dates indicated in Unit 9 under Income Tax Procedures.

2.

```
12-1-78
8900 PROVISION FOR INCOME TAXES              48,500 (1)
8400 SECURITY G/L—(NET)                       66,000 (2)
      2941  INCOME TAXES PAYABLE—FEDERAL                 19,300 (3)
      2951  INCOME TAXES PAYABLE—STATE                   36,000 (4)
      29XX DEFERRED INCOME TAXES PAYABLE                 59,200 (5)
```

(1) This debit would bring the balance in account 8900 to $80,000 ($31,500 + $48,500).

(2) This is the amount of income tax applicable to the security gains per the given data in SAMPLE BANK's financial statements. This is covered in Unit 11.

(3) This is the $50,800 tax liability less the estimated tax payments of $31,500.

(4) I am assuming that none of the state tax liability has been paid.

(5) See Exhibit 14-6.

UNIT 15

1. See Exhibit E-5.

2. These are the factors (in thousands of dollars) that I used. You should be able to plug these into the formulas given in the unit and come up with the same answers.

NET INCOME	$1,435
AVERAGE ASSETS (for 1978)	104,505
AVERAGE SHAREHOLDERS' EQUITY (for 1978)	9,471
INTEREST INCOME ($7,011 + $1,306) =	8,317
AVERAGE EARNINGS ASSETS (for 1978)	95,623
OPERATING EXPENSES (net of service & fee income) ($4,059 + $1,983 − $187 − $106 − $74) =	5,675
NET INTEREST INCOME ($8,317 − $4,059) =	4,238
OPERATING EXPENSE ($4,059 + $60 + $1,983) =	6,102
OPERATING INCOME ($7,011 + $541) =	7,552

3. The indicated market value would be $84. (P.S.: Had the PE ratio remained at 10, the indicated market value would have been $70.)

The FIRST TYPICAL BANK Financial Statement Project

ASSETS

```
CASH & DUE FROM BANKS:
     1000                                    $ 9,000
     1021                                       -0-
     1023                                       -0-
     1024                                       -0-
     1099                                       300
     1101                                    32,250
     1200                                     8,000    $      49,550
                                            --------

INVESTMENTS
     1301                       $ 20,000
     1302                          1,950
     1303                       (    -0-) $21,950
                                ---------

     1398                                      -0-
     1399                                      -0-    $      21,950
                                                      --------

LOANS
     1401                       $ 39,500
     1402                       (    -0-)
     1403                       (    -0-)
     1404                          -0-    $39,500
                                ---------

     1421                       $ 17,100
     1423                       ( 1,100) $16,000
                                ---------

     1440                                 $    -0-
     1461                                      -0-
     1464                                      -0-
     1465                                      170
                                         --------
                                         $55,670
     1490                                 (1,000)    $      54,670
                                         --------

FIXED ASSETS
     COST                                 $ 9,000
     LESS ACCUMULATED DEPRECIATION        (   560)   $       8,440
                                          --------

OTHER ASSETS
     1800 & 1900 ACCOUNTS                            $      11,105
                                                     ----------
          TOTAL ASSETS                               $     145,715
                                                     ==========
```

LIABILITIES

```
DEPOSITS
     2010-2101                          $ 73,235
     2201                               $ 56,400    $ 129,635
                                        --------

SHORT-TERM BORROWINGS
     2410 & 2440                                    $      -0-

ACCRUED INTEREST & OTHER LIABILITIES
     2600-2990                                      $    2,350

SUBORDINATED DEBT
     2999                                           $      -0-
                                                   ---------
              TOTAL LIABILITIES                     $ 131,985
```

SHAREHOLDERS' EQUITY

```
     3100                           $      -0-
     3200                                5,000
     3300                                5,000
     3400                                3,730    $   13,730
                                        --------   ---------
     TOTAL LIABILITIES & SHAREHOLDERS' EQUITY     $ 145,715
                                                   =========
```

After completing this worksheet, you should again review Project 1 in Unit 6.

EXHIBIT E-3

The FIRST TYPICAL BANK Capital Statement for 1984

	Total	Capital Stock	Surplus	Retained Earnings
Initial sale of stock	$ 10,000	$ 5,000	$ 5,000	
Net Income	4,230			$ 4,230
Cash Dividends	(500)			(500)
Balance, 12-31-84	$ 13,730	$ 5,000	$ 5,000	$ 3,730

The FIRST TYPICAL BANK—Multiple Step Income Statement

```
Interest Income
     Loans ($11,400+$1,500)              $ 12,900
     Investments                              700    $13,600
                                         --------

Interest Expense                                       4,600
                                                     -------
          Net Interest Income                          9,000

Provision for Loan Losses                              1,500
                                                     -------
          Net Interest Income after
             provision for loan losses                 7,500

Other Income ($60+$5)                                     65

Other Expenses
     Salaries and Wages                  $   1,000
     Employee Benefits                         530
     Occupancy Expense ($365+$256)             621
     Furniture & Equip Expenses ($15+$304)     319
     Other Operating Expense                   765    3,235
                                         --------   -------

Income before tax and security gains                   4,330
Applicable income taxes                                  500
                                                     -------
Income before security gains                           3,830

Security gains, net of $50 tax                           400
                                                     -------

          NET INCOME                                 $ 4,230
                                                     =======
```

EXHIBIT E-5

The FIRST TYPICAL BANK—Funds Statement

```
FUNDS PROVIDED FROM:
    Operations ($4,230+$560+$1,500)        $   6,290
    Increase in other liabilities              2,350
    Sale of common stock                      10,000
    Increase in deposits                     129,635   $148,275
                                            --------


FUNDS APPLIED TO:
    Purchase of fixed assets               $   9,000
    Dividends paid                               500
    Increase in:
        Loans, net                            56,170
        Investments                           21,950
        Other assets                          11,105   $ 98,725
                                            --------   --------


INCREASE IN CASH AND DUE FROM BANKS                    $ 49,550
                                                       ========
```

This project completes your preparation of the financial statements for "TYPICAL." The 51 transactions (16 prior to 6-30 and 35 after 6-30) were not designed to give "TYPICAL" financial statements that are representative of actual banks, such as SAMPLE BANK in Appendix C. My thrust was to make individual entries realistic and to make sure that all accounts had normal balances. I also made sure that "TYPICAL" showed a profit. Other than that, I let the numbers fall where they might.

F

THE FIRST TYPICAL BANK
GENERAL LEDGER

This is a continuation of THE FIRST TYPICAL BANK general ledger started in Unit 2. The year, 1984, is TYPICAL's first year of business. The activity in the general ledger in Unit 2 occurred in the first six months of 1984. The beginning balance of the general ledger, in this appendix, are TYPICAL's 6-30-84 ending balances.

The 35 general journals in this appendix occurred in the last six months of 1984. The trial balance and balance sheet, in this appendix, are as of 12-31-84. The current period column in the profit and loss statement covers the last six months of 1984 and the year-to-date column is for all of 1984.

The following table references the journal entry projects in Units 3 through 10 to the 35 entries in the General Journal in this appendix. This will serve as your key in checking your solutions to the unit projects.

KEY TO UNIT REVIEW JOURNAL ENTRY PROJECTS

UNIT #	UNIT PROJECT TRANSACTION LETTER	GENERAL JOURNAL #
3	A	1
	B	2
	C	3
	D	4
	E	5
	F	6
	G	7
4	A	8
	B	9
	C	10
	D	11
	E	12
5	A	13
	B	14
	C	15
	D	16
	E	17
	F	18
	G	19
	H	20
6	A	21
	B	22
	C	23
7	A	24
	B	25
	C	26
8	A	27
	B	28
9	A	29
	B	30
	C	31
	D	32
	E	33
10	A	34
	B	35

GENERAL JOURNALS

DATE	JE#	ACCOUNT	DEBIT	CREDIT
07/01/84	1	1000 CURRENCY & COIN	11,000.00	
		2010 DDA-INDIVIDUALS/COS		7,000.00
		2201 SAVINGS & TIME DEPOSITS		4,000.00
		TO RECORD CASH DEPOSITS		
07/01/84	2	2010 DDA-INDIVIDUALS/COS	6,000.00	
		1000 CURRENCY & COIN		6,000.00
		TO RECORD CASHING OF ON US CHECKS		
07/01/84	3	1101 DUE FROM BANK A---Z	3,000.00	
		1000 CURRENCY & COIN		3,000.00
		TO RECORD TRANSFER OF CASH		
07/05/84	4	1021 REDEEMED SAVINGS BONDS	150.00	
		1101 DUE FROM BANK A---Z	12,000.00	
		1024 TRANSIT ITEMS	1,500.00	
		1023 UNPOSTED DEBITS	200.00	
		2201 SAVINGS & TIME DEPOSITS		3,450.00
		2010 DDA-INDIVIDUALS/COS		9,000.00
		1421 INSTALLMENT LOANS		600.00
		2081 UNPOSTED CREDITS		800.00
		TO RECORD A BATCH OF OUTCLEARING ITEMS		
07/15/84	5	1200 RESERVE ACCT (FED/ST)	8,000.00	
		1101 DUE FROM BANK A---Z		8,000.00
		TRANSFER TO RESERVE ACCOUNT		
07/15/84	6	1101 DUE FROM BANK A---Z	1,650.00	
		1024 TRANSIT ITEMS		1,500.00
		1021 REDEEMED SAVINGS BONDS		150.00
		CLEAR IN TRANSIT ITEMS		
07/03/84	7	1101 DUE FROM BANK A---Z	200.00	
		2081 UNPOSTED CREDITS	800.00	
		1023 UNPOSTED DEBITS		200.00
		1421 INSTALLMENT LOANS		300.00
		2010 DDA-INDIVIDUALS/COS		350.00
		2201 SAVINGS & TIME DEPOSITS		150.00
		TO CLEAR UNPOSTABLES FROM 7-5		
08/01/84	8	1301 INVESTMENT SEC-FACE	10,000.00	
		1901 INT REC-INVESTMENTS	100.00	
		1101 DUE FROM BANK A---Z		9,100.00
		1303 UNAMORTIZED DISCOUNT-INV		1,000.00
		PURCHASE OF BONDS		
09/30/84	9	1901 INT REC-INVESTMENTS	200.00	
		4010 INT INCOME-INVESTMENTS		200.00

252

THE FIRST TYPICAL BANK

GENERAL JOURNAL
AS OF 12/31/84

DATE	JE#	ACCOUNT	DEBIT	CREDIT
		TO ACCRUE INTEREST ON BONDS		
12/31/84	10	1303 UNAMORTIZED DISCOUNT-INV	50.00	
		4010 INT INCOME-INVESTMENTS		50.00
		TO AMORTIZE DISCOUNT ON BOND		
09/30/84	11	1099 OTHER ITEMS IN COLL	300.00	
		1901 INT REC-INVESTMENTS		300.00
		TO COLLECT INTEREST ON BOND		
12/31/84	12	1101 DUE FROM BANK A---Z	9,500.00	
		1303 UNAMORTIZED DISCOUNT-INV	950.00	
		1301 INVESTMENT SEC-FACE		10,000.00
		8400 SECURITY G/L-(NET)		450.00
		TO RECORD SALE OF BOND AT A GAIN		
07/01/84	13	1401 COMMERCIAL LOANS	10,000.00	
		2010 DDA-INDIVIDUALS/COS		9,500.00
		2084 UNDISBURSED LOAN PROCEEDS		500.00
		TO RECORD A COMMERCIAL LOAN		
07/15/84	14	2084 UNDISBURSED LOAN PROCEEDS	500.00	
		2010 DDA-INDIVIDUALS/COS	5.00	
		2061 OFFICIAL CHECKS (ALL TYPES)		500.00
		8030 OTHER MISC INCOME		5.00
		ISSUE CHECK TO CLEAR UNDISBURSED LOAN PROCEEDS		
12/31/84	15	1931 INT (& FEES) REC-LOANS	900.00	
		4020 INT & FEES ON LOANS		900.00
		ACCRUE INTEREST ON LOAN		
12/31/84	16	2010 DDA-INDIVIDUALS/COS	10,900.00	
		1401 COMMERCIAL LOANS		10,000.00
		1931 INT (& FEES) REC-LOANS		900.00
		TO RECORD COLLECTION OF LOAN AT MATURITY		
12/31/84	17	4020 INT & FEES ON LOANS	1,500.00	
		1490 RES FOR POSS LN LOSSES		1,500.00
		TO RECORD ESTIMATED LOAN LOSSES		
09/15/84	18	1490 RES FOR POSS LN LOSSES	500.00	
		1401 COMMERCIAL LOANS		500.00
		TO WRITE OFF AN UNCOLLECTABLE LOAN		
09/15/84	19	1421 INSTALLMENT LOANS	3,000.00	
		1423 UNEARNED DISCOUNT-INST LNS		600.00
		2010 DDA-INDIVIDUALS/COS		2,400.00
		DISBURSEMENT OF INSTALLMENT LOAN		

DATE	JE#	ACCOUNT	DEBIT	CREDIT
========	===	=================================	==========	==========
		PROCEEDS		
12/31/84	20	1423 UNEARNED DISCOUNT-INST LNS	4,000.00	
		4020 INT & FEES ON LOANS		4,000.00
		TO RECORD INTEREST INCOME ON		
		INSTALLMENT LOANS		
12/31/84	21	6200 DEPRECIATION EXPENSE	550.00	
		1502 ACCUM DEPR-BLDG		250.00
		1522 ACCUM DEPR-F&F		300.00
		TO RECORD DEPRECIATION EXPENSE		
08/01/84	22	1952 PREPAID FDIC ASSESSMENT	180.00	
		2061 OFFICIAL CHECKS (ALL TYPES)		180.00
		PAYMENT OF FDIC ASSESSMENT		
12/31/84	23	6900 OTHER OPERATING EXPENSES	75.00	
		1952 PREPAID FDIC ASSESSMENT		75.00
		TO RECORD EXPIRATION OF FDIC		
		ASSESSMENT		
08/01/84	24	2010 DDA-INDIVIDUALS/COS	3,000.00	
		2031 US TT&L ACCOUNT		3,000.00
		TT&L DEPOSIT		
12/31/84	25	1465 OVERDRAFTS	170.00	
		2010 DDA-INDIVIDUALS/COS		170.00
		TO RECLASSIFY OVERDRAFTS TO LOANS		
12/31/84	26	2010 DDA-INDIVIDUALS/COS	60.00	
		8000 DDA SERVICE CHARGES		60.00
		TO RECORD SERVICE CHARGES		
12/31/84	27	5000 INT EXP-DEP & DEBT	2,600.00	
		2841 INT PAY-SAV & TIME DEPOSITS		2,600.00
		TO ACCRUE INTEREST ON SAVINGS		
10/01/84	28	2841 INT PAY-SAV & TIME DEPOSITS	1,200.00	
		2201 SAVINGS & TIME DEPOSITS		800.00
		2061 OFFICIAL CHECKS (ALL TYPES)		400.00
		PAY INTEREST ON SAVINGS		
07/01/84	29	2980 ACCOUNTS PAYABLE	600.00	
		6900 OTHER OPERATING EXPENSES		600.00
		TO REVERSE 6-30 ACCOUNTS PAYABLE		
07/05/84	30	6900 OTHER OPERATING EXPENSES	600.00	
		2061 OFFICIAL CHECKS (ALL TYPES)		600.00
		PAYMENT OF INVOICES FROM 6-30		

THE FIRST TYPICAL BANK

GENERAL JOURNAL
AS OF 12/31/84

DATE	JE#	ACCOUNT	DEBIT	CREDIT
12/31/84	31	6030 GROUP INSURANCE	30.00	
		6100 OCCUPANCY EXPENSES	65.00	
		6300 FURNITURE & EQUIP EXPENSES	15.00	
		6900 OTHER OPERATING EXPENSES	90.00	
		2980 ACCOUNTS PAYABLE		200.00
		TO RECORD ACCOUNTS PAYABLE		
		AS OF 12-31		
09/15/84	32	8900 PROVISION FOR INCOME TAXES	300.00	
		2061 OFFICIAL CHECKS (ALL TYPES)		300.00
		ESTIMATED INCOME TAX PAYMENT		
12/31/84	33	8900 PROVISION FOR INCOME TAXES	200.00	
		8400 SECURITY G/L-(NET)	50.00	
		2941 INCOME TAXES PAYABLE-FEDERAL		250.00
		ACCRUAL OF INCOME TAXES		
		AS OF 12-31		
12/31/84	34	3400 UNDIVIDED PROFITS	500.00	
		2820 DIVIDENDS PAYABLE		500.00
		DECLARATION OF CASH DIVIDENDS		
12/31/84	35	3500 CURRENT YEAR EARNINGS	4,230.00	
		3400 UNDIVIDED PROFITS		4,230.00
		FINAL CLOSING ENTRY FOR THE YEAR		
		TOTAL DEBITS	111,420.00	
		TOTAL CREDITS		111,420.00

GENERAL LEDGER

ACCT NO	ACCOUNT NAME	FOLIO	FORWARD	MONTH	BALANCE
1000	CURRENCY & COIN		7,000.00		
	JE # 1	GJ		11,000.00	
	JE # 2	GJ		6,000.00CR	
	JE # 3	GJ		3,000.00CR	
	CHECKS FOR MONTH	CD		0.00	
					9,000.00
1021	REDEEMED SAVINGS BONDS		0.00		
	JE # 4	GJ		150.00	
	JE # 6	GJ		150.00CR	
					0.00
1023	UNPOSTED DEBITS		0.00		
	JE # 4	GJ		200.00	
	JE # 7	GJ		200.00CR	
					0.00
1024	TRANSIT ITEMS		0.00		
	JE # 4	GJ		1,500.00	
	JE # 6	GJ		1,500.00CR	
					0.00
1099	OTHER ITEMS IN COLL		0.00		
	JE # 11	GJ		300.00	
					300.00
1101	DUE FROM BANK A---Z		23,000.00		
	JE # 3	GJ		3,000.00	
	JE # 4	GJ		12,000.00	
	JE # 5	GJ		8,000.00CR	
	JE # 6	GJ		1,650.00	
	JE # 7	GJ		200.00	
	JE # 8	GJ		9,100.00CR	
	JE # 12	GJ		9,500.00	
					32,250.00
1200	RESERVE ACCT (FED/ST)		0.00		
	JE # 5	GJ		8,000.00	
					8,000.00
1301	INVESTMENT SEC-FACE		20,000.00		
	JE # 8	GJ		10,000.00	
	JE # 12	GJ		10,000.00CR	
					20,000.00
1302	UNAMORTIZED PREMIUM-INV		1,950.00		1,950.00
1303	UNAMORTIZED DISCOUNT-IN		0.00		
	JE # 8	GJ		1,000.00CR	
	JE # 10	GJ		50.00	

ACCT NO	ACCOUNT NAME	FOLIO	FORWARD	MONTH	BALANCE
	JE # 12	GJ		950.00	
					0.00
1401	COMMERCIAL LOANS		40,000.00		
	JE # 13	GJ		10,000.00	
	JE # 16	GJ		10,000.00CR	
	JE # 18	GJ		500.00CR	
					39,500.00
1421	INSTALLMENT LOANS		15,000.00		
	JE # 4	GJ		600.00CR	
	JE # 7	GJ		300.00CR	
	JE # 19	GJ		3,000.00	
					17,100.00
1423	UNEARNED DISCOUNT-INST		4,500.00CR		
	JE # 19	GJ		600.00CR	
	JE # 20	GJ		4,000.00	
					1,100.00CR
1465	OVERDRAFTS		0.00		
	JE # 25	GJ		170.00	
					170.00
1490	RES FOR POSS LN LOSSES		0.00		
	JE # 17	GJ		1,500.00CR	
	JE # 18	GJ		500.00	
					1,000.00CR
1501	BANK BLDG & IMPR'S-COST		5,000.00		5,000.00
1502	ACCUM DEPR-BLDG		6.00CR		
	JE # 21	GJ		250.00CR	
					256.00CR
1521	FUR & FIX-COST		3,000.00		3,000.00
1522	ACCUM DEPR-F&F		4.00CR		
	JE # 21	GJ		300.00CR	
					304.00CR
1541	LAND		1,000.00		1,000.00
1901	INT REC-INVESTMENTS		2,000.00		
	JE # 8	GJ		100.00	
	JE # 9	GJ		200.00	
	JE # 11	GJ		300.00CR	
					2,000.00
1931	INT (& FEES) REC-LOANS		6,000.00		
	JE # 15	GJ		900.00	

ACCT NO	ACCOUNT NAME	FOLIO	FORWARD	MONTH	BALANCE
	JE # 16	GJ		900.00CR	
					6,000.00
1951	PREPAID INSURANCE		3,000.00		3,000.00
1952	PREPAID FDIC ASSESSMEN		0.00		
	JE # 22	GJ		180.00	
	JE # 23	GJ		75.00CR	
					105.00
2010	DDA-INDIVIDUALS/COS		59,000.00CR		
	JE # 1	GJ		7,000.00CR	
	JE # 2	GJ		6,000.00	
	JE # 4	GJ		9,000.00CR	
	JE # 7	GJ		350.00CR	
	JE # 13	GJ		9,500.00CR	
	JE # 14	GJ		5.00	
	JE # 16	GJ		10,900.00	
	JE # 19	GJ		2,400.00CR	
	JE # 24	GJ		3,000.00	
	JE # 25	GJ		170.00CR	
	JE # 26	GJ		60.00	
					67,455.00CR
2031	US TT&L ACCOUNT		0.00		
	JE # 24	GJ		3,000.00CR	
					3,000.00CR
2061	OFFICIAL CHECKS (ALL TY		800.00CR		
	JE # 14	GJ		500.00CR	
	JE # 22	GJ		180.00CR	
	JE # 28	GJ		400.00CR	
	JE # 30	GJ		600.00CR	
	JE # 32	GJ		300.00CR	
					2,780.00CR
2081	UNPOSTED CREDITS		0.00		
	JE # 4	GJ		800.00CR	
	JE # 7	GJ		800.00	
					0.00
2084	UNDISBURSED LOAN PROCEE		0.00		
	JE # 13	GJ		500.00CR	
	JE # 14	GJ		500.00	
					0.00
2201	SAVINGS & TIME DEPOSITS		48,000.00CR		
	JE # 1	GJ		4,000.00CR	
	JE # 4	GJ		3,450.00CR	
	JE # 7	GJ		150.00CR	
	JE # 28	GJ		800.00CR	
					56,400.00CR

260

ACCT NO	ACCOUNT NAME	FOLIO	FORWARD	MONTH	BALANCE
2820	DIVIDENDS PAYABLE		0.00		
	JE # 34	GJ		500.00CR	
					500.00CR
2841	INT PAY-SAV & TIME DEPO		0.00		
	JE # 27	GJ		2,600.00CR	
	JE # 28	GJ		1,200.00	
					1,400.00CR
2941	INCOME TAXES PAYABLE-FE		0.00		
	JE # 33	GJ		250.00CR	
					250.00CR
2980	ACCOUNTS PAYABLE		600.00CR		
	JE # 29	GJ		600.00	
	JE # 31	GJ		200.00CR	
					200.00CR
3200	COMMON STOCK		5,000.00CR		5,000.00CR
3300	SURPLUS		5,000.00CR		5,000.00CR
3400	UNDIVIDED PROFITS		0.00		
	JE # 34	GJ		500.00	
	JE # 35	GJ		4,230.00CR	
					3,730.00CR
3500	CURRENT YEAR EARNINGS		4,040.00CR		
	JE # 35	GJ		4,230.00	
					190.00
4010	INT INCOME-INVESTMENTS		1,950.00CR		
	JE # 9	GJ		200.00CR	
	JE # 10	GJ		50.00CR	
					2,200.00CR
4020	INT & FEES ON LOANS		6,500.00CR		
	JE # 15	GJ		900.00CR	
	JE # 17	GJ		1,500.00	
	JE # 20	GJ		4,000.00CR	
					9,900.00CR
5000	INT EXP-DEP & DEBT		2,000.00		
	JE # 27	GJ		2,600.00	
					4,600.00
6010	SALARIES & WAGES		1,000.00		1,000.00
6030	GROUP INSURANCE		0.00		
	JE # 31	GJ		30.00	
					30.00

ACCT NO	ACCOUNT NAME	FOLIO	FORWARD	MONTH	BALANCE
6040	OTHER EMPLOYEE BENEFITS		500.00		500.00
6100	OCCUPANCY EXPENSES		300.00		
	JE # 31	GJ		65.00	
					365.00
6200	DEPRECIATION EXPENSE		10.00		
	JE # 21	GJ		550.00	
					560.00
6300	FURNITURE & EQUIP EXPEN		0.00		
	JE # 31	GJ		15.00	
					15.00
6900	OTHER OPERATING EXPENSE		600.00		
	JE # 23	GJ		75.00	
	JE # 29	GJ		600.00CR	
	JE # 30	GJ		600.00	
	JE # 31	GJ		90.00	
					765.00
8000	DDA SERVICE CHARGES		0.00		
	JE # 26	GJ		60.00CR	
					60.00CR
8030	OTHER MISC INCOME		0.00		
	JE # 14	GJ		5.00CR	
					5.00CR
8400	SECURITY G/L-(NET)		0.00		
	JE # 12	GJ		450.00CR	
	JE # 33	GJ		50.00	
					400.00CR
8900	PROVISION FOR INCOME TA		0.00		
	JE # 32	GJ		300.00	
	JE # 33	GJ		200.00	
					500.00
9999	INCOME TRANSFER		4,040.00		4,040.00
	TOTALS		0.00	0.00	0.00

ACCT NO	ACCOUNT NAME	FOLIO FORWARD	MONTH	BALANCE

NET INCOME(CR) OR LOSS(DB):   190.00CR

RESULTING EARNING AND INCOME TRANSFER ACCOUNTS:

3500	CURRENT YEAR EARNINGS	4,040.00CR	4,040.00	0.00
9999	INCOME TRANSFER	4,040.00	190.00	4,230.00

TRIAL BALANCE

TRIAL BALANCE
AS OF   12/31/84

ACCOUNT NUMBER	TYPE	ACCOUNT NAME	BALANCE
1000	ASSETS	CURRENCY & COIN	9,000.00
1021	ASSETS	REDEEMED SAVINGS BONDS	0.00
1023	ASSETS	UNPOSTED DEBITS	0.00
1024	ASSETS	TRANSIT ITEMS	0.00
1099	ASSETS	OTHER ITEMS IN COLL	300.00
1101	ASSETS	DUE FROM BANK A---Z	32,250.00
1200	ASSETS	RESERVE ACCT (FED/ST)	8,000.00
1301	ASSETS	INVESTMENT SEC-FACE	20,000.00
1302	ASSETS	UNAMORTIZED PREMIUM-INV	1,950.00
1303	ASSETS	UNAMORTIZED DISCOUNT-INV	0.00
1398	ASSETS	FEDERAL FUNDS SOLD	0.00
1399	ASSETS	SEC PUR/RESELL AGREE	0.00
1401	ASSETS	COMMERCIAL LOANS	39,500.00
1402	ASSETS	PART SOLD-COM'L LNS	0.00
1403	ASSETS	UNEARNED DISCOUNT-COM'L LNS	0.00
1404	ASSETS	PART PURCHASED-COM'L LNS	0.00
1421	ASSETS	INSTALLMENT LOANS	17,100.00
1423	ASSETS	UNEARNED DISCOUNT-INST LNS	1,100.00-
1440	ASSETS	REAL ESTATE LOANS	0.00
1461	ASSETS	CREDIT CARD LOANS	0.00
1464	ASSETS	IMMEDIATE CR COLL ITEMS	0.00
1465	ASSETS	OVERDRAFTS	170.00
1490	ASSETS	RES FOR POSS LN LOSSES	1,000.00-
1501	ASSETS	BANK BLDG & IMPR'S-COST	5,000.00
1502	ASSETS	ACCUM DEPR-BLDG	256.00-
1521	ASSETS	FUR & FIX-COST	3,000.00
1522	ASSETS	ACCUM DEPR-F&F	304.00-
1541	ASSETS	LAND	1,000.00
1551	ASSETS	LEASEHOLD IMPROVEMENTS	0.00
1552	ASSETS	ACCUM AMORTIZATION-LH IMPR	0.00
1801	ASSETS	REAL ESTATE OWED (NET)	0.00
1840	ASSETS	REPOSSESSIONS	0.00
1850	ASSETS	CASH ITEMS-NOT IN COLL	0.00
1901	ASSETS	INT REC-INVESTMENTS	2,000.00
1921	ASSETS	INT REC-FED FUNDS SOLD	0.00
1922	ASSETS	INT REC-SEC PUR/RESELL	0.00
1931	ASSETS	INT (& FEES) REC-LOANS	6,000.00
1951	ASSETS	PREPAID INSURANCE	3,000.00
1952	ASSETS	PREPAID FDIC ASSESSMENT	105.00
1957	ASSETS	PREPAID RENT	0.00
1979	ASSETS	OTHER PREPAID EXPENSES	0.00
2010	LIABILITIES	DDA-INDIVIDUALS/COS	67,455.00-
2031	LIABILITIES	US TT&L ACCOUNT	3,000.00-
2039	LIABILITIES	OTHER US DDA	0.00
2040	LIABILITIES	DDA-STATE & LOCAL GOVT	0.00
2061	LIABILITIES	OFFICIAL CHECKS (ALL TYPES)	2,780.00-
2081	LIABILITIES	UNPOSTED CREDITS	0.00
2084	LIABILITIES	UNDISBURSED LOAN PROCEEDS	0.00
2101	LIABILITIES	DUE TO BANK A---Z	0.00
2201	LIABILITIES	SAVINGS & TIME DEPOSITS	56,400.00-
2410	LIABILITIES	FEDERAL FUNDS PURCHASED	0.00

THE FIRST TYPICAL BANK

TRIAL BALANCE
AS OF 12/31/84

ACCOUNT NUMBER	TYPE	ACCOUNT NAME	BALANCE
2420	LIABILITIES	SEC SOLD-REPUR AGREE	0.00
2600	LIABILITIES	MORTGAGE DEBT	0.00
2610	LIABILITIES	OTHER LIAB FOR BORROWED MONEY	0.00
2620	LIABILITIES	BORROWINGS FROM FED RES BK	0.00
2820	LIABILITIES	DIVIDENDS PAYABLE	500.00-
2841	LIABILITIES	INT PAY-SAV & TIME DEPOSITS	1,400.00-
2931	LIABILITIES	INT PAY-FED FUNDS PUR	0.00
2932	LIABILITIES	INT PAY-SEC SOLD/REPUR AGR	0.00
2935	LIABILITIES	INT PAY ON BORROWED MONEY	0.00
2941	LIABILITIES	INCOME TAXES PAYABLE-FEDERAL	250.00-
2951	LIABILITIES	INCOME TAXES PAYABLE-STATE	0.00
2976	LIABILITIES	REAL ESTATE TAXES PAYABLE	0.00
2978	LIABILITIES	OTHER TAXES PAYABLE	0.00
2980	LIABILITIES	ACCOUNTS PAYABLE	200.00-
2990	LIABILITIES	OTHER ACCRUED LIABILITIES	0.00
2999	LIABILITIES	SUBORDINATED DEBT	0.00
3100	CAPITAL	PREFERRED STOCK	0.00
3200	CAPITAL	COMMON STOCK	5,000.00-
3300	CAPITAL	SURPLUS	5,000.00-
3400	CAPITAL	UNDIVIDED PROFITS	3,730.00-
3500	CAPITAL	CURRENT YEAR EARNINGS	0.00
4010	INCOME	INT INCOME-INVESTMENTS	2,200.00-
4020	INCOME	INT & FEES ON LOANS	9,900.00-
5000	EXPENSES	INT EXP-DEP & DEBT	4,600.00
6010	EXPENSES	SALARIES & WAGES	1,000.00
6020	EXPENSES	PAYROLL TAXES	0.00
6030	EXPENSES	GROUP INSURANCE	30.00
6040	EXPENSES	OTHER EMPLOYEE BENEFITS	500.00
6100	EXPENSES	OCCUPANCY EXPENSES	365.00
6200	EXPENSES	DEPRECIATION EXPENSE	560.00
6210	EXPENSES	AMORTIZATION-LH IMPR'S	0.00
6300	EXPENSES	FURNITURE & EQUIP EXPENSES	15.00
6900	EXPENSES	OTHER OPERATING EXPENSES	765.00
8000	INCOME	DDA SERVICE CHARGES	60.00-
8010	INCOME	OTHER S/C ON DEPOSITS	0.00
8020	INCOME	OTHER S/C & FEES	0.00
8030	INCOME	OTHER MISC INCOME	5.00-
8400	INCOME	SECURITY G/L-(NET)	400.00-
8800	EXPENSES	OTHER MISC EXPENSE	0.00
8900	EXPENSES	PROVISION FOR INCOME TAXES	500.00
9999	INCOME	INCOME TRANSFER	4,230.00
	TOTAL		0.00

BALANCE SHEET

```
                    THE FIRST TYPICAL BANK
                        BALANCE SHEET
                     DECEMBER 31, 1984


ASSETS
    CASH & EARNING ASSETS
        CURRENCY & COIN                    9,000.00
        OTHER ITEMS IN COLL                  300.00
        DUE FROM BANK A---Z               32,250.00
        RESERVE ACCT (FED/ST)              8,000.00
        INVESTMENT SEC-FACE               21,950.00
        COMMERCIAL LOANS                  39,500.00
        INSTALLMENT LOANS                 16,000.00
        OVERDRAFTS                           170.00
        RES FOR POSS LN LOSSES           <1,000.00>
            TOTAL CASH & EARNING ASSETS                126,170.00

    FIXED ASSETS
        BANK BLDG & IMPR'S-COST            4,744.00
        FUR & FIX-COST                     2,696.00
        LAND                               1,000.00
            TOTAL FIXED ASSETS                           8,440.00

    OTHER ASSETS
        INT REC-INVESTMENTS                2,000.00
        INT (& FEES) REC-LOANS             6,000.00
        PREPAID INSURANCE                  3,105.00
            TOTAL OTHER ASSETS                          11,105.00
                                                     --------------
        TOTAL ASSETS                                   145,715.00
                                                     ==============
```

```
                  THE FIRST TYPICAL BANK
                     BALANCE SHEET
                  DECEMBER 31, 1984


LIABILITIES
    DEPOSIT LIABILITIES
        DDA-INDIVIDUALS/COS            67,455.00
        US TT&L ACCOUNT                 3,000.00
        OFFICIAL CHECKS (ALL TYPES)     2,780.00
        SAVINGS & TIME DEPOSITS        56,400.00
            TOTAL DEPOSIT LIABILITIES                129,635.00


    OTHER LIABILITIES
        DIVIDENDS PAYABLE                 500.00
        INT PAY-SAV & TIME DEPOSITS     1,400.00
        INCOME TAXES PAYABLE-FEDERAL      250.00
        ACCOUNTS PAYABLE                  200.00
            TOTAL OTHER LIABILITIES                    2,350.00
                                                    --------------
        TOTAL LIABILITIES                           131,985.00

CAPITAL
        COMMON STOCK                    5,000.00
        SURPLUS                         5,000.00
        UNDIVIDED PROFITS               3,730.00

        TOTAL CAPITAL                                13,730.00
                                                    --------------
        TOTAL LIABILITIES & CAPITAL                 145,715.00
                                                    ==============
```

PROFIT AND LOSS STATEMENT

```
                    THE FIRST TYPICAL BANK
                   PROFIT AND LOSS STATEMENT
                      DECEMBER 31, 1984

                      CURRENT    %      YEAR-TO-DATE    %


INTEREST INCOME
   INT INCOME-INVESTMENTS      250.00              2,200.00
   INT & FEES ON LOANS       3,400.00              9,900.00
                            ------------           ------------
      TOTAL                  3,650.00  100.0      12,100.00  100.0


INTEREST EXPENSE
   INT EXP-DEP & DEBT        2,600.00   71.2       4,600.00   38.0
                            ------------           ------------
GROSS PROFIT                 1,050.00   28.8       7,500.00   62.0


OPERATING EXPENSES
   SALARIES & WAGES             0.00    0.0        1,000.00    8.3
   GROUP INSURANCE             30.00    0.8           30.00    0.2
   OTHER EMPLOYEE BENEFITS      0.00    0.0          500.00    4.1
   OCCUPANCY EXPENSES          65.00    1.8          365.00    3.0
   DEPRECIATION EXPENSE       550.00   15.1          560.00    4.6
   FURNITURE & EQUIP EXPENSES  15.00    0.4           15.00    0.1
   OTHER OPERATING EXPENSES   165.00    4.5          765.00    6.3
                            ------------           ------------
      TOTAL                   825.00   22.6        3,235.00   26.7
                            ------------           ------------
INCOME <LOSS>                 225.00    6.2        4,265.00   35.2


OTHER INCOME
   DDA SERVICE CHARGES         60.00    1.6           60.00    0.5
   OTHER MISC INCOME            5.00    0.1            5.00    0.0
   SECURITY G/L-(NET)         400.00   11.0          400.00    3.3
                            ------------           ------------
      TOTAL                   465.00   12.7          465.00    3.8


OTHER EXPENSES
   PROVISION FOR INCOME TAXES 500.00   13.7          500.00    4.1
                            ------------           ------------
NET INCOME <LOSS>             190.00    5.2        4,230.00   35.0
                            ============           ============
```

274

G
BIBLIOGRAPHY

As noted in the Preface, there is no lack of literature for the banking industry. In fact, the real problem in researching many professional areas is in the selection of the information relevant to one's needs from the vast quantity of data that is available. Keeping this in mind, I have selected bibliography material that was helpful in preparing this text and/or is geared to the needs of the users of this text. The bibliography is organized by topics as follows:

- Accounting and Auditing
- Income Taxes
- Regulations
- Management, Systems, and Controls
- General

ACCOUNTING AND AUDITING

Bank Audits and Examinations, A Detailed, Step-by-Step Program for CPA's, Bank Internal Auditors, Bank Directors, and Bank Examiners. John H. Savage, Bankers Publishing Company, Boston, 1973.

Comptroller's Handbook for National Bank Examiners. Comptroller of the Currency, Washington, D.C. (March 1977; Supp.#7, Sept. 1979).

EDP Examination Handbook. Comptroller of the Currency, Washington, D.C. (November 1976; Supp.#1, December 1977; presently in revision 1980).

Computer Control and Audit (2nd ed.). William C. Mair, Donald R.Wood, and Kengle W. Davis, Institute of Internal Auditors, 1976.

Customer Confirmation. Bank Administration Institute, Park Ridge, 1967. Discusses in detail all types of confirmation, methods of choosing accounts, procedures for confirming accounts, and follow-up procedures.

Financial Reporting Trends—Banking. Ernst & Whinney, Cleveland. Published annually. A survey of banking industry reporting practices as disclosed in annual reports and filings with the Securities Exchange Commission.

Modern Bank Accounting and Auditing Forms. Warren, Gorham & Lamont, Boston, 1978. Periodic supplements.

Principles and Presentation. Peat, Marwick, Mitchell & Co., New York, updated annually. An annual study of the Annual Reports of one hundred largest commercial banks in the United States.

Proposed Audit Guide: Audits of Banks. Banking Committee of the AICPA, 1980.

Simplified Guide to Bank Call Preparation. Bank Administration Institute, Park Ridge, 1979.

Standards of Internal Bank Auditing in an Electronic Data Processing Environment. Bank Administration Institute, Park Ridge, 1972. Detailed description of the following guidelines: proficiency, independence, performance, scheduling, internal control, documentation, and reporting.

INCOME TAXES

The Bank Tax Report. (Includes Annual Special Reports, Bank Tax Planning Ideas.) Management Reports, Incorporated, Research Affiliate of Banking Law Journal. 6 pp.—semimonthly loose- leaf fillers.

Federal Income Taxation of Banks and Financial Institutions. Banking Law Journal, Warren, Gorham & Lamont, Boston. (loose-leaf)

REGULATIONS

Annual Report of the Federal Deposit Insurance Corporation. Federal Deposit Insurance Corporation, Washington, D.C.

Control of Banking. Prentice-Hall, Inc., Englewood Cliffs, N.J. 1 vol. Bimonthly updates.

Comptroller's Manual for National Banks. Comptroller of the Currency, Treasury Department, Washington, D.C. (January 1979; Supp.#1, May 1979).

Duties and Liabilities of Directors of National Banks. Comptroller of the Currency, Treasury Department, Washington, D.C., June 1972. 30 pp. Booklet outlines laws and directors' examinations.

Federal Deposit Insurance Corporation—Law, Regulations and Related Acts. Federal Deposit Insurance Corporation, Washington, D.C.

Federal Banking Laws (4th ed.). Warren, Gorham & Lamont, Boston, 1979.

MANAGEMENT, SYSTEMS, AND CONTROLS

Bank Costs for Decision Making. Costing Procedures for Pricing Bank Services. John R. Walker, Bankers Publishing Company, Boston, 1970.

Bank Capital: Determining and Meeting Your Bank's Capital Needs. Bank Study Series, Bankers Publishing Co., Boston, 1976.

Bank Management (2nd ed.). American Bankers Association, New York, 1970. Using actual cases, presents new trends that have emerged in the philosophy and practice of management.

A Financial Information System for Community Banks. Bank Administration Institute, Park Ridge.

- No. 1 Chart of Accounts (1979)
- No. 2 Financial Reporting
- No. 3 Accrual Accounting
- No. 4 Cost Accounting
- No. 5 Budgeting
- No. 6 Responsibility Accounting
- No. 7 Profit Planning

Modern Banking Checklists. Warren, Gorham & Lamont, Boston. Annual supplements. (loose-leaf)

GENERAL

Bank Cards. American Bankers Association, Washington, D.C., 1976. History of bank cards, bank card operations, and applications.

Bank Administration Institute Index of Bank Performance. Bank Administration Institute, Park Ridge, 1978.

Bank Administration Manual. Bank Administration Institute, Park Ridge, 1974. 2 vols. Covers all aspects of bank administration: Auditing, controllership, personnel administration, automation and technology, regulatory changes, current administrative practice. Encyclopedic format.

A Banker's Guide to Financial Statements. Thomas F. O'Malia, Bankers Publishing Company, 1976.

Bank Operating Statistics. Federal Deposit Insurance Corporation. Published annually.

How to Analyze a Bank Statement (6th ed.). Bank Study Series, F.L. Garcia, Bankers Publishing Company, Boston, Spring 1978. For use by analysts, investors, and the public interested in banks and bank stocks, Text supported by many tables, exhibits, and a bibliography.

The Thorndike Encyclopedia of Banking and Financial Tables. David Thorndike, Warren, Gorham & Lamont, Boston, 1973, 1980 supp. Comprehensive financial tables in all areas of banking.

INDEX

Liquidity, **G**, 36, 37
Loan, **G**
  types, 50
Loan amortization schedule, 60
Loan classifications, **G**
Loan commitment fees, 62
Loan fees, 62
Loan losses, 63
  provision for, 159
Loan status, 63
Local items, **G**

Mail deposit, **G**
Maker, **G**
Memorandum account, **G**
MICR (Magnetic Ink Character
  Recognition), **G**, 139
Microcomputer applications, 140
Microfilm, **G**
Money order, **G**
Monthly payment loan, **G**
Mortgage, **G**
Mortgage participation certificate
  (PC), **G**
Multiple step income statement, 109

National banks, 2
Negotiable instrument, **G**
Net interest margin, 6, 168
Net occupancy expense or net
  occupancy income, **G**
Net proceeds, 55
Net of tax items, 112
Night depository, **G**
Nonaccrual loans, 64
Noncollateralized loans, 52
Nonearning assets, 5
Note, **G**
N.S.F., **G**

Obligation, **G**
Off line processing, 137
Official check, **G**, 77
On line processing, 138
On us checks, **G**
Operating cycle, 51, 167
Operating expense to operating
  income, 168
Ordinary cash dividends, 101
Other loans, 62
Overdraft, **G**, 76

Paid in capital, 98
Par value, 98
Participation loans, 53
Passbook, **G**
Pass-through certificate, **G**
Payee, **G**
Pay-off balance, 58
Permanent differences, 153
Pockets, 28
Post, **G**
Post dated check, **G**
Preferred stock, 104
Premium, 41
  accounting for, 42
  amortizing methods, 42
Prepaid expenses, 71
Price earnings ratio, 168
Principal, **G**
Prior period adjustments, 111
Problem loans, 64
Profit and loss statement (P&L),
  5, 109
  sample of, 25
Profitability, 164
Proof, **G**, 28
Proof department, **G**, 28
Provision for loan losses, 159
Purchased interest, 40